"Give of thy sons to bear the message glorious,
Give of thy wealth to speed them on their way.
Pour out thy soul for them in prayer victorious,
And all thou spendest Jesus will repay."

*

The parents of the five men have, in a very literal sense fulfilled the words of this hymn. This book is dedicated to them.

GLOSSARY

(All a's are pronounced halfway between the a in father and the a in cat.)

ARAJUNO a-ra-*hoo*-no. An abandoned Shell Oil Company base in the eastern jungle. The station where the McCullys worked; also the base from which the rescue party set out.

ATSHUARA at-*shwa*-ra. A group of Jivaro Indians among whom Roger Youderian established an outstation.

AUCA *ow* (rhymes with cow)-ka. A group of savage Indians inhabiting the eastern jungle. The word is a Quichua term meaning "savage."

CURARAY coo-ra-*rye*. The river on which the five missionaries established their "beachhead."

DAYUMA dye-*u*-ma. An Auca woman who escaped from her tribe several years ago. She furnished Jim Elliot with the data used on the initial contact.

JIVARO *he*-va-ro. A group of Indians known for their ancient practice of head-shrinking, who live in the southeastern jungles of Ecuador.

MACUMA ma-*coo*-ma. Home base of the Youderians. A jungle station among the Jivaros.

PUYUPUNGU pu-yu-pungu (all four *u*'s are long). Outstation opened by the Elliots; later the home of the Flemings.

QUICHUA *keech*-wa. Any of a number of groups of Indians in Ecuador who were conquered by the Incas. Also the language spoken by these people now (it was forced on them by the conquerors). This is the Ecuadorian spelling of Kechua, or Quechua. In this book, Quichua refers to the Lowland Quichuas—those who live in the eastern forests, among whom Jim Elliot, Ed McCully, and Pete Fleming worked.

QUITO *key*-toe. The capital of Ecuador.

SHANDIA *shan*-dya. The station where Peter Fleming and Jim Elliot worked when they first went into the forest. The McCullys lived here for a time, and later only the Elliots.

SHELL MERA shell-*meh*-ra. The base of operations of the Missionary Aviation Fellowship in Ecuador, at the edge of the jungle. It is accessible by road from Quito. Home of the Saint family.

CONTENTS

Acknowledgments vi

Map: The Territory of "Operation Auca" ....vii-viii

I   "I Dare Not Stay Home" 1

II   Destination: Shandia 13

III   "All Things to All Men" 21

       Picture section 23–30

IV   Infinite Adaptability 39

V   "Expendable for God" 49

VI   Missionary to the Head-Shrinking Jivaros 65

VII   Breaking Jungle Barriers 73

VIII   The Aucas 89

IX   September 1955 99

       Picture section 101–116

X   Operation Auca Begins 123

XI   A Line from Plane to Ground 129

XII   The Savages Respond 139

XIII   The Search for "Palm Beach" 151

XIV   An Auca on the Path 161

XV   Why Did the Men Go? 167

XVI   "We Go Not Forth Alone" 173

XVII   Success on Friday 185

XVIII   Silence 191

       Picture sections 197–228, 237–244

XIX   "Yet Have We Not Forgotten Thee" 245

       Epilogue (November 1958) 253

       Picture section 256–260

       Epilogue II (January 1996) 261

       End of the Spear preview chapters 269

       Back to the Stone Age 271

       Can Cowodi Hunt? 281

ACKNOWLEDGMENTS

Many people, scattered from the jungles of Ecuador to the skyscrapers of New York, have helped in the writing of this story. The four other widows, Barbara Youderian, Marj Saint, Marilou McCully, and Olive Fleming, when they suddenly found themselves with doubled responsibility, took time to gather their husbands' diaries, letters, and other writings, and were willing to share them. Abe C. Van Der Puy, of the missionary radio station HCJB in Quito, Ecuador, spent many months assembling material for *The Reader's Digest* article, prepared by Clarence W. Hall, which appeared in the issue of August, 1956. I have freely drawn on this material in the expanded version of the story. Cornell Capa, of Magnum Photos, flew to Ecuador for *Life* magazine within hours after the news of the martyrdom of the missionaries was radioed to the American press. With his perceptive and sensitive pictures, he tells a story which words could not have told. His skillful guidance could not have been bought with money. *Life* has generously made available the photographs taken for them by Cornell Capa. Jozefa Stuart, of the Magnum research staff, made a special trip to Ecuador for the publishers to collect extensive additional data which I needed in writing the book. Many of the facts on the Auca Indians came from Rachel Saint, sister of the missionary pilot, who learned them from an escaped member of the tribe. Nate Saint's brother Sam played a unique role as adviser and official representative for the five of us widows. Decisions which would have been beyond our ability to make, Sam made, consulting with us by overseas telephone, personal conference, and mail. The hours and the miles of travel he devoted on our behalf cannot be counted. The editors of Harper & Brothers were unstinting in giving of themselves to make this book what it ought to be. Their counsel and encouragement have been invaluable. To all of these people I am deeply grateful. With Barbara, Marj, Marilou, and Olive, I thank God for allowing us to share so intimately in the lives recorded in these pages. And to Him who made them what they were, we repeat the words which our husbands sang a few days before they died:

> "*We rest on Thee, our Shield and our Defender,*
> *Thine is the battle, Thine shall be the praise*
> *When passing through the gates of pearly splendor*
> *Victors, we rest with Thee through endless days.*"

Elisabeth Elliot
Quito, Ecuador
February, 1957

SOUTH AMERICA

Equator

Quito
ECUADOR

See detail
map→

PERU

PACIFIC

OCEAN

The Territory of
"OPERATION AUCA"

Map above shows the location of Ecuador
on the Northwest coast of South America

Air routes used by missionary plane — — — — —

CHAPTER I
"I Dare Not Stay Home"

The *Santa Juana* is under way. White stars breaking through a high mist. Half moon. The deep burn of phosphorus running in the wake. Long, easy rolling and the push of steady wind."

It was hot in the little cabin of the freighter. Jim Elliot, who was later to become my husband, was writing in the old cloth-covered ledger he used for a diary. It was a night in February, 1952. Pete Fleming, Jim's fellow missionary, sat at a second desk. Jim continued:

"All the thrill of boyhood dreams came on me just now outside, watching the sky die in the sea on every side. I wanted to sail when I was in grammar school, and well remember memorizing the names of the sails from the Merriam-Webster's ponderous dictionary in the library. Now I am actually at sea—as a passenger, of course, but at sea nevertheless—and bound for Ecuador. Strange—or is it?—that childish hopes should be answered in the will of God for this *now?*

"We left our moorings at the Outer Harbor Dock, San Pedro, California, at 2:06 today. Mom and Dad stood together watching at the pier side. As we slipped away Psalm 60:12 came to mind, and I called back, 'Through our God we shall do valiantly.' They wept some. I do not understand how God has made me. Joy, sheer joy, and thanksgiving fill and encompass me. I can scarcely keep from turning to Pete and saying, 'Brother, this is great!' or 'We never had it so good.' God has done and is doing all I ever desired, much more than I ever asked. Praise, praise to the God of Heaven, and to His Son Jesus. Because He hath said, 'I will never leave thee nor forsake thee,' I may boldly say, 'I will not fear. . . .' "

Jim Elliot laid down his pen. He was a young man of twenty-five, tall and broad-chested, with thick brown hair and blue-gray eyes. He was bound for Ecuador—the answer to years of prayer for God's guidance concerning his lifework. Some had thought it strange that a young man with his opportunities for success should choose to spend his life in the jungles among primitive people. Jim's answer, found in his diary, had been written a year before:

"My going to Ecuador is God's counsel, as is my leaving Betty, and my refusal to be counseled by all who insist I should stay and stir up the believers in the U.S. And how do I know it is His counsel? 'Yea, my heart instructeth me in the night seasons.' Oh, how good! For I have known my heart is speaking to me for God! . . . No visions, no voices, but the counsel of a heart which desires God."

Jim's mood of the moment was felt by Pete. Pete was shorter than Jim with a high forehead and dark wavy hair. The two had learned to understand and appreciate each other long before, and their going to Ecuador together was, to them, one of the "extras" that God threw in. Pete, too, had met with raised eyebrows and polite questions when he made it known that he was going to Ecuador. An M.A. in literature, Pete was expected to become a college professor or Bible teacher. But to throw away his life among ignorant savages—it was thought absurd.

Only a year or two before, the problems of Ecuador, on the northwest bulge of South America, had seemed remote. The two young men had talked with several missionaries who had been there, who described the enormous problems of transportation, education, and development of resources. Missionary work had done much to help the country bridge the cultural span of a millennium between primitive jungles and modern cities. But progress was pitifully slow. Evangelicals had been working among the head-shrinking Jivaros for twenty-five years, among the Quichuas of the high Andes, and among the red-painted Colorados of the western forest. The Cayapas of the northwestern river region had also been reached with the Gospel, and advances were soon to be made into the Cofan tribe of the Colombian border.

But there remained a group of tribes that had consistently repelled every advance made by the white man: the Aucas. They are an isolated, unconquered, seminomadic remnant of age-old jungle Indians. Over the years, information about the Aucas has seeped out of the jungle: through adventurers, through owners of haciendas, through captured Aucas, through missionaries who have spoken with captured Aucas or Aucas who have had to flee from killings within the tribe. Whatever Jim and Pete had been able to learn about them was eagerly recorded, so that by now the very name thrilled their young blood. Would they someday be permitted to have part in winning the Aucas for Christ?

They were aware that the first missionary to have entered Auca territory—Pedro Suarez, a Jesuit priest—had been murdered by spears in an isolated station near the confluence of the Napo and Curaray. That was in 1667. His murderers were Indians who might have been the ancestors of some present-day Aucas. For about two hundred years after this the Indians had been left in peace by the white man. Then the coming of rubber hunters wrote a dark page in the history of this jungle area. For some fifty years—from about 1875 to 1925—these men roamed the jungles, plundering and burning the Indian homes, raping, torturing, and enslaving the people. It was a time when the concept of "lesser breeds without the law" was almost universally accepted. For the Aucas to have no love for the white man was understandable. Could Christian love wipe out the memories of past treachery and brutality? This was a challenge to Jim and Pete as they hoped to bring the message of God's love and salvation to these primitive people. It was a challenge and leading for which they had both been prepared since childhood.

God *had* led Jim—since boyhood, when, in his home in Portland, Oregon, he learned that the Book of all books is the Bible, and that to follow its teaching is not necessarily to live a cloistered, dull life. Now as he sat in his cabin on shipboard his mind went back to his family house on a hillside facing snow-covered Mt. Hood. Jim's father, a red-haired, iron-jawed Scotsman, would gather his four children each morning after breakfast and read to them out of the Bible, trying always to show them that this Book was to be lived, and that the life it depicted was a happy and rewarding one. The children would squirm in their seats in the little breakfast nook, but some of the truths sank in, and Jim, third of the Elliot sons, soon received Jesus Christ as Saviour and Lord.

When he entered high school, Jim, following the example of the Apostle Paul, was "not ashamed of the gospel of Christ." A Bible always rested on top of his stack of textbooks when he entered the classroom. Academically his early interest was in architectural drawing. His talent in this was exceptional, and his drawings were kept by the teacher to be used as examples to future classes. Before finishing Benson Polytechnic School, however, he began orienting his life toward the mission field.

While at Wheaton College in Illinois, Jim limited his extracurricular activities, fearing that he might become occupied in nonessentials and miss the essentials of life. He refused requests that he run for several offices on the campus. He did, however, go out for wrestling, explaining his choice in a letter to his mother:

"I wrestle solely for the strength and co-ordination of muscle tone that the body receives while working out, with the ultimate end that of presenting a more useful body as a living sacrifice. This God knows, and even though He chose to allow it to be strained, the motive was for His glory and the faith He honors. Simplicity of heart and freedom from anxiety He expects of us, and gives grace to have both."

During his sophomore year in college Jim came to the conclusion that God wanted him in a Latin-American country, preaching the Gospel to those who had never heard it. This decision was immediately followed by action; he began the informal study of Spanish. He chose Greek as his major, preparatory to translating the Bible into some unwritten language. His professors remember the vigor, if not always the accuracy, with which he translated some of the ancient classics—Xenophon, Thucydides, patristic literature. It was a thrill to him to read for the first time in Greek the old stories of the New Testament, so familiar in English.

"Today I read the story of the Cross in John 19 for the first time in the original," he wrote to his parents. "The simplicity and pathos made me almost weep; something which has never occurred in my English reading. Surely it is a wonderful story of love."

In November, 1947, Jim wrote a letter to his parents which showed where his ambition lay: "The Lord has given me a hunger for righteousness and piety that can alone be of Himself. Such hungering He alone can satisfy, yet Satan would delude and cast up all sorts of other baubles, social life, a name renowned, a position of importance, scholastic attainment. What are these but the objects of the 'desire of the Gentiles' whose cravings are warped and perverted. Surely they can mean nothing to the soul who has seen the beauty of Jesus Christ. . . . No doubt you will hear of my receiving preliminary honors at school. They carry the same brand and will lie not long hence in the basement in a battered trunk beside the special gold 'B' pin, with the 'ruby' in it for which I studied four years at Benson. All is vanity below the sun and a 'striving after wind.' Life is not here, but hid above with Christ in God, and therein I rejoice and sing as I think on such exaltation."

Jim and my brother, Dave Howard, were both members of the class of 1949 at Wheaton, but although I was also at Wheaton, I had not met Jim until Christmas, 1947, when Dave brought him home with us for the holidays. I smiled later when I learned Jim had written his parents about "a tall, lean girl, far from beautiful, but with a queer personality-drive that interests me."

His junior year at college completed, Jim wrote to his parents: "Seems impossible that I am so near my senior year at this place, and truthfully, it hasn't the glow about it that I rather expected. There is no such thing as attainment in this life; as soon as one arrives at a long-coveted position he only jacks up his desire another notch or so and looks for higher achievement—a process which is ultimately suspended by the intervention of death. Life is truly likened to a rising vapor, coiling, evanescent, shifting. May the Lord teach us what it means to live in terms of the end, like Paul who said, 'Neither count I my life dear unto myself, that I might finish my course with joy. . . .' "

During that summer, after preaching to a group of Indians on a reservation, Jim wrote: "Glad to get the opportunity to preach the Gospel of the matchless grace of our God to stoical, pagan Indians. I only hope that He will let me preach to those who have never heard that name Jesus. What else is worth while in this life? I have heard of nothing better. 'Lord, send me!' "

In his diary of the summer he wrote: " 'He makes His ministers a flame of fire.' Am I ignitable? God deliver me from the dread asbestos of 'other things.' Saturate me with the oil of the Spirit that I may be a flame. But flame is transient, often short-lived. Canst thou bear this, my soul— short life? In me there dwells the Spirit of the Great Short-Lived, whose zeal for God's house consumed Him. 'Make me Thy Fuel, Flame of God.' "

The man who wrote these words was no recluse. He was an American college senior, school-champion wrestler, consistent honor student, president of the Student Foreign Missions Fellowship, amateur poet, and class representative on the Student Council. Jim was warmly admired by fellow students. He was known as "one of the most surprising characters" on campus. Able to recite such poems as "The Face on the Barroom Floor" and Robert Service's "The Cremation of Sam McGee," he was at the same time recognized as a man of spiritual stature above his classmates. George Macdonald said, "It is the heart that is not yet sure of its God that is afraid to laugh in His presence." Jim spoke of "joking with God." "Every now and again," he said, "I ask for something—a little thing, perhaps, and something answers. Maybe it's only me, but something answers, and makes the request sound so funny that I laugh at myself and feel that He is smiling with me. I've noticed it several times lately, we two making fun of my 'other self' who does so hate to be laughed at!"

Sure that he belonged to God by faith in His Son Jesus Christ, Jim was equally sure that the God who had redeemed him would also guide him. "I am as sure of His direction as I am of His salvation," he used to say. During his senior year a large convention was held at the University of Illinois for students who were interested in foreign missionary work. Jim attended and asked God to show him what He wanted him to do.

At the end of the convention he wrote: "The Lord has done what I wanted Him to do this week. I wanted, primarily, peace about going into pioneer Indian work. And as I analyze my feelings now, I feel quite at ease about saying that tribal work in South American jungles is the general direction of my missionary purpose. One more thing: I am quite confident that God wants me to begin jungle work single. Those are good-sized issues to get settled finally in a week, but just now I am happy about them."

Toward the end of the summer of 1950, Jim's "general direction" became specific. He met a former missionary from Ecuador who told him of the needs in that field, and mentioned the great challenge of the dread Aucas. This was the climax to several years of seeking direction from God. Jim devoted ten days largely to prayer to make sure that this was indeed what God intended for him. He was given new assurance, and wrote to his parents of his intention to go to Ecuador. Understandably, they, with others who knew Jim well, wondered if perhaps his ministry might not be more effective in the United States, where so many know so little of the Bible's real message. He replied:

"I dare not stay home while Quichuas perish. What if the well-filled church in the homeland needs stirring? They have the Scriptures Moses, and the prophets, and a whole lot more. Their condemnation is written on their bank books and in the dust on their Bible covers."

This feeling is reflected in his diary account of Gospel meetings that he and his college pal Ed McCully conducted in southern Illinois: "Sterile days. Have had thirty-two nights of 'Youth Rallies' in Sparta, with fifty or sixty out in the public school gymnasium. There is little interest, and very few young people are reached in this way, I'm beginning to see. This problem of meeting a culture with truth from God is the most difficult kind of thing. One comes as a renovator, a conditioner of society, and society is in no mood to be conditioned. The fixedness of the human mind is the 'wall of Jericho' to Gospel preaching. *God* must shake, or there will be no shaking.

"There has been a sense of discouragement and doubt come over me through this. . . . There is a strong pull to the philosophy that 'chaos created this lump of clay in his own image'—and to let fall the whole gamut of theological arguments. Again, I'm held by the resurrection of Jesus Christ. Were it not that I believed that Jesus was seen of men and proved Himself to be supernatural in outwitting death, I would throw the whole system back to the troubled skies and take a raft down the Mississippi today. But the fact is founding, settling, establishing. It holds as nothing else, and gives the sense that there *are* answers, not yet discovered, for which I must wait."

It was typical of Jim that, once sure of God's leading, he did not turn aside easily. The "leading" was to Ecuador, so every thought and action was bent in that direction. Jim practiced what he preached when he wrote in his diary: "Wherever you are, *be all there*. Live to the hilt every situation you believe to be the will of God."

Jim had been praying for some time that God would give him a comrade with whom to go to the mission field, a single man ready to enter tribal work with him. For a while he thought that it might be Ed McCully, but when Ed married in June, 1951, Jim began to pray for another. In August he saw an old friend, Pete Fleming, who had just obtained his master's degree and was at that time seeking God's direction for his lifework. Jim later wrote to him:

"I would certainly be glad if God persuaded you to go with me, but if the Harvest-Chief does not move you, I hope you remain at home. To me, Ecuador is an avenue of obedience to the simple word of Christ. There is room for me there, and I am free to go. Of this I am sure. He *will* lead you too, and not let you miss your signs. The sound of 'gentle stillness' after the thunder and wind have passed will be the ultimate word from God. Tarry long for it. Remember the words of Amy Carmichael: 'The vows of God are on me. I may not stay to play with shadows or pluck earthly flowers, till I my work have done and rendered up account.' "

Jim's hopes were to be fulfilled when he and Pete set sail from San Pedro in 1952.

Their paths had crossed when groups of young people interested in studying the Bible had gotten together from Seattle and Portland for conferences and mountain-climbing expeditions.

Pete had once gone east to join Jim Elliot in a series of speaking engagements at religious conferences and other meetings. Six weeks of traveling together brought them into a deeper comradeship than they had known before. Driving back across the country to the northwest, Jim wrote:

"Pete is a most engaging traveling partner, interested in all the things that I notice—geology, botany, history, and the sky and all the good things God has scattered through the west in such extravagant variation."

Pete, who was born in Seattle, Washington, in 1928, early learned to appreciate the Bible and to hold it as his supreme rule of life and conduct. Those who knew him in his late teens and early twenties were impressed by his intelligent grasp of Scripture, and by the breadth of his spiritual knowledge. Converted at the age of thirteen after hearing the testimony of a blind evangelist, Pete, like Enoch, "walked with God" in a way that set him apart in the eyes of fellow high school students. He earned his letters in basketball and golf, and the members of the letter club asked him to be their chaplain. In his valedictory speech at graduation he said: "Where shall we look? Where shall we go? I believe that we have a right to go back to the Bible for our anchorage. Here we have a recognized foundation . . . let us build upon it."

This conviction stood Pete in good stead when, in the fall of 1946, he entered the University of Washington as a philosophy major. He was a man with a critical mind, and the study of philosophy challenged him to re-examine his whole view of life and of the world around him. For a while he almost foundered on the shoals of conflicting thought, but at last the God to whom he had long since "committed the keeping of his soul" brought him back to the harbor of truth, His eternal Word.

Pete worked part time, studied hard, and was president of the University Christian Fellowship. He was a man who drove himself, yet in his busy schedule he took time for prayer and study of the Bible. In 1951 he received a master's degree, his thesis being on Melville's *The Confidence Man*.

In the meantime, having seen and corresponded with Jim, he reached a decision about his lifework. He surprised his friends by announcing that he believed God was calling him to Ecuador.

"I think a 'call' to the mission field is no different from any other means of guidance," he once wrote to his fiancée, Olive Ainslie. "A call is nothing more nor less than obedience to the will of God, as God presses it home to the soul by whatever means He chooses."

He had known Olive since childhood; the two of them had attended the same worship group on Sundays. When he responded to God's call to Ecuador, however, he went with the intention of serving Him without the responsibilities of home life—at least for the first year or so.

On September 6, 1951, he wrote to Dr. Wilfred Tidmarsh, an English missionary with twelve years' service in the Ecuadorian jungle, who had addressed many Christian groups in the States:

"Since your visit I have been very much in prayer about going to Ecuador. In fact, I have never prayed so much before the Lord about anything. Jim and I have exchanged several letters in which I told him of the increased desire to go forth, and of the Scriptures which God seemingly had brought to mind to confirm it. My thinking, both in and outside of the Scriptures, was directed toward the stringency of Christ's words to His disciples, when he sent them forth: 'I send you forth as sheep among wolves. . . .' 'He that loveth father or mother more than me is not worthy of me. . . .' 'He that taketh not up his cross, and followeth after me is not worthy of me. . . .' 'He that findeth his life shall lose it: and he that loseth his life for My sake shall find it.' It has seemed that the severe requirements of a difficult field like Ecuador are matched on a spiritual level by the severe requirements placed on real disciples. Ecuador, as it seems, is a God-given opportunity to place God's principles and promises to the extreme test.

"This door seems to be opening at a time when I was looking to the Lord regarding the future, and thus is the Lord's answer to my prayers."

On the verge of his sailing from the States, Pete said to one of his college friends: "Remember the last few verses of I Corinthians 3: 'For *all things* are yours . . . and ye are Christ's; and Christ is God's.' Throughout all our personality we are God's, and since God has made our whole selves, there is great joy in realizing who is our Creator. This realization is to permeate every area and level of life. In appreciation of beauty, mountains, music, poetry, knowledge, people, science—even in the tang of an apple—God is there, to reflect the joy of His presence in the believer who will realize God's purposes in *all things*."

CHAPTER II
Destination: Shandia

After eighteen days at sea Jim Elliot and Pete Fleming arrived in Guayaquil, Ecuador. "About half-way up the Guayas River," wrote Pete, "I finally comprehended that this, *this* was Ecuador. I felt a tingling sensation for the first time. Jim and I sang quietly, 'Faith of our Fathers,' as the boat pulled into the harbor:

> *"'Faith of our Fathers, holy faith*
> *We will be true to thee till death.'"*

Leaving the ship, the two young men made their way through the stacks of baggage out into the hot sunlight on the Malacon, the parkway beside the Guayas River. The tide was coming in, and out in the center of the current, great masses of water hyacinths rode swiftly upriver. A gleaming white fruit ship stood at anchor, and beside it crowded the barges and long slim dugout canoes of banana vendors. A ferry was disgorging its sweating, shouting multitudes, with their straw suitcases, cloth bundles, chickens, and baskets. Jim and Pete stopped to watch the faces until the crowd dissipated in all directions; then they turned and crossed the street. Portals over the sidewalk shaded them from the tropical sun, and they gazed at the store windows with their astonishingly heterogeneous displays: sweaters and typewriters, frying pans and automobile tires, fake shrunken heads from the Jivaro Indians, and Camay soap. In one side street, cocoa beans were spread out like a nubbly red-brown carpet to dry in the sun. Businessmen, dressed in crisp white suits and Panama hats, were coming out of the buildings for their two-hour lunch break. Cadillacs and donkeys, nudging each other for the right of way, epitomized this land of contrasts.

With a growing population of over three hundred thousand, Guayaquil is the country's largest and most modern city, with wide streets and imposing office buildings. The streets are crowded, as owners, managers, and clerks from the various importing and exporting firms bustle about their business. Guayaquil is the banana capital of the world, and also from here, since World War II, more than three million bags of coffee, some seventy million pounds of cocoa, and more than three hundred million pounds of rice have annually been loaded for the export market. An air of prosperity prevails, production is constantly rising, and this port city serves as the country's trade barometer.

Pete and Jim spent their first night in a third-class hotel. Heat, mosquitoes, the occasional bray of a burro, and the Latin rhythm of a dance band nearby made the night a memorable one. The next day they took a plane to Quito, traveling up over the western cordillera of the Andes, crossing a 13,000-foot pass, and landing in the capital of Ecuador. Quito is 9,300 feet above sea level, and to the west rises the volcanic mountain Pichincha.

Here was a new opportunity to "live to the hilt." This old-world city, with its adobe houses, high mud walls, cobblestone streets, ornate churches, with its red geraniums and eucalyptus trees, was to be their home for the next six months. For before they could get to the Oriente—the eastern jungle area of Ecuador, goal of their tireless preparation and planning—there remained this last requirement, the learning of Spanish, the national language of Ecuador.

They signed up for Spanish lessons with a *señorita* who expected nothing short of perfection, and they also engaged a room in the home of an Ecuadorian doctor who had five children. Here was an unparalleled opportunity for practice. They were forced to speak Spanish, and the children were quite uninhibited in pointing out the mistakes and peculiarities of their guests.

"Señor Jaime," said little Moquetin, a bright-eyed imp of six, "why is it that your face is always red?" Jim countered, "Why is it that *your* face is always brown?" "Because it is much prettier that way," was the unexpected reply.

"Language is a tyranny of frustration," Pete once said. But learn it they must. During those months of study Pete wrote in his diary: "I am longing now to reach the Aucas if God gives me the honor of proclaiming the Name among them. . . . I would gladly give my life for that tribe if only to see an assembly of those proud, clever, smart people gathering around a table to honor the Son—gladly, gladly, gladly! What more could be given to a life?

"These almost six months have been crammed full of goodness and God has given us special privileges by way of having not set responsibilities, of giving us the money and the freedom to live with a national family and undoubtedly we have learned things that will stand us in good stead all our missionary lives. And it has been a terrific boon; praying together and seeing God give us faith, getting more and more from the Spanish Bible, gradually finding Spanish easier and getting useful phrases fixed in my mind so I didn't have to think out every one. It has all been good and we have learned things; how to cope with situations and how to keep our mouths shut on some subjects, how to get along with the nationals, what their perspective on missionaries is. . . . God is going to give us Spanish by one means or another, and Quichua as well."

Finally the day came when Jim and Pete were to leave Quito. They saw their gear thrown up on top of a fat, ungainly vehicle that served as a bus. An American truck bed had been surmounted by an amazing superstructure that protruded on both sides accommodating perhaps thirty or more passengers inside, and as many as dared cling on the outside. Squeezing themselves and their cameras, hall-mark of the missionary as well as of the tourist, in among the other riders, they each found a seat—a board perhaps ten inches wide, with as much room again for the legs, between it and the next seat. They were fortunate indeed to be in a bus with an aisle, for in some vehicles passengers cheerfully clamber over the backs of the seats to their places. And they were able to sit up straight and still see out of the low windows. To have one's knees close to one's chin is not the most comfortable position, but then, they could take turns sitting by the aisle to stretch their legs.

"*Vamos!*" called the driver. Jim and Pete rejoiced that the bus was going to start on schedule. But no such luck this time—for this is the land of *mañana*. Everywhere there are unexplained delays, and perhaps the most trying thing of all to an outsider is the fact that no one seems to be the least interested in giving an explanation. No questions are asked. Silence. In this case, the delay lasted only ten minutes or so; and, without warning, the driver gunned his motor and the bus lurched to a start.

Leaving the city, the bus climbed up over the paramo, where a cold drizzle added to the bleakness of great stretches of brown grass. An occasional Indian galloped by on horseback, red wool poncho flying in the strong wind. A woman dressed in a heavy wool skirt and embroidered blouse passed at a dog trot, the usual gait of the Indian of the high Andes. Her baby, dressed exactly as she was, complete with fedora, joggled in a cloth on her back. The mother's hands moved nimbly, spinning wool on a spindle.

At 12,000 feet the men could see the small grass huts of the high-land Quichuas. They eke out a living herding cattle and sheep, grow-ing potatoes and certain grains. This scene was soon replaced by the arid territory surrounding Ambato, the city of the earthquake of 1949, and the "gateway to the Oriente." Here the bus stopped, and was immediately besieged by women with their trays of fried pork, meat pies, glasses of fruit drink, or slices of pineapple piled into an enamel basin. Each called her wares in a peculiar singsong.

The trip was resumed once more, with the bus climbing up between lofty, snow-clad peaks, then tipping forward to swoop down in dizzy, hairpin turns into the vast gorge cut by the Pastaza River through the eastern cordillera of the Andes, past the cone-shaped Tungurahua, an extinct volcano. With startling suddenness the desert of the western slope and the high mountain pass were replaced by lush greenness on the breathtaking eastern descent. Purple orchids nodded out over the road as the bus swayed and jerked along the narrow shelf of road, a precipice on the right, a steep wall of rock shouldering up on the left. Toward late afternoon the bus rounded another curve, and the Pastaza spread itself out before them, flowing in broad ribbons over black beaches. This was the western extreme of the mighty Amazon basin, which terminates three thousand miles to the east, as the river empties into the Atlantic Ocean. Another little town or two, and Shell Mera was reached. A former base of the Shell Oil Company for prospecting operations in the area, it is now an unpretentious huddle of dilapidated wooden buildings; houses, a hotel, and stores on one side of the road, and an army base and mission-sponsored Bible school on the other.

The Ecuador base of the Missionary Aviation Fellowship was at the southern end of town. Here Jim and Pete met Dr. Tidmarsh, the missionary with whom they had corresponded before coming to Ecuador. And with him they were soon flying north from Shell Mera, over the green sea of jungle, following the Ansuc River toward the Atun Yaku, headwaters of the Napo.

They were headed for Shandia, the Quichua mission station which Dr. Tidmarsh had had to abandon because of his wife's health. They planned to reopen the station, Dr. Tidmarsh staying till they could get established. Shandia did not at this time have an airstrip, so the three flew to another station nearby. Here they landed and set out on foot through the jungle. It was late in the afternoon when they started, and knowing that it was normally a three-hour hike, they raced against the sudden tropical twilight. Slipping on grassy roots, stumbling and struggling through deep mud at times, they pressed eagerly on to the place that would be their home for months to come. They were full of anticipation for what lay ahead, but at the same time they drank in the beauties of the great Amazon rain forest through which they passed.

It was virgin jungle. Trees with buttress-shaped roots grew to tremendous heights, often with no branches except at the top. Under these umbrellas an incredible variety of flora thrives. It was often impossible for Jim and Pete to distinguish the leaves which belong properly to the trees, for the huge tangle of lianas, air plants, and fungus that sponge a living from them. Orchids everywhere lent their soft colors to the living green. Fungus grew in vivid colors and bizarre shapes—vermilion, shaped like the ruffle on a lady's dress; turquoise, shaped like a shell, half hidden under a rotten log.

Just as the moon rose over the forest, the three men burst into the clearing that was Shandia.

"Indians immediately gathered around," wrote Pete, "and I remembered a couple of faces from Tidmarsh's pictures, and felt a kind of pride in remembering. My first thought was, 'Yes, I can love these people.' The ink-colored designs on the women's faces interested me and the pitiful drape of the faded blue skirts. Lots of children were about, smiling shyly. Babies sucked on big, tremulous breasts, and the young, eager faces of boys looked up at us. Heard Tidmarsh's first conversation in Quichua; wondered how I would ever learn it."

At the same time Jim wrote: "We have arrived at the destination decided on in 1950. My joy is full. Oh, how blind it would have been to reject the leading of these days. How it has changed the course of life for me and added such a host of joys!"

At the far end of the clearing stood the small thatched house in which Dr. Tidmarsh had lived. It was walled with split bamboo, floored with boards, and set on posts to insure circulation of air and to give protection from both the damp ground and the invasion of insects.

"At my first glance the house looked spacious and comfortable,"

Pete wrote in his diary, "and I thought how easily Olive and I could live in such a set-up, feeling joy in the knowledge and anticipation. Afterwards we got cleaned up a bit, washed our muddy feet in the ice-cold Napo, took a look around, and settled down to a meal of rice soup, plantain, manioc, and rice, with coffee. Now by the light of the kerosene lamp I am writing on the dining room table . . . tired but full of thankfulness to the Father, who leads on. In reality, this is not an end but a beginning."

CHAPTER III
"All Things to All Men"

In Shandia, Jim and Pete became full-fledged missionaries for the first time. They had come to reach the Quichuas with the Word of God, a task for which they were prepared but could accomplish only if they gained the Quichuas' confidence and love. So by living among them, sharing in their lives and thus laying the foundations of mutual trust they hoped to open the minds and hearts of the Indians to the Christian message. And Jim and Pete knew that whatever knowledge they gained from their experiences among the Quichuas would prepare them for work among other tribes further removed from today's civilization.

The two young missionaries learned quickly that the Quichuas hunt a little, farm a little, and work occasionally for a neighboring hacienda owner. They are subject to a variety of diseases and debilitating intestinal parasites. They are caught between two cultures—the disappearing one of the forebears and the rising white man's world of today. They are a gentle people, unlike their neighbors to the south, the headhunting Jivaros, and to the northeast the feared Aucas. Every facet of the lives, health, language, education, birth, and death of the Indians was of immediate interest to Jim and Pete.

Night after night they sat in their little hut, listening to the jungle tuning up its nocturnal orchestra, and recording their experiences in diaries and letters. Moths and flies swarmed against the lantern, dropping to the paper and clogging penpoints. Great beetles zoomed at their faces, which glistened with sweat from the heat of the lamp. Every evening they were surrounded by a circle of dark, laughing faces—schoolboys who came in to watch whatever the missionaries might be doing.

"Don't white people ever get tired of paper?" said one to Dr. Tidmarsh in Quichua. "These two, all they do is look at paper and write on paper. My father says white men smell like paper. He gets mad at me for smelling like paper when I come home from school."

Pete Fleming smiled as Dr. Tidmarsh translated. How was a man to concentrate for five minutes? But then—he loved these Quichua boys. This is what he had bargained for—this is why he had renounced the solitude and silence for study, which had been his pleasure before.

I was by this time in the western jungle of Ecuador, and Jim kept in touch with me as frequently as jungle mail service would permit. Soon after he reached Shandia he wrote: "Days begin at 6 A.M. with the swooshing of the gas stove on which Dr. Tidmarsh heats his shaving water. The box we use for a wash stand sits on the corner of the front porch, and the drain is over the wall, where you aim the basin at a ditch which runs right around the house. Breakfast, usually consisting of a bowl or two of banana soup or ground corn, a fresh banana and a cup of coffee, has so far been interrupted at 7:15 each morning to make radio contact with the other mission stations of the region. At meal-time we speak only in Spanish. Breakfast is followed by a reading of Daniel in Spanish, and morning prayer.

"So far my mornings have been consumed in watching the doctor do medical work, studying, or making some gadget to bring things

Airstrip at Shell Mera—home base of the Missionary Aviation Fellowship. *Lower right:* MAF quarters, house occupied by the Saint family, and hangar. *Left:* the Pastaza River. *Top:* foothills of the Andes.

OVERLEAF: With a playmate, five-year-old Stevie Saint (left) watches his father taxi down the runway in the MAF's bright yellow Piper Cruiser after a flight over the danger-filled jungle.

ABOVE: In 1953, long before they were to launch Operation Auca, three of the missionaries made a survey trip down the Bobonaza River. *Left to right:* Ed McCully, Pete Fleming, Jim Elliot. The tame parrot was a gift from friendly Quichuas.

LEFT: This picture of Roger Youderian, and similar pictures of the other missionaries, was dropped to the Aucas to familiarize them with the faces of their sky-borne friends. To aid in the identification, Roger holds a feathered headdress, a gift from the Aucas; in addition, a plane was sketched on the edge of the picture.

RIGHT: Nate Saint, the pilot among the five men, whose development of a bucket-drop system from his plane made possible the interchange of gifts between the missionaries and the Aucas.

TOP LEFT: Roger Youderian, using a language chart developed by the missionaries, teaches Jivaro Indians to read in their own language.

LOWER FAR LEFT: In Puyupungu, Pete Fleming translates the Bible into Quichua for Atanasio, the local chief.

LOWER LEFT: Nate Saint pauses during a welding job at Shell Mera.

ABOVE: Jim Elliot baptizes an Indian woman.

Mission station at Arajuno, with Ed McCully, Marilou, and their son Stevie. Aluminum sheets for the roof were flown in by Nate Saint, while boards for the walls were salvaged from the abandoned Shell Oil community. Gasoline barrels at the right catch rain water.

to a little better state for comfort, and interspersed with visits to the airstrip to see if the men are working. Today, as a herd of wild pigs upriver sent most of them scurrying to the hunt, there were only a dozen or so working. They had arrived at that part of the strip which was planted in patches of plantain [a tropical fruit, 'cooking cousin' of the banana] and they were loath to cut them down. I helped them push over the trees to get them started. It's like destroying food to them, and it hurt me a little, too, but there are other plantains and no other airstrips.

"Our room is exceedingly pleasant; a huge window looks out on a beautiful view. Door is monk's cloth curtain, between our room and the living room. Two throw rugs and the two aluminum chairs make the place look very civilized and the Indian, Venancio, sweeps it daily to clean out the mud and dead cockroaches."

Old Venancio, a typical Quichua, was Dr. Tidmarsh's right-hand man. He dresses as the white man does, in ordinary pants and shirt, his parents having years ago left the old costume of the Quichuas, the *kushma*. Travel on jungle trails, sometimes in knee-deep mud, makes shoes an absurdity for him, though a few others wear them on special occasions as a sign of prestige. A safety pin adorns a conspicuous spot on the front of his unironed shirt, handy for removing chonta palm thorns from his feet. As he travels the trails, he carries a well-worn machete, which he swings aimlessly at trees. If he comes to a steep or slippery bank, he can cut steps for his toes as he ascends. If a vine hangs in his way, one swipe removes it. His wife Susanna trudges behind him, carrying her baby in a cloth on her side, and a great basket containing cooking pot, chickens, blanket, and plantains. This basket is strapped with a jungle "rope," a strip of bark or a long, fibrous leaf, which is passed around the basket and up over Susanna's forehead. She, too, carries her machete, with which to dig and peel the manioc which is their main diet, trim

31

her fingernails, or discourage the weeds around their front door. The machete is their most valued implement—indeed, often the only implement. It makes an excellent hoe, shovel, ax, knife, scissors, or what have you. Jim and Pete soon learned that it is indispensable in the jungle, and wondered how they had ever done without one in the States.

Venancio spends much of his time making small baskets for storing eggs, trumpet-shaped traps and nets for scooping fish, woven sieves, and monkey-skin drums. His wife does all of the heavy work, such as clearing the land of trees and other jungle growth, planting, carrying water and firewood, washing of clothes on the rocks by the river, hauling of heads of plantains, which may weigh up to one hundred pounds each.

Venancio's bed is made of a few slabs of split bamboo laid across a few poles. For chairs he has chunks of wood, five or six inches in height, on which he squats by the fire. A soup plate and spoon make up his eating utensils, and he uses half-gourds for drinking, along with the clay bowls. The staple food of Venancio and his fellow tribesmen is a drink known as chicha. This is made from manioc, a starchy tuber dug daily by the womenfolk, peeled with deft whacks of the machete, and steamed in a clay pot. When it is cooked, the women pound the manioc with a wooden pestle to the consistency of mashed potato, but coarser and heavier. Taking mouthfuls of this, they chew it and spit it into a tray, thus beginning the fermentation which continues as the mass is put back into the great clay urns. It is left for a day or two, or even a week if strong chicha is desired. The Quichuas literally live on this stuff for most of their lives, supplementing it when they can with wild meat or fish, perhaps a little jungle fruit, and eggs.

Day by day in their observation of the Indians as individuals and in a group, Jim and Pete learned to fit themselves into this new fabric of living. One night as the two men, with their senior worker Dr. Tidmarsh, sat with the schoolboys in their little bamboo house, running steps were heard outside.

"Doctor! Doctor! *Tiangichu?* Are you there?"

"*Ikui. Ikui.* Come in."

"My sister-in-law is dying!"

This, in Quichua, may mean anything from a headache to a snakebite. If one is in excellent health, he is "living." Otherwise, he is "dying."

"What is the matter with your sister-in-law?"

"She is causing a child to be born. Will you come?"

Unless there is some complication, the missionary is not usually called to attend a delivery, but Dr. Tidmarsh knew that in this case the woman had lost five babies. He was a doctor of philosophy, not a medical doctor, although he had studied homeopathy. So he collected the simple equipment he had for such emergencies, and with Pete, started down the river. Venancio, serving as guide, plunged ahead in the darkness, while they swung their flashlights to try to augment the little circle of light they threw on the muddy trail. The Talac River, a shallow stream perhaps fifty feet wide, had to be crossed two or three times, and finally the house was reached, a rectangular building constructed of split bamboo and palm-leaf roof, woven beautifully and evenly. As they entered the narrow doorway, stepping over a low sill designed to discourage pigs and chickens, they could see several fires glowing dimly through the smoke that always fills the house and incidentally acts as a preservative for the roof leaf, coating it with tars that resist insects. In one corner sat a man, weaving a string fishing net. Another sawed away on a homemade violin.

"The woman was lying on a bamboo board," Pete wrote later in his diary, "partly shielded from public view by two loosely hung blankets, and was attended by the 'midwife.' Gradually all became dark, the smoldering fires died to embers, and the families went to their boards for the night, the little children with their parents, older boys together in one corner, girls in another. They gave Tidmarsh and me a bed and we lay down as there was no sign of the baby's arrival, labor pains still seven minutes apart. As the bamboo had none of the usually-associated attributes of flexibility which it has in the minds of many, and as our shoes and pants were still wet from walking in the river, we soon chilled, and later rose and sat on small log seats around a smoky fire which refused to stay alight. In company of two mangy skeleton-ribbed dogs we sat listening to the whine of the crickets, the strange goose-like honking of the tree toads, the occasional waking cry of a child, the creaking of the bamboo as someone rolled over, and the periodic moans of the woman which rose shrilly to a short scream.

"Gradually as the pains increased and intensified the girl rose to her knees and reached for the vine-rope which hung from the ceiling above, intertwining her hands in the rope and lifting her body when the pains came. For me, those small brown hands held high over the head, and the arms, lined with taut tendons, communicated something of the simplicity and yet binding custom of their means of giving birth. After she had passed the water, the pains waned and finally the baby began to descend. The midwife gave a word, everybody woke up and moved sleepily to the corner and stood peering over the curtains. Privacy is a word and concept unknown. They prepared a drink for the mother by scraping the claw of a sloth and mixing the powder with water. I think this is suppose to hasten the arrival of the baby.

"Venancio, our cook, then stepped inside, grasped the girl by the shoulders and began shaking her violently which he continued to do until the baby arrived, dropping half onto the banana leaves, half on the earthen floor, a tiny white frail thing attached to an intestine-like cord, motionless in the flickering kerosene light. It burped a couple of times, sputtered and cried, then adopted normal breathing. Tidmarsh stepped in to tie off the cord, and the midwife cut it with the sharp edge of a bamboo stick. The midwife then took the baby, took a mouthful of water from an iron pot, and spat it out over the baby, thus washing it. Then wrapping it in an old dirty cloth and tying it with a woman's embroidered belt, she handed it to a small naked child who tottered across the floor with it. A woman took it, laid it on a bamboo plant, where it was apparently forgotten. Meanwhile the mother continued in her martyr-like position, wincing and writhing under the continuing contractions. Tidmarsh committed the baby to the Lord in prayer."

Slowly the men became more familiar with the language. They were never without their little black notebooks and pencils. Since the language was not a written one, they had only to write down what they heard, try to find out by one means or another what it meant, and then memorize.

"I find the language fascinating," Jim wrote home. "The freshness of discovering a language from the speaker's mouth, without the aid of a textbook, is most stimulating. And an especially interesting feature to me now is the onomatopoeic value of certain words. For example, I heard it said of a free-swinging broken wrist, 'It goes whi-*lang*, whi-*lang*.' The word has no dictionary meaning, so far as we can discover. Or a lamp flickering goes 'li-*ping*, li-*ping*, tiung, tiung, and dies.' The word 'tukluk, tukluk' describes rapid swallowing and gulping. And there are myriads more."

As Pete and Jim's knowledge of the language grew, so grew the Indians' confidence in them, and they began to invite the missionaries to greater participation in their life and customs. "You speak Quichua better than we do," said Wakcha, a proud young Indian who always wore a pith helmet, a sign of great prestige among his people. "You hear us too well. We are talking away, saying to ourselves, 'They do not hear,' and then you answer us!"

Dr. Tidmarsh eventually left the forest to return to his family in the mountains, but before he went he gave Jim and Pete a few simple instructions about caring for the sick. On their own, they would have to give what medical aid they could with the help of medical books and prayer. Sick calls had to be answered. One night in January a distraught father came to them on behalf of his baby who was ill.

"Will you not stick it with medicine?" he pleaded. It had not taken the Indians long to learn the healing power of antibiotics for their frequent tropical infections, and they soon began to feel that unless they were injected, the missionary had really done nothing at all. It was useless for the missionary to try to explain that if a man had a bad case of worms, penicillin would not cure him. "Drinking-medicine" was not nearly so effective, in the Indian mind, as "sticking-medicine." This time, however, the baby's case seemed to be pneumonia, so Jim gave penicillin. The parents were satisfied that he had done what he could—but the baby did not show immediate signs of recovery. They fell back, then, on the greatest power they knew, the witch doctor. Jim asked if he might stay to watch the ceremony. "A bed was pointed out to me," he recalled later. "I was told they were going to drink *ayak waska* and that I was to stay on the cane bed and not turn on my flashlight.

"All lamps were extinguished by 8:30, and the three Indians who were to drink the herb, *ayak waska,* could be heard speaking across the room occasionally. I feigned sleep and drowsed but woke when one of the watchers sleeping on the floor beside me was roused to be alert to listen as the drinking passed and the 'swoon speech' expected. I heard the quick, steady, swish beat of what sounded like a bunch of dry leaves being shaken, and from somewhere, I cannot say if it was from the same source, the rather melodious whistle of the three-tone pattern so usual among them. This was interspersed with a spitting, retching sound, and the curious pop of the smoke blowing on the patient's head, as I had seen done earlier. (I had offered another injection of penicillin and been refused at supper time. The witch doctor insisted that we wait till morning.) The swishing and blowing and whistling were joined by an occasional heavy snore and I dropped off to sleep.

"At eleven I was awakened by an Indian playing a violin. We chatted. I checked the baby at midnight and was told that the witching had not amounted to much as the drinkers had not taken enough to do much talking. Fever seemed a little higher, breathing and general condition had not changed. Around one I fell asleep again. The mother and an old woman were awake, making applications of leaves and tobacco. Lamps and kerosene lanterns made things somewhat less eerie than earlier. I slept until the death wail awakened me at three. No struggle; just quit breathing. Made our third small coffin this morning."

These happenings gave insight into the life of these people. Superstition and fear bound them tightly. Would the New Testament answer the longing of the Quichua for freedom from fear, peace of heart, deliverance from evil spirits? The missionaries prayed and discussed these problems, but still they felt themselves foreigners—felt that they would always be foreigners. The Indian himself must be the answer—he must learn the Scriptures, be taught, and in turn teach his own people. To this end Pete and Jim reopened the missionary school at Shandia that Dr. Tidmarsh had been forced to close. Here in a one-room schoolhouse the youngsters of the community were taught to read and write so that ultimately they could read the Scriptures for themselves.

But there were others, Indians who had as yet never had one chance to hear the story which these boys listened to daily. Would God send Jim and Pete to take the message to the Aucas?

"The thought scares me at times," wrote Pete, "but I am ready. We have believed God for miracles, and this may include the Aucas. It has got to be by miracles in response to faith. No lesser expedient is a short-cut. O God, guide!"

CHAPTER IV
Infinite Adaptability

Ever since their college days, Jim Elliot and Ed McCully had wondered if someday they might work together on the mission field. When Ed, his wife Marilou, and their towheaded toddler Stevie arrived in Quito in December, 1952, it seemed that their hopes would be realized. The McCullys planned to stay in Quito for their required Spanish study and then join Jim and Pete in Shandia. In June, 1953, Ed left his family in Quito and made a quick trip to his future home in the jungle. He wrote to his folks in the States of the scenes he had witnessed:

"I have just returned to Quito, after spending twelve days in the jungles with Jim Elliot and Pete Fleming among the lowland Quichua Indians. If the Lord permits, we hope to be located there in a few months. During these twelve days, after viewing the Indian boys in school and the endless line of people seeking medical aid, after visiting Indian homes, after hearing the weird chant of witch calling, and the hopeless cry of the death mourners, I praise God for bringing us to this land to work with these people. I pray that we might be faithful to our calling and that God will use us to bring many of these Indians to Himself.

"I stood by the bed of an eighteen-year-old Indian boy in the eastern jungle. I watched him vomit blood and in a few minutes I watched him die. In that hour, as I stood looking at his lifeless form lying on bamboo sticks on the dirt floor of the hut, I was to realize more fully what Paul meant in I Thessalonians 4, 'Ye sorrow not, even as others which have no hope.' I will not soon forget the screaming-chanting wail of these heathen folk as they beat their breasts and mourned for two days and nights. It was a pathetic picture of 'no hope.' Tonight I pray a peculiar prayer . . . that God will spare the lives of these Indians until He enables us to bring to them the message of hope, of eternal life, of salvation in their own language."

Oldest son of a Milwaukee bakery executive, Ed McCully grew up in the Midwest, in a home which knew something of sacrifice for the work of the Lord. Ed's father was active in preaching, traveling throughout the United States, speaking of Christ to his business associates at every opportunity, and to Christian groups in many places. When Ed entered Wheaton College in the fall of 1945, it was not with the idea of becoming a foreign missionary. He chose business and economics as his major.

Six feet two inches tall, weighing one hundred and ninety pounds, he soon distinguished himself as star end on Wheaton's championship football team. His surprising speed for so big a man made him a track star as well. His track coach, the national champion miler, Gil Dodds, tells of an incident in Ed's senior year. Ten 440-yard men were in training for a special meet in Boston; from the ten, five would be picked to go. Ed wanted to go to Boston. So, in spite of the fact that he was a 100-220-yard man and had never run a 440 in his life, he asked if he could try out with the others. It was typical of Ed that he made the relay team by one-tenth of a second. "He was always coming through with the impossible when the chips were down," was Dodds' concluding comment.

Ed was at his best on the platform. His simple, direct approach to his audience enabled him, with no formal training whatever in public speaking, to win the 1949 championship in the National Hearst

Oratorical Contest in San Francisco, a competition in which over ten thousand students had competed. His essay on Alexander Hamilton was nearly memorized by his classmates, who insisted on his reciting it at every class gathering. When he came to the climax,

> *"And like a silver clarion rung,*
> *The accents of that unknown tongue,"*

the class would rise simultaneously and shout with Ed,

> *"Excelsior!"*

Such was the spirit which Ed, senior class president, had generated. Of his election my brother Dave wrote: "Ed was elected (or shouted in) without a contrary vote. I frankly doubt if anyone even entertained the idea of proposing anyone else for the position. It was a foregone and unanimously accepted conclusion."

The following year Ed McCully, having turned his thinking toward the bar, entered the law school at Marquette University. At the beginning of his second year there he took a job as hotel clerk at night, intending to spend the time studying. But God, who ordains men of His own choosing and moves in them to the accomplishment of His eternal purposes, had other plans. Ed told his Wheaton classmate Jim about it in a letter dated September 22, 1950:

"Since taking this job things have happened. I've been spending my free time studying the Word. Each night the Lord seemed to get hold of me a little more. Night before last I was reading in Nehemiah. I finished the book and read it through again. Here was a man who left everything as far as position was concerned to go do a job nobody else could handle. And because he went the whole remnant back in Jerusalem got right with the Lord. Obstacles and hindrances fell away and a great work was done. Jim, I couldn't get away from it. The Lord was dealing with me. On the way home yesterday morning I took a long walk and came to a decision which I know is of the Lord. In all honesty before the Lord I say that no one or nothing beyond Himself and the Word has any bearing upon what I've decided to do. I have one desire now—to live a life of reckless abandon for the Lord, putting all my energy and strength into it. Maybe He'll send me someplace where the name of Jesus Christ is unknown. Jim, I'm taking the Lord at His word, and I'm trusting Him to prove His Word. It's kind of like putting all your eggs in one basket, but we've already put our trust in Him for salvation, so why not do it as far as our life is concerned? If there's nothing to this business of eternal life we might as well lose everything in one crack and throw our present life away with our life hereafter. But if there *is* something to it, then everything else the Lord says must hold true likewise. Pray for me, Jim.

"Man, to think the Lord got hold of me just one day before I was to register for school! I've got my money put away and was all set to go. Today was registration day so I went over to school to let them know why I wouldn't be back. I really prayed like the apostle asked the Ephesians to pray, that I might 'open my mouth boldly.' I talked to all the fellows that I knew well. Then I went in to see a professor I thought a lot about. I told him what I planned to do, and before I left he had tears in his eyes. I went in to see another professor and talked to him. All I got was a cold farewell and a good luck wish.

"Well, that's it. Two days ago I was a law student. Today, I'm an untitled nobody. Thanks, Jim, for the intercession on my behalf. Don't let up. And brother, I'm really praying for you too as you're making preparation to leave. I only wish I were going with you."

Ed's period of boot-training came when he went with Jim Elliot to Chester, Illinois, in the winter of 1951. Besides the tent meetings and children's classes which they held in an attempt to preach the Gospel in that town, Ed frequently preached on a weekly radio broadcast which he and Jim shared. As the Apostle Paul wrote, "I am debtor both to the Greeks, and to the Barbarians; both to the wise, and to the unwise. So, as much as in me is, I am ready to preach the gospel to you that are at Rome also. For I am not ashamed of the gospel of Christ: for it is the power of God unto salvation to every one that believeth. . . ." So Ed believed and so he preached.

On May 16, 1951, he used civic law as an illustration in one of these radio messages. Ed's sermon explains better than most theological statements the belief shared by all five of the men who were ultimately to combine forces in Operation Auca.

"The fate of the criminal," Ed said, "is to fulfill the condemnation by being punished—for some this means serving a term of years, for others it means imprisonment for life, for others it means death. God's condemnation upon all sinners is death. 'The wages of sin is death. . . .' One sentence, and one punishment for those who do not believe.

"But, you say, God is a God of love. He will not punish anyone eternally. It is true that He is a God of love. And His condemnation does not in any way alter the fact. God is not willing that you or I experience the punishment we justly deserve. Therefore He offers us an escape, if we choose to accept it. At the price of His only begotten Son, God provided pardon.

"This is the simple, plain, and clear Word of God from His book, the Bible. 'He that believeth on My Son,' says God, 'is not condemned, but he that believeth not is condemned already, because he has not believed on my only begotten Son.'"

As in the days when the Lord Himself walked on the earth, the results were not startling. A few wrote to the radio station for further information. A handful of people professed conversion as a result of the meetings held in school auditoriums and tents. But Ed knew that he had been obedient to God in the work of those months. Just prior to going to Chester, Ed had accepted an invitation to speak at a young people's banquet in Pontiac, Michigan. God had more in mind than Ed had imagined. It was there that he met Marilou Hobolth, a pretty dark-haired pianist in the church where he was to speak. During the months in Chester, Ed sent more letters, no doubt, to Marilou than he had posted to others in several years. Early in the correspondence he wrote:

"I'm praying definitely for two things: first, that the Lord will give us wisdom in our relationship—even in the business of letter writing. Second, that as long as we've got anything to do with each other, that each of us will be an influence upon the other for closer fellowship with the Lord. I don't mean that we'll be *preaching* to each other—but just that our attraction for each other will be a means of attracting us more to the Lord. I know that's the way you feel too."

Their friendship ripened fast and in April Ed and Marilou became engaged. A few days later Ed wrote her:

"When you pray, ask the Lord definitely to show us where He wants us to spend our lives, and that we'll be willing to spend them there, even anxious to."

Ed's love for the girl he was going to marry was wholehearted: "When anybody speaks to me, it takes everything I've got to stay with them in conversation. It's the craziest sensation! I'm beginning to believe everything the poets and songwriters have to say about love!"

On May 29, 1951, he was writing: "One month from today you will have lost all your freedom and will be subject to my iron rule, my unflinching law, and my cruel command. You have exactly thirty-one days to reconsider. Do you think you'll really be able to put up with me for the rest of your life? It won't be easy. There'll be plenty of times you'll wonder why on earth you married me. Have you reconsidered? Now, let me tell you that I love you with all of my heart."

Marilou did not reconsider. They were married in June in her home church, the First Baptist of Pontiac, Michigan.

Ed's decision to become a foreign missionary led him to enroll at the School of Missionary Medicine in Los Angeles, where he spent a year of intensive study in tropical diseases and their treatment, obstetrics, dentistry, learning the fundamentals in order not only to be of help to the Indians, but also to keep himself and family in shape.

On December 10, 1952, with eight-month-old son Stevie, Ed and Marilou sailed for Ecuador, the country where God had indicated He wanted them to spend their lives.

In the jungle, Jim and Pete had been looking forward to the day when the McCullys would join them. They were building a house for them, along with other mission buildings. In the meantime, the McCullys were living in a stucco house in Quito with an Ecuadorian family, learning Spanish. It was not an easy life and they found themselves subject to discouragement and a sense of uselessness. "We ask in prayer that we might have aptness and accuracy in the studies, and grace to carry us over the 'hump' so we will be able not only to converse but also speak the Word of Life." Ed wrote to friends who had promised to pray for them. He and Marilou were eagerly looking forward to having their own home down in the jungle, and to getting into the work which they longed to do. One day Ed was called to the short-wave radio.

"I didn't read that transmission too well—did you say *all* of the buildings?" he asked. "Over."

"All of the buildings at Shandia have been destroyed by flood. *All* of the buildings at Shandia have been destroyed by flood. Jim and Pete would like you to come down as quickly as possible. Over."

"Okay. Okay. Tell them I'll be right down."

Ed McCully handed the microphone back to the short-wave operator. The message had been relayed to him from Shell Mera. Jim and Pete had sent a runner to Dos Rios, a mission station six hours' walk from Shandia. The missionaries there had informed Shell Mera by radio of the flood.

Ed was dazed. He walked over to the window and stood looking out across the valley of Quito, toward Antisana, the mighty snowcap between him and the little mission station he had visited only a few weeks before.

The mission station at Shandia had been wiped out. In one day of thunderous rising water, followed by a nightmare that lasted through the long hours of darkness, the rampaging river destroyed

45

everything. Five hundred hand-planed boards—each representing one full day's work for one man—stacked up for a new house, a new clinic, and a new school kitchen had disappeared in the night. Most of their personal belongings were saved but Jim and Pete's invaluable Quichua vocabulary manuscript was strewn all over the ground and tracked in mud. Three hundred and thirty feet were sliced off the end of the airstrip. It was a poignant reminder to the men of the temporal quality of their present "city."

Just as they had instinctively sought Ed's help, so now he turned to Marilou. "Babe, the whole station at Shandia has been destroyed by flood!"

Marilou was incredulous. Ed told her of the disaster and of Jim and Pete's having asked him to go down to the forest. She agreed immediately that this was the right course of action.

"But—what about you and Stevie?" he asked.

"Oh, we'll be fine," Marilou replied. "We'll just stay right here, and you let us know by radio whatever you plan to do. I'm sure it'll work out okay."

As usual, Ed was cheered by her spirit, and began making preparations for the trip. "Elliot," he had said one day to Jim, "I've married an efficient wife. She plans—and she makes me plan. And we get it done!"

She got him ready in record time, and soon thereafter he was seated on a canvas chair in the tent which Jim and Pete had pitched in Shandia. Discouragement gave way to planning and the young men quickly turned to rebuilding the mission station and getting things ready for the McCullys. As soon as possible, Ed went to Quito to move his family down. An excerpt from Ed's diary tells of their first days in the rain forest:

"September, 1953. We are well settled by now. Life gets to be a routine of buying, selling, treating sick, fixing kerosene and gasoline appliances, trying to learn a language. It's a fight to try to get time for the latter. Also time for Bible study and prayer. It's hard to stay on top of it all, hard to keep rejoicing, hard to love these ungrateful Indians.

It's hard to keep our primary purpose in view when we get so swamped with secondary things."

The life of a missionary calls for infinite adaptability—from winning a national oratorical contest to struggling with an unwritten language . . . from starring on the college football field to teaching a bunch of small Indians to play volleyball . . . from prospects of a law career in a North American city to a life in the jungle of South America Marilou, who had been director of music in a large church, slowly and carefully taught Indian children to sing two-line songs which she and Ed had written in the Quichua language. With all this, they were ready. They were fully prepared to be "fools for Christ's sake."

CHAPTER V
"Expendable for God"

A *vioneta uyarimun!* The little plane is coming into hearing!"

These words, shouted by the Indians, announced to Jim, Ed, Pete, and other missionaries in the Oriente that the bright yellow Piper of the Missionary Aviation Fellowship was about to land on the station airstrip. The most welcome sound in the jungle was the approaching hum of its engine. The missionary would interrupt his business for the morning—treating a baby for impetigo, selling a bottle of worm medicine, teaching a Bible class, or sawing boards for a building. There would be a grand scramble to clear the strip, the missionary would pace it for a final check of the surface, and then, when dogs and children were at a safe distance, the plane would glide onto the grass. As the prop stopped spinning, the door would swing open, and a sunburned, sandy-haired man with a wide grin and frank, blue eyes would hop out—Nate Saint, the man whose vision had changed missionary life in the jungle.

Nate would dig out the cargo listed for that station, checking aloud the list which his wife, Marj, had made out for him beforehand:

"Let's see—a sack of flour, fifteen gallons of diesel oil, meat, vegetables, two brooms, and the mail. Your penicillin is in the mail sack. Guess that's it. How's it going, Ed?"

As the two men talked beside the plane, Indians would eagerly gather round. One would stand rubbing one leg down the back of the other continually, to keep off the flies. A baby would cry, or a dog would escape from the captivity of a child—nothing would distract the Indians from looking at the plane, no matter how many times they had seen it.

And then, without warning, a tiny alarm would sound—Nate's watch! A methodical man, he had figured out exactly how much time he could spend in that station and still make his deadline home before sundown, or, if he had another flight scheduled, he would know precisely when he must take off for that. After piling and lashing down the empty diesel oil cans in the back of his plane for re-filling at his headquarters in Shell Mera, and rechecking his list, he would jump in, fasten safety belt and shoulder harness, wave good-bye, and take off. It was a bright spot in the week for the isolated missionary.

"Man, there's nobody like old Nate," Ed would say to Marilou, as they walked back to the house.

Truly the coming of Nate Saint with the Piper had marked the beginning of a new way of life on the isolated mission stations of this jungle area. Heretofore the missionary and his family would be completely cut off from the outside world long months at a time—four, six, eight days of heartbreaking struggle on dangerous jungle trail separated him from medical and other help. Then, one by one, airstrips were hacked from the jungle. Radio transmitters and receivers were installed, and the airplane, when it came, covered in five minutes the distance of a long hard day on the trail. Housing was vastly improved—from vermin-ridden bamboo and short-lived thatch to boards cut and planed by machinery brought in by air. Nate worked out a special frame underneath his plane for hauling sheets of aluminum. These provided a durable and easily-constructed roof. Electric light plants and fuel to run them, kerosene refrigerators, filing cabinets, stoves, power saws, and cement—all helped to make life in the jungle safer, healthier, and more efficient.

Nate and his wife, Marj, arrived in the Oriente in September, 1948. His first job there was to set up some kind of living quarters for himself and Marj in Shell Mera. A tent sufficed during the weeks he was building a small frame house, which soon became "warehouse-dormitory-toolshed." But the job of serving the missionaries was not allowed to wait until the Saints were comfortably settled. Nate had come down as a pilot of the Missionary Aviation Fellowship, an inter-denominational organization founded by two ex-Navy pilots whose aim it was to transport evangelical missionaries, their supplies, their sick, to and from remote outposts. Thus, by lightening the physical burden which the missionary carries because of the primitive nature of his surroundings, the MAF could give him more time and energy for his spiritual ministry.

Almost at once Nate started ferrying missionaries in his plane, transporting their cargo, making courtesy flights, and handling all the maintenance on the plane himself. Marj began entertaining all the missionaries and their visitors who came through Shell Mera. These were numerous and she was the only available hostess for miles around. She never knew whether supper should be cooked for two or twelve. "And they eat like harvest hands!" she said. "I cook what I think ordinary people would eat, and then double it."

For the stringent requirements of their unique job, Nate and Marj were eminently suited. Nate's appreciation of Marj's role was once expressed in a letter: "How glad I am to have you working at my side *always*. I have felt that I had sufficient 'snort' and drive for the sprints, but God knew I would need a flywheel to steady me for the long haul."

Nate's first concern in flying was that it should be safe, efficient, and economical: "Missionaries who used to travel the old trails made sure they weren't carrying anything that wasn't necessary. Today, in the airplane, we, too, make sure we don't carry anything that isn't necessary. When our mission bought the plane, it had nice, soft seats in it. But we found that these seats weighed almost eight pounds each So we decided to use harder seats that weighed only one pound, and take seven pounds of extra food and cargo."

Every ounce counted in a plane of this type. When Nate found that the streamlined wheel covers were collecting mud, he took them off. Characteristically, Nate turned this to spiritual illustration: "When life's flight is over, and we unload our cargo at the other end, the fellow who got rid of unnecessary weight will have the most valuable cargo to present to the Lord."

Nate had always regarded himself as "expendable" for the cause of Christ. In a short sermon delivered over the missionary radio station HCJB—The Voice of the Andes in Quito—he shared his belief with others:

"During the last war we were taught to recognize that, in order to obtain our objective, *we had to be willing to be expendable*. . . . This very afternoon thousands of soldiers are known by their serial numbers as men who are expendable. . . . We know there is only one answer to our country's demand that we share in the price of freedom. Yet, when the Lord Jesus asks us to pay the price for world evangelization, we often answer without a word. We cannot go. We say it costs too much.

"God Himself laid down the law when He built the universe. He knew when He made it what the price was going to be. God didn't hold back His only Son, but gave Him up to pay the price for our failure and sin.

"Missionaries constantly face expendability. Jesus said, 'There is no man that hath left house, or brethren, or sisters, or mother, or wife, or children, or lands for my sake and the Gospel's but shall receive a hundred fold now in this time and in the world to come eternal life.' "

However, Nate's convictions about expendability did not lessen that sense of caution which is ingrained in the fiber of any first-rate flier. On the contrary, his brain teemed with ideas for improving the safety of his plane. "I am trying to steer clear of gimmicking for the sake of gimmicking," he wrote. "Nevertheless, I can't help the gadgets that run through my head, but I do try to sort out stuff that might have some value."

One of the devices of real value which he put into operation was an alternate fuel system. He often tried out his ideas on his older brother Sam, an airline pilot with long experience in the field of aeronautics.

"As I sit about the jungle listening for the symptoms of trouble that I never want to hear," Nate wrote to Sam, "I have in the back of my mind little things like the fuel line that fell off in my hand in Mexico a few years back. The flare had broken off one end of the tubing, but natural spring tension had kept it in place. I also think of the quick work of mud wasps when they decide to plug up a fuel vent. To be sure, I am also impressed by the dire consequence to my passengers, not to mention my own bones, if I should come out on the short end somewhere over these tall trees."

While turning over in his mind methods of eliminating a breakdown in the fuel system, Nate was working one day at the hangar at Shell Mera when he noticed a truck en route to Ambato, high in the Andes. Trucks in that region were not common and this one had an additional attention-catcher. A small boy was clinging to the roof of the cab holding a five-gallon can of gas and a syphon, while an older boy sat on the front fender holding the lower end of the syphon, pointed in the direction of the carburetor under the partially opened hood. Whatever had caused the failure of the regular fuel system, here was a truck preparing for an ascent of six thousand feet, most of the way in second or third gear with a great deal of shifting, while a boy metered gas to the engine through a rubber hose!

Nate's lively imagination immediately transferred this method of feeding gas to his own need. He lifted the cowl of his plane, removed the temperature-gauge fitting from the intake manifold, and squirted in gasoline. Each squeeze on the gas-loaded tube produced a burst of power. Encouraged by his experimentation, he went into the kitchen and borrowed one of Marj's cooking-oil tins to use as an auxiliary three-gallon tank. To provide a streamlined fairing for the tank he sent an Indian boy for a piece of balsa wood, which the lad obtained by chopping down an eight-foot balsa tree. The tank and fairing were then strapped to the struts under the left wing. Salvaged fittings, strainers, and a screw-type valve finished the rig. Nate mounted the valve on the fire wall and extended a control rod to the instrumental panel. So far so good, but darkness forced him to wait until morning to test his homemade safety device.

He put in a sleepless night, thinking of various reasons why his idea was totally impracticable—but still there *was* that truck racing along in second gear without its normal fuel source. Then, too, from his long experience as a mechanic he knew that the complexity of a modern carburetor arises from the need to accelerate smoothly from slow speeds to higher speeds. And a dead engine in the air, he told himself, will windmill fast enough to stay out of those critical lower speeds.

The next morning, first tests proved that the alternate fuel system could work without a hitch on the ground. The moment had come to test it in the air. He described the experience:

"Two thousand feet above the landing strip I pulled the mixture control to idle-cut-off. It was quite a novel experience for a fellow who had listened so long, hoping never to hear it happen. But a turn of the new little T-handle on the instrument panel brought with it a wonderful feeling as the engine wound back up to smooth full-power. For the next twenty minutes the normal fuel source was shut off tight. Even though the carburetor was by-passed completely the engine never missed. It picked up from the windmilling condition without a cough.

"I put the plane into every imaginable attitude at various power settings. It never faltered. 'Feeling' for the best mixture setting with the emergency T-handle was no more difficult than 'leaning' the engine with the regular mixture control. Same thing.

"The whole rig, tank and all, weighs only four pounds. The only thing it has in common with the ship's fuel system is the engine. It takes care of all the common troubles such as clogged vents and broken lines. With the simplicity and low cost of a deal like this, why do we fly along with our only source of fuel supply in jeopardy at several points between tank and engine, and no alternative? We are all sold on dual *ignition*: why not an alternate fuel system for emergencies?"

With government permission, every MAF plane now goes out to the jungle a safer machine because it is equipped with Nate's alternate fuel system.

Another ingenious invention of Nate's has astonished many in the aviation world. He developed a method of lowering a canvas bucket from an airplane in full flight into the hands of a person on the ground. This "spiraling-line technique," as he called it, later made possible the first direct contact with the Aucas. A canvas bucket is let out behind the airplane on a line about fifteen hundred feet long. As the airplane goes into a tight turn, the bucket moves toward the center of the circle—the drag of the cord across the circle overcoming the centrifugal force tending to throw the bucket outward. As the bucket moves toward the center it falls until it eventually hangs almost motionless at the bottom or vortex of an inverted cone. Not only could the person on the ground receive mail, medicine, and small parcels, but, more important, could send messages or other things back to the airplane as the bucket is pulled up again. Sometimes Nate substituted a telephone wire for the cord, with a field telephone in the bucket. In this way he could talk by telephone to a missionary on a sandbar or in a jungle clearing in areas where there was no landing strip.

One of the essential safety measures was the maintenance at all times of short-wave contact with the plane. This was Marj's job. Whenever the plane was in the air, she stood by for regular checks of location, altitude, and fuel load. She checked on weather conditions in Shell Mera, and kept in touch with the missionary to whose station Nate was flying for a check from that end. Each missionary station was equipped with transmitter and receiver, and at seven o'clock every morning the missionaries called in to Shell Mera. If a medical emergency had arisen since the previous call, help could be obtained, and flights arranged for evacuating the patient. Routine supplies were ordered, and flights scheduled by means of this contact. It meant hours and hours of sitting by the radio, but Marj was as convinced that this was her share of missionary work as Nate was that flying was his. Thus on any morning a visitor to Shell Mera might have heard something like this:

"Shell Mera is standing by for Macuma, Macuma. Over."

"Macuma standing by. We'd just like to know how many carriers to have at the airstrip when our cargo arrives. Over."

"Good morning, Macuma. I think two will be enough. Over."

"Okay, thanks. And how is the boy we sent out to the clinic? Over."

"I'll phone the clinic and find out if he can come home on Thursday's flight. Incidentally, you'll be having a visitor on Thursday. A missionary just came in on the bus and would like to see a typical jungle station. Over."

"Okay, Marj. We'll be glad to have him. Better send us a little more food than our usual order this week, though. Over."

"Okay. Okay Macuma. Shell Mera calling Shandia, Shandia. Do you have any traffic? Over."

"Shandia standing by. No traffic, Marj. Over."

And so the morning would pass, Marj taking orders for food, supplies for the Indian schools, medicine for the dispensaries, standing by while one station talked with another, relaying messages from missionaries to the doctor, getting his answer by telephone and relaying it back to the missionary, and calling "56 Henry," Nate's plane, as he flew out over the jungle, carefully noting down his position every five minutes.

There were those back home who smiled at Nate's constant concern for safety. "After all," they said, "a missionary is supposed to trust the Lord!"

"Perhaps my reasoning *is* pagan, as I've been told," Nate wrote home. "I do believe in miracles. They are nothing to God, surely. But the question is one of finding the pattern that the Lord has chosen us to conform to. I wouldn't be here if I weren't trusting the Lord. Chances are that those who shrug it off by saying, 'The Lord will take care of you,' are the same ones who would hardly expose themselves to the bacteriological risks of working in a downtown rescue mission. Forgive me if I feel a little strongly at this point. I'm concerned about safety, but I don't let it keep me from getting on with God's business. Every time I take off, I am ready to deliver up the life I owe to God. I feel we should be quick to take advantage of every possible improvement in carrying out the job before us."

Besides facilitating the work of the jungle missionaries, Nate had a direct influence on the Ecuadorians at his own doorstep. He never appeared to be hurried, and many a national came to him just to talk, recognizing in him a love for God and a sympathetic heart which drew them. He improved steadily in the Spanish language, and was respected for this effort. Street meetings, Sunday school and literacy classes, personal chats—these things made Nate a missionary as well as a pilot.

Small contrivances to add to the convenience and pleasure of his family also took his attention. He built a concrete cistern to catch rain water from the roof, and also built up a lower outer wall so that the children—Kathie born in 1949 and Stevie born in 1951—could have a place to wade in the overflow from the larger tank. He put a bell-ringing timer on the washing machine to save Marj steps while she was at the radio. Dampness is a major problem in Shell Mera, so Nate created a drying room behind the kitchen by building the kerosene refrigerator flush with the kitchen wall and backing the heating unit into the little room, into which he also put the hot water heater. Thus clothes and other equipment could be kept dry.

What had brought a man with this inventive, ingenious turn of mind, with these modern technical skills, into the primitive jungle of Ecuador? Like Ed, Pete, and Jim, Nate came from a family whose guiding principles of life were rooted deep in the teachings of the Scriptures. As a small boy, he understood the personal implications of the New Testament, and placed his faith in Christ as the only ground for his hope of salvation. In the Saint home in Philadelphia, where Nate was born in 1923, movies and dancing were not allowed, nor any form of gambling, from pitching pennies to playing poker. But it was no monastery. The children went fishing, trapping, sledding in wintertime, and were allowed such adventures as sleeping out-of-doors. Nate blueprinted and built model gliders, boats, and locomotives. His older sister Rachel was "like a little mother" to him, reading him missionary books about Africa, Japan, India, and South America. His imagination fastened eagerly onto these stories, and he once said, "I don't expect ever to be a preacher, but someday I would like to talk to someone who has never heard about Jesus."

His older brother Sam took him flying when Nate was seven—so small that he had to stand on the seat to see out of the cockpit of the old biplane. From that time on he was captured by wings and the wide sky.

At thirteen he suffered a severe case of osteomyelitis in his leg, and enforced inactivity gave him time to think. Could it be that God wanted him to be a missionary?

Later he recorded: "Through high school everything was evaluated in terms of flying machines and all emotions were tuned to imagined air adventures. All else became almost unbearably confining, in fact, any occupation that keeps me where I can't see the sky for a day is still one of my rougher tribulations."

The four walls of the classroom finally did become unbearable, and in his senior year Nate took a daytime job in a welding shop and went to night school, completing his high school course in a few months. A job at a small airport, where he learned to fly small planes, took up the next six months. After this he worked in an airline overhaul shop and gained a mechanic's license. The next step was to sign up for the Air Force pilot cadet program. "It looked as though the Eagle was about to lay the golden egg!" he said. "Twenty-five thousand dollars' worth of pilot training!" By this time he had piloted a 40-horsepower light plane about eighty hours, but he had dreamed long of flying the big powerful planes of the military.

The night before he was to report for his first military flying instruction he became aware of pain around his old osteomyelitis scar. Yanking up his trouser leg, he knew the truth. It was inflamed. All his boyhood ambitions of the past years, wrapped up and focused on this shining opportunity to get into big-time flying, suddenly collapsed. "I didn't say a word to my roommate, but jumped into bed and turned out the light without a word. There I barred myself into the small, dark confines of my heart, which had now become a dungeon for solitary confinement. Except for the tossing, and choked, then sighing, respiration, no one would have known the thing that was almost overwhelming me. No fooling; I was heartbroken."

The shock of losing the opportunity of getting out of the flying "put-puts" into real airplanes left Nate in a state of numbness, not caring much about anything. When he came out of the hospital, the Air Force made him a maintenance crew chief. On this job he had time to burn and he used it for Bible reading, which he had neglected. One year after he was grounded, he was sent to Detroit on detached service to study new and larger engines that were soon to be on the line, and there, at a New Year's Eve worship service, he felt that the Lord was turning his heart to the mission field. "What was going on in the service wasn't important," he recalled later. "I wasn't hearing anything with my ears, anyhow. I pleaded helplessly with my Heavenly Father for the answer that stood between me and the peace that Jesus had said should be ours. Now, you've heard about people being spoken to by God. I don't know about the other fellow, but that night I saw things differently . . . BING . . . like that. Just as though a different Kodachrome slide had been tossed onto the screen between my ears. As soon as I could, I stepped out of the building and started out . . . just to get away from people. It was snowing and there was already a deep virgin snow on the ground, and the moan of city traffic had been muffled as it is when deep snow is around. A joy, such as I had never known since the night I accepted Jesus' forgiveness for my sins, seemed to leave me almost weak with gratitude. It was the first time that I had ever really heard that verse: 'Follow me, and I will make you to become fishers of men.' The old life of chasing things that are of a temporal sort seemed absolutely insane."

It was at this juncture, when Nate thought that he would have to say good-bye to planes and flying and buckle down to a couple of years of college in preparation for the mission field, that he heard of the Missionary Aviation Fellowship. He wrote to his mother: "Methinks the aircraft industry has suffered the loss of a 'big operator,' and the Lord has won for Himself a 'li'l operator.' "

Shortly after V.E. Day he was shipped out to Salinas, California, to work as crew chief with the Fourth Air Force. There he met the two ex-Navy pilots who had founded MAF. It sounded like the perfect, made-to-order spot for Nate Saint. He got hold of an old, beaten up, 40-horsepower airplane, fixed it up, and began flying in every spare minute—practicing, always practicing.

While he was still in the Army he met Marj Farris, whom he later described in a letter: "Among other blessings, the greatest. She had just finished her State exams and is now a practicing registered nurse in California. She is a graduate of U. of California at Los Angeles, an ardent student of the Word, and has a challenging love for the lost. She is the most selfless person I have met in my life except my Mother. She is a meek girl of deep conviction ready for service for the Lord of the Harvest. . . ."

When Nate was discharged from the Air Force he asked God specifically to show him his next move. Suddenly, he found himself with his first assignment with MAF. Early in July, 1946, he was asked to go down to Mexico to repair a plane that had crashed there during a landing. "When God took over my life a couple of years before," Nate said, "He had not defined my duties but somehow it seemed immediately clear that this was to be my first [missionary aviation] assignment." Less than two weeks after he accepted the job, he found himself near the Guatemalan border, in the town of Tuxtla Gutiérrez, with a knowledge of Spanish "limited to my childhood acquaintance with the Lone Ranger."

He knew he was something of a sight, with a duffel bag containing forty pounds of tools, plus all his worldly goods. He wondered, too, if he might have difficulty at the customs office—"It's not exactly usual for tourists to carry seven-foot airplane propellors under their arms."

"I tried to imagine the damaged plane. It wouldn't be too bad—a damaged landing gear, and probably a splintered prop. Little did I dream that I would later find two completely demolished wings in a bushel basket." The plane had crashed in the bush at the edge of a jungle airstrip. Pieces of wing struts, landing gear, and the panels had been brought out to the Tuxtla airport for Nate to rebuild. With the help of a Mexican cabinetmaker to whom everything had to be explained by drawings, he set to work to put the pieces together again. He was impeded by the fact that the blueprint he had been given did not match the plane and that a factory-made wing spar sent down as a replacement matched neither the blueprint nor the plane. When he had finally reassembled the parts, the problem arose of taking the wing panels out to the airstrip in the bush where the wrecked plane lay. It was not feasible to crate them and send them on the trail, where narrow canyon walls had to be scaled; the crates would never make the turns. So the wings were built up like a model plane kit, piece by piece without any glue, then each piece labeled, the whole works disassembled, tied up in bundles, and flown out to the jungle airstrip. When Nate got to the wrecked plane, he found that some parts had been stolen and that mud wasps had lodged in the fuel tank and lines. For lack of rigging data, he had to prop the tail up on a stump and rig the new wings to match the old by eye, just as he used to rig model planes as a child. Thus he finished his first MAF assignment, the plane being flown out barely within the work-permit time limit.

Later Nate went to Los Angeles and spent ten happy days with his little nurse. As he bade her good-by he said, "Well, Marj, as far as I'm concerned, it's all settled but the hardware!"

The winter of 1947–48 found him enrolled at Wheaton College, and in January Marj took a nursing job in a nearby town, studying Bible at the college in preparation for the missionary life they anticipated together. They started a Bible club for teenagers. Nate called the program "a sort of candy-box, loaded with Gospel dynamite."

But their training practice period was shorter than they had expected. The need of a pilot in Ecuador was presented to them. They cut short their courses, pooled their funds, bought an engagement ring and Model-A Ford, and set out one midnight for Long Island, New York, nearly a thousand miles away. They stayed with his brother Sam, and were married. After a four-day honeymoon, they headed their old Ford west, all their worldly goods stacked up in the back seat. Meals were cans of food heated on the engine. Finally they reached California and Nate began final work on a plane that had been purchased by the MAF for its operation in Ecuador. Marj took another nursing job.

On September 8, the plane was ready and Nate, with another MAF pilot, flew it to Ecuador, leaving Marj to follow later that month by commercial transportation.

The years at Shell Mera passed quickly. The house grew into a large chalet of dark wood, with spacious porches, wide eaves for protection against tropical rains, a running water system for kitchen and shower, connected with the rain pipes from the aluminum roof and with tanks under the eaves. After they raised the roof and built in a second story, there were ten bedrooms to accommodate the many guests who came through, and a radio room where Marj could work efficiently and where radio repairs for the missionaries could be made.

Another pilot, Johnny Keenan, arrived with a second airplane to help in the work, and Nate soon had a comfortable house well on the way for the Keenans, plus accommodations in the hangar for the two planes. He installed a hydroelectric plant down by the river behind his house to furnish electricity for the establishment.

They were now set up to operate with the greatest efficiency; jungle stations were all being supplied, and Nate and Marj began to ask God in what new way they might forward His work in the Ecuadorian jungle.

Nate, despite the unceasing load of responsibility that weighed on him, had never forgotten that the Auca Indians lived only some sixty air miles from Shell Mera. Shortly after arriving in South America Nate had written home: "Not long ago we talked with another missionary who is longing to reach a tribe of killers, the Aucas. Few white persons have contacted them in a friendly way and lived to tell about it. We expect the airplane to play an essential part in reaching these people with the Gospel." Nate used his plane to make an occasional survey flight over Auca territory, but not much was located on any of the flights—only a house or two which had been abandoned. He was beginning to wonder where they were. Then one day in July, 1954, the jungle grapevine carried the news that there had been another Auca killing and this time Nate became personally involved. He wrote home his own account of what happened:

"Yesterday I landed at Villano, about 45 miles west of here. Just after I got on the ground a runner came up and told me of an Auca raid. Later two Quichua survivors arrived at the airstrip. The woman was being carried on a bamboo stretcher and had a serious-looking lance puncture under the armpit. They told us that the lance broke off in the wound. Her attacker was going to jab her again but she grabbed the end of the lance and hung on to save her life. She is about six or seven months pregnant. The man arrived under his own power although considerably crippled up with chest punctures, a hole all the way through one thigh and a hole through his hand where he had apparently tried to stop one of the deadly shafts. We loaded the two patients onto the plane. Once in the air I told Marj what had taken place so that when we arrived here in Shell Mera she had cots set up and, with another woman helping, the Indians got the best care that local facilities would permit.

"We can't talk directly to our patients but our hired couple speak Quichua and converse easily with them. Last night our hired man read the Bible to them in Spanish, interpreting into Quichua as he went along. They had never heard of the Bible. Apparently the truth had not yet found its mark because this morning the man asked if I couldn't fly back out there in the plane and kill at least one of the Aucas for him. Again the hired man explained that we were not interested in taking life but rather in saving it through the Lord Jesus Christ."

Greatly as this incident intensified Nate's sense of urgency about reaching the Aucas, there were also other tribes whose ignorance of the Gospel offered a spiritual challenge to missionaries. In 1954 came an unusual opportunity for Nate to help push deeper into the dark reaches of the jungle. One of the key figures in this new page of missionary history was Roger Youderian.

CHAPTER VI
Missionary to the Head-Shrinking Jivaros

At Macuma, a mission station in the southern jungle served by the little yellow plane, lived Roger Youderian, his wife, Barbara, and their two children, Bethy and Jerry. Macuma, run since 1945 by Frank Drown, is reminiscent of a busy farm in the United States. As the plane comes in, chickens scatter off the airstrip, while cows continue chewing their cud undisturbed. Buildings are made, not of split bamboo, but of sturdy wooden planks, and an atmosphere of stability and permanence pervades the compound. Macuma is located in Jivaro territory. The Jivaros, whose lives are punctuated by fierce interfamily feuds, are famous the world over for their custom of shrinking human heads. They live throughout seven thousand square miles in the southern part of the jungle, independent of the white man who has nominally ruled their country for four hundred years.

Roger, tall and thin, with a shock of black hair, had been born on January 21, 1924, on a ranch near Sumatra, Montana, the seventh child of a ranching family. From his mother he received a devoted and thorough Christian training. Roger had been an active youngster, and on the way to becoming a good pianist, when polio struck him at the age of nine. This crippled him so that he not only lost his musical touch but for the rest of his life walked and ran like an old man.

In high school in Lewistown, Montana, he overcame the effects of polio sufficiently to play basketball. From high school, Roger went to Montana State College with three scholarships. He planned to become a teacher in agriculture. He was chosen the outstanding freshman of his year in 1942 and worked during the following summer drawing maps of farms around Lewistown that are still used by the Federal Land Bank. In October, 1943, Roger enlisted in the Army, eventually becoming a paratrooper. He was stationed in England where he became assistant to Army Chaplain Paschal Fowlkes, who wrote to Roger's parents: "Christian work in the Army is not greatly different from Christian work outside, in that the leader must learn to depend on a comparatively small number to carry the load and give inspiration to others. I thought you would be proud and happy to know that I count Roger one of those 'strong pillars.' " During this time in England, Roger's faith was deepened and strengthened and in December, 1944, we find him writing to his mother:

"The happiest day of my life was the day I accepted Jesus Christ as my Savior for the remission of my sins, duly repented for, and with God's help I hope and pray for the faith and strength to glorify our Father through my daily living as a witness and follower of Christ. Searching the Scriptures is my greatest source of hope and inspiration, having yet to learn the full power of prayer. I used to say, 'This is a great world.' With this new faith, this feeling has increased a thousandfold and I fairly ache within from happiness and rejoicing in sharing God's manifold blessing which He gives to this world with Infinite mercy and grace."

Roger survived the Rhine jump of 1944 and was decorated for action in the Battle of the Bulge. The idea of dedicating his life totally and completely to the Lord was taking root in Roger's mind and in August, 1945, he wrote from Berlin: "I've a secret to tell you, Mother, in this more than anything in the world I want the action to precede the announcement. Ever since I accepted Christ as my personal Saviour last fall and wanted to follow Him and do the will of the Lord, I've felt the call to either missionary, social, or ministerial work after my release from the service. Can't say now what the calling will be but I want to be a witness for Him and live following Him every second of my life."

Roger returned to Montana in January, 1946, and during that winter his conviction that he had been called to the mission field was confirmed. He enrolled in the College of Liberal Arts at Northwestern Schools in Minneapolis, where he met Barbara Orton, a quiet, fair-haired girl who was also studying Christian Education with the mission field in mind. She came from a Baptist family in Lansing, Michigan, and all her childhood she had heard of mission work, listened to missionaries speak at her church, and met them in her home. "I believe that the Lord just spoke to me, while I was a child," she says now, "and made me feel that that was what I should do." In September, 1950, Barbara and Roger enrolled in the missionary medicine course at Northwestern Schools. All winter they sat next to each other in a little classroom with nine other students, learning how to set bones, deliver a baby, give injections. They were engaged on Easter Day, 1951, and married in September. They were accepted as candidates by the Gospel Missionary Union, a nondenominational board, and left immediately for six months' probation work in Kansas City. Here they had Spanish classes, learned how to approach some of the practical problems of a mission station, took turns leading Sunday services, and worked with groups of children from the city slums.

In January, 1953, they set out with six-month-old Beth Elaine for Ecuador. After a period of Spanish study in Shell Mera, the Youderians went to Macuma. Frank and Marie Drown, senior missionaries at the Macuma station, had come to Ecuador eight years before from the farm country of Iowa. It was through letters written back to the States by Marie that Roger became interested in working with the Jivaros.

Once settled on the station to which God had sent them, Roger and Barbara plunged into a study of the Jivaro language and were soon able to help in the development of a method of teaching the Jivaros to read and write their own language. Roger made little pen-and-ink drawings of familiar sights—a sloth hanging upside down on a branch, a blow gun, a lizard lazing on a tree trunk—and next to the drawing he printed the sound of the Jivaro words.

Although Roger had come to preach the Gospel there is much a missionary must accomplish and learn before he can expect to make successful contact with a primitive tribe. And even after he has mastered the language, built himself a home, gained the confidence of the Indian, he still has to spend a large amount of time in what is best described as maintenance. The jungle grows with incredible speed and therefore has to be kept at bay by the constant use of the machete. The generators that are used for current at the bigger stations break down with irritating frequency, roofs leak in the hard tropical rain, and the only person who can cope with all this is the missionary himself. Roger's skill as a carpenter and his pleasure in this kind of work stood him in good stead when he first came to Macuma. Barbara wrote: "Roj is in his glory in Macuma; they have two men sawing boards, two fellows are planing, two are grooving, two more sawing and planing 2 by 4's. Roj has his power saw going and they have poured pillars to set the house on. Roj has planted 74 tomato plants from the seeds he got from the station in Costa Rica."

It was not to do construction work, however, that Roj had left his home. Soon he was driving himself to reach the Jivaro Indians with the Gospel. A fiercely independent people, the Jivaros combine warlike hostility and a boisterous sense of humor. "All they do is laugh and spit," said one missionary in describing them. They seem to laugh with little provocation, and have a way of punctuating their conversation by spitting through the second and third finger with an explosive sound. Like the Quichua, the Jivaro never tires of pressing his face to the screen of the missionary's window, watching all that goes on inside. Roj became accustomed to this after a short time, though he found their *sotto voce* comments and sudden outbursts of smothered giggles upsetting at first.

Wearing shorts, a sweat shirt, cotton cap, and canvas leggings and sneakers, Roger spent much of his time visiting Jivaro houses. He followed the twisting and exhausting jungle trails, more often than not knee-deep in mud. He might pause sometimes, arrested by an indescribably sweet fragrance, sweeter than orange blossom, but because of the forest, he would be unable to locate the source. The most striking flowers are found high up in the treetops, nearly smothered by the ubiquitous green foliage. He would also have to be on his guard against the most dangerous of jungle fauna, the snakes. Protective coloring renders many varieties almost impossible to detect. The tiny viper may lie in the center of the path, but the dappled pattern of its skin so blends with the pattern of sunlight on fallen leaves that the traveler seldom sees it. The bushmaster carries enough poison in his sacs to kill one hundred men. The coral snake, whose poison attacks the central nervous system and causes death without previous symptoms in twenty-four to forty-eight hours, is one of the smaller species, and therefore more difficult to see. Suddenly, the forest path would end and Roger would step into a clearing, his eyes blinded by direct sunlight after the twilight zone of the jungle. Each Jivaro house stands in its own clearing. It is oblong-shaped, a narrow slit about five feet high at either end serving as window and door, and covered with a palm-thatched roof of pointed leaves whose fringe almost touches the ground.

Strict rules of etiquette govern the behavior of the Jivaro host and the visitor who enters his clearing. A formal greeting, which may take ten or fifteen minutes, is proper. It is a series of utterances which may go something like this:

"I have come."

"You've come?"

"Yes, I've come to your house."

"You have come well."

Roj learned that no matter how many people are present, the newcomer goes through this dialogue with each one.

Bending his head to get his five feet eleven inches through the slit, he would enter the murky interior through which he could just barely see the dim figures of women moving about at the far end of the house, trailed by several little naked children. Hard-packed earth serves as a floor in these houses and small fires glow at intervals down the long thirty-foot interior, the smoke creating an acrid odor and adding to the lack of visibility. The Jivaro house is strictly divided between the men's section, the front part, known as the *tangamash*—somewhat the equivalent of the small-town front porch, a place where men can sit and gossip for hours on end— and the back part of the house, which is exclusively for the use of women. The women wear a long piece of cloth that hangs down straight to the knees, the two ends tied at one shoulder. The men are bare-chested but wear a cloth tied around their waists. Like the Quichuas, the Jivaros have long, straight black hair. It hangs loosely around the women's faces, little attempt being made at any kind of coiffure. The men, as befitting their position as superior beings, go in for an elaborate hair-do. The waist-long hair is combed and then dressed in bright red, yellow, or blue tropical bird feathers.

Roger would be invited to sit down on a bench alongside the wall, and facing him, on a low stool, sat the head of the house. If the man were trying to impress his visitor with his position, he would go through an elaborate charade for the first five minutes before he permitted conversation to begin. One of his two or three wives would bring him a bowl of water, from which he took a mouthful but not to swallow. He spat it out over his hands and then washed his face with his wet hands. After that he combed his hair slowly and deliberately. The entire performance was carried through wordlessly and with dignity and deliberation. He would then be served his chicha, the bowl offered to his guest and conversation begun. Thus Roger spent many hours talking to the Jivaros in their houses, slowly acquiring their language, absorbing their way of life, and above all, telling them the story of Jesus.

Among the Jivaros, witchcraft and sorcery, hate and murder, take deep roots early in life. Children as they fall asleep at night are taught to repeat a list of names of those they must learn to hate. Writing of the tribe, Nate said: "They aren't cruel except that they are made that way by the religion of fear and evil spirits with which they hope somehow to cope with their sin problem. For instance, a witch visited the Macuma Indians a couple of months ago. He was from another section of the forests. For some reason or other he got mad and cursed a certain woman. Usually Jivaro difficulties are over women, who are soulless possessions of the man and are frequently stolen or traded in business deals. At any rate, the woman that had been cursed died within twenty-four hours. Her husband, brothers, and father then felt duty bound to avenge her blood because the witch was as guilty as if he had shot her outright. They went over to the other tribe and brutally killed the witch and another fellow. The thing is a couple of months old now so life goes on as usual but one of these days there will be another killing. It's routine in the Jivaria. There's no end to the killings. The miserable part is that to pay off these debts, as they call them, they don't necessarily have to kill the very murderer himself—any relative will do. Their consequent fear determines even the construction of their houses which are very much like military fortresses. They often put traps in the trails for their suspected enemies. Not long ago one missionary in the Jivaria was out doing visitation work in the jungles. His barefoot carrier was in front and as they approached a Jivaro clearing, he pulled up to a sudden, painful halt. A needle-sharp palm wood spike was sticking out of the top of his bloody foot."

These were the people with whom Roger had lived for over a year. He had learned their language on the Macuma station, and helped make up primers for the literacy program. At times the atmosphere of vengeance and murder affected Roger deeply, but with typical energy he kept driving ahead. Nate Saint once said of him: "Roj is one of the few missionaries I know who display a real sense of urgency in the task of winning souls."

Now this sense of urgency was prompting Roger to consider making a move. Knowing that Frank Drown could carry on the work of this established station alone, Roj began to pray for a wider sphere of service, as the Apostle Paul wrote: "[It is] my ambition to preach the Gospel, not where Christ has already been named, lest I build on another man's foundation."

CHAPTER VII
Breaking Jungle Barriers

Among the tribes where Christ had not yet been named were the Atshuaras, first cousins of the Jivaros but their deadly enemies. Roger prayed often for an opening in this group and talked it over with Nate, who had shared his concern for some time. Frank and another missionary had tried to contact them five years before. On that occasion, Frank and his colleague had almost reached the house of the chief when they were met by a boy carrying a verbal message: "If you do not turn around at once, you will be killed." The reputation of the chief was such that there was no doubt about the accuracy of the message. The missionaries turned around.

Roger finally decided to move closer to the Atshuaras. On June 5, 1954, he left Macuma and traveled southeast two days on foot to a place called Wambimi, where the Shell Oil Company had abandoned an airstrip and a few dilapidated houses.

"This location is particularly important as a possible doorway [to the Atshuaras]," he wrote. "It was marvelous how the Lord worked for us in preparing this outstation. He enabled us to erect a new building 20 by 60 feet, with a permanent roof to augment the small houses already available on the spot. He protected us in those eleven days from snakes (I stepped on one), scorpions, tarantulas, injury, complications from nails, from roofs caving in while dismantling old buildings, et cetera."

The airstrip needed only a little grass-cutting, and was ready for Nate's plane to land. Nate recorded the subsequent events on magnetic tape: "We flew in Barb and the two children, and they set up housekeeping, started language study and literacy work among the local Jivaros as well as evangelism. While Roj was down there, as any missionary does, he carried on medical ministry. One of the sicknesses that plagues the Jivaro is leishmaniasis. It affects nasal cavity, nose and the back of the throat, the roof of the mouth. It's a hideous disease that is long and drawn out, eventually kills them and, of course, is very shameful—it disfigures the face terribly and the Indians dread it with a passionate dread. Several years ago missionary doctors ran down a cure, a drug called 'Repodral.' Roj had some with him and he scored a couple of notable cures among the local Jivaros. Despite the continual running feuds that go on between the Jivaros and Atshuaras, as well as within both groups, there is some li-aison on the trail and word of the cures got across the line to the Atshuaras. One of the chiefs over there in the Atshuara country was called Santiaku (a chief in this case as in most jungle situations is just a Number One man in a given small area; Jivaros and Atshuaras don't group up; they're scattered all over Timbuktu and the fellow that's the strongest or the most feared in a small area is a chief). The chief, Santiaku, had come down with this dread disease, and despite fear and happenings of the past, he finally showed up at Wambimi. And, of course, it was a milestone and a cause for great rejoicing because it was an answer to prayer. Roj did help him; the Repodral helped his nose condition and he showed up again later and invited Roj to go back to his house. Of course, this is what everybody had been waiting for, but as in the case of the spider and the fly, Roj wasn't going to accept this offer carelessly. So he said to Santiaku, 'Okay, I'll come over to visit you at your house if you come and take me over there.' And so, good enough, the escort did come and escorted Roj

Youderian, Frank Drown, and another missionary into Atshuara country.

"Somewhere along the way Frank coughed and the Atshuaras stopped right there; that was as far as they were going to go because they are deathly afraid of catching cold. Apparently it's a cold or grippe—what we call flu—that kills them off because they haven't much resistance to it, the disease never having touched their group while the generation was younger. It was with great difficulty that Frank convinced them that he was just clearing his throat. Frank says that that night when they were camping along the trail somewhere he felt a tickle in his throat again and he just didn't know what in the world to do, so he feigned that he had business off in the bush and got away from them and cleared his throat, fearing, of course, that he might break up the whole expedition by coughing and being heard by the Atshuaras.

"When they got to Santiaku's place it turned out to be a great big house, about three times the size of the long Jivaro houses. Roj says it was just big enough to put a basketball floor inside. The Atshuaras speak a somewhat different dialect but understand Jivaro, their facial features are different, and the women have narrow hips, instead of wide hips like Jivaro women. When they got there, Frank started to give them the Gospel in Jivaro, telling them of the love of Christ and how he had died for us. It was a question of giving these Indians a story from scratch that they had never before heard any suggestion of. Frank talked until he was hoarse and exhausted. They had a little wind-up phonograph with them and they played Gospel recordings made in the Jivaro language and they would play these until Frank got his voice back and then the Atshuaras would say: 'All right now, Panchu (an affectionate Spanish nickname for Frank), tell us more.' And for three days, the Atshuaras went on like that—just sitting around, listening to the story of Christ, a most amazing opportunity and Santiaku showed real interest.

"Because of the isolation of the Atshuaras and the tense situation with the neighboring Jivaros, it seemed as though the key to getting in there and actually doing some good was air communication. Frank suggested right off the bat that they build themselves an airstrip. It seems to me that it was a really bold stroke of genius and I'm sure I wouldn't have had the faith to suggest it the very first time. The idea took hold—the Lord blessed the suggestion and brought it to fruition, because they started cleaning an airstrip; the missionaries, while they were there, showed them where they could cut down the trees in line with their manioc patches, so that they would have some natural approaches to take advantage of the forest they had already cleared. Then the missionaries retired.

"After several months, we thought it time to encourage the Atshuaras, so we flew down over there to see how they were coming along and found that they had cleared about 100 yards of the jungle floor for an airstrip. But 300 feet with trees standing all around it, trees that grow to 100, maybe 120 or 150 feet, is hardly an airstrip. So we dropped them a couple of pieces of cloth to encourage them, and then we went away again and a few more months went by.

"The other day we went down and had a look again. And to our disappointment we found that the direction of the strip in the forest was such that it was lining right up with the great big house, and, of course, it's not ideal to have a house sitting right on one end of a strip in the approach. And the work didn't seem to have gone very far— looked like they needed help at this point. So we went back and had a short council of war and Roj said: 'Well, it sounds to me like they need help and I think I should go.' He had a little hand-crank radio, but he didn't have enough provisions. He really hadn't contemplated such a trip at all. Well, I guess he had a machete. But the need was there, the opportunity was there, and he could be there within two days' walk. He decided to try to get some Jivaro to help him carry the radio and guide him over the trail from Wambimi to the Atshuara country.

"We left Roj at Wambimi on a Wednesday and on Thursday we listened on the radio for him. We thought it might just be that he would have set it up along the trail somewhere or maybe he was still in Wambimi. We didn't hear from him on Thursday, Friday, or Saturday. Monday we thought surely we'd hear from him—that he'd be with the Atshuaras and surely be on the air. We still didn't hear a word from him and there he was with no other missionary, but with those unconverted Jivaros who were known to be rascals. And, I guess many of them out there have killed—they're killers and some have survived killings—not the choicest group to have for company on a dangerous trail. At any rate, we decided on Monday when we didn't hear from him that we ought to go in and check on him and make sure he was all right. So we assembled provisions, notes to drop him, food, and medicine. And we took out the air-to-ground telephone. Frank and I went together in the airplane. We flew with the door off, of course, so we could operate the telephone if necessary. We got down there and when I first saw the strip my heart sank. In the first place, because I couldn't see right off the bat that anything at all had happened to it—and I knew that if Roj had gotten there, something would have happened to that strip, because Roj just doesn't have anything in hand very long before something happens to it—especially if it needs something to happen to it. Then I started looking around for a white shirt. We looked for several anxious minutes before we finally distinguished him down there on the airstrip. I'll tell you for sure, I hadn't realized how anxious I was about his safety until that moment when I looked for him and the thing was in the balance—either yes or no. Then I realized how concerned we had been about him on the trail, with just a Jivaro guide and a few provisions. There are snakes out there. But we saw him and our hearts were very rejoiced by seeing him.

"We made a couple of low passes over the field. First we flew low over and throttled back the engine to quiet it down and I shouted down to Roj to ask him to get the Indians off the strip, that we had some stuff to drop to him. He heard us perfectly and cleared the Indians out of the way. We made about four runs, dropping the food and some axheads and cloth to the Indians as gifts for them. We needed to know what the situation was down there, so we pulled up and put out the telephone on a double-wire cable, using the spiraling-line technique. We reeled out about 1,500 feet of telephone cable and then started to circle. The telephone on that long line duplicated our circling, then slowly slid toward the center and began to drop. Finally it hovered, drifting around in a slightly unruly way, its horizontal velocity perhaps six or eight miles an hour, while we above were circling at sixty miles an hour. With a little trial and error and compensating for the drift, we were able to finally get the phone down close to Roger. I heard Frank's voice saying: 'Hello, Roj; hello Roj,' and I knew that we had contact with him down there.

"Frank talked with Roj for about ten minutes there on the phone, getting data from him. And then he apparently had all the information he needed and we started to pull up to put tension on the line. Meanwhile, Roj had tied his mailsack on to the cable—his outgoing mail and a note to his wife—and turned the phone loose. It went soaring up just about vertically, cleared all trees and we had it trailing behind us on the end of 1,500 feet of wire that we then had to reel in. We waved good-bye to Roj and shoved off for Wambimi."

When Nate landed again in Wambimi, Frank informed him that Roger had asked for a landing on the following Friday. "It's impossible!" said Nate. "The strip won't be ready. But then," he added, "I guess that's not my department. I'd better get in there as requested and then decide whether or not the strip is landable."

Roger had also explained over the ground-to-air telephone that he needed medicine. The Atshuaras had contracted the flu from a group of soldiers who had passed through. This accounted for Roger's not having a radio. The Jivaro who had promised to carry it in had gotten wind of the sickness among the Atshuaras, and knowing how deadly flu can be, refused to go near the place.

"Friday came along and I was getting kind of keyed up about this business of inaugurating a new field," Nate continued on the tape recorder. "It isn't child's play; it isn't a Sunday school picnic, as they say; it is a very serious business, where you have to do your best possible calculating and double checking on everything and then trusting the Lord—go in and do your duty.

"Friday morning woke up, as they say in Spanish, raining. By noontime we knew that it was out of the question for the day; the field would be wet anyway, and we can't add mud to the other unavoidable hazards of such an operation, so we canceled out for that day. We took it that it was God's indication that it was not the day to go and we left it pending for the next day. The next morning we made the preparations and Frank and I flew down to Wambimi after lunch. Frank got out and we unloaded the extra cans of gasoline and I took off alone with a very limited supply of gas. The airplane was completely stripped, with even the right seat taken out, so that it was as light as you could possibly get and have enough gasoline to be safe. I had a safe reserve—perhaps an hour and a half of gasoline aboard, and the round trip over to Santiaku's place and back would have been about forty minutes; so I had a hundred percent reserve."

Taking off, Nate headed for a little river halfway between the Macuma River and the Pastaza, which was the only landmark for Santiaku's place. When he found it, figuring he must be south of the spot, he turned north, scanning the horizon near and far in search of the little island in the sea of green. Nothing. Suddenly, just below him, he saw a little house—of the square stockade style, but without a *chacra* [an agricultural clearing in the forest].

"That's strange," thought Nate. "Maybe it belongs to some Indian who's just killed somebody and is lying low here for a while. Probably his *chacra* is off somewhere else, to confuse the enemy."

Mystified, he kept on. Ah—there it was! He called in to Marj on the radio:

"56 Henry—I'll be over Jimmy's place in two minutes. 56 Henry—I'll be over Jimmy's place in two minutes. Over." Since Santiaku is a form of the Spanish name for James, they had nicknamed the spot for secrecy.

"Lo and behold," Nate's record continued, "when I got over it two minutes later, there was no airstrip there! Looked just like his place, but no strip. That was a little disconcerting, because I didn't have a great deal of gas along, so I flew a little farther north and climbed on up, gaining altitude, trying to decide what I should do. I decided I'd better beat a track for Wambimi. Landed there around four-thirty. I hadn't been in a hurry before, because I wanted to get to Jimmy's place late in the afternoon when the air is cool and buoyant. It's steadier for this type of operation. Frank was a little surprised to see me back so soon. I described the house I'd seen and he recognized it as one they'd passed on the trail to Santiaku's. He passed me about five gallons of gas, and I took off, heading due east, picked up the little river and turned south."

Nate's blue eyes squinted through the plexiglass. Visibility that day was about a hundred miles, and "you can almost imagine you see steamship smoke on the horizon," but in all that expanse there was not a sign of life.

"I went south," he continued. "I went farther south. I was really beginning to make bets that I had never seen anything before, and goodness, I thought, there's no percentage in this! About that time I stumbled onto a house that was on a river bank, well stockaded, and the way that house was situated you just wouldn't see it unless you flew directly over it, that's all. Tucked down there in the forest, it was made differently from the other houses that I'd seen, Quichua or Jivaro. I didn't feel that I was exactly in a friendly neighborhood. I decided that the Lord's hand must be in this somehow (I was farther south than I had ever flown on survey)."

Even though Nate by this time was greatly concerned about finding Roger, he looked this new house over carefully and made a mental note about its location, "because they would need to hear the Gospel, too, way out there in their isolated places. You feel convinced that it is the will of the Lord that we do everything possible, that each Indian have an opportunity to know of the grace of God, and to hear that Name that is above all other names.

"So I went on. I felt buoyed up by the challenge of the very isolation of these people and the challenge to help other missionaries to get the Gospel to them, so the risk involved seemed to be offset and justified by the spiritual challenge of the situation."

Nate kept on flying till he figured the gas load was getting down. Then he switched on his transmitter:

"56 Henry to Shell Mera. I've looked up and down the river. Can't find Jimmy's place. I'm turning around now, heading upstream, gaining altitude. Do you read, Shell Mera? Over."

"Okay, Okay," came Marj's answer, and Nate started looking for smoke on the horizon, for surely he must be in Atshuara country, and if Roj had heard he'd get a smudge going.

Presently he saw it—there, apparently to the southwest, was a column of smoke. But it seemed to be in the wrong direction. Was his compass off? Or was it that he was not as well oriented as he had thought he was? The situation seemed incongruous, but, Nate thought, "once in a while you get in a situation like that, and the answer, when it comes, is a kind of surprise. So with that in mind, and with the fact also that where there's smoke there's fire, and where there's fire there are people, I decided to trust the Lord and head out across the stuff and see what in the world was producing that smoke. When I got there, I was well rewarded, but not in the way I'd expected.

"Down a steep bank that had been cleared, in a little hidden river, set in the trees, there was a little flat place. And down in the flat place, sunken way down deep, was a big house, with rounded ends, and Indians all over the clearing." Again Nate made a mental record for future use. After a quick look, with gas getting low, "I rolled out of the turn and started climbing and looked to the left, and, I'll be switched, there was a great big house, bigger than the one on the bank of the river, tucked down in there just off to one side. I just don't know how in the world it is that you can't see something until you're right on it. It's like hunting needles in a haystack."

Nate then started climbing, still circling. "I thought it just possible that if I got up really high, where I could look down into those little barrels of isolated pockets of mankind," he said, "I just might see some more interesting things. I was all eyes and quite excited over these finds and thrilled to find myself completely thrust into the arms of the Almighty, because down there there's no question at all about that. If that old engine had quit up there, God alone could have saved me. I might just as well admit it frankly right here; I don't like to fly over stuff like that and I have to have a pretty good reason to be over it without a good position-check and a good river to identify my position by. But these are people for whom Christ died, and you have to find them before you can take the Gospel to them, so I was happy to have stumbled on them.

"I had one last look around before turning over to Wambimi and on that inspection I noticed a little blemish, off to the east, and I thought I could afford to fly a minute or two and see what it turned into. And so I did. And within two minutes I could distinguish a house and then a few seconds later I could see a clearing; some solid earth behind some trees, some tall trees that indicated that it was Jimmy's place, and there, completely hidden behind those tall trees, was the runway. I finally realized I'd had all this trouble finding the place because the late afternoon sun was hitting the low ridges at a different angle than I had been used to on previous trips over the area. Anyway, when I saw that clearing I got on the radio, but quick, and started down. That old airplane really let down in a hurry and when I looked over at the vertical speed indicator I was clocking about 1,500 feet a minute. I was spiraling down at a good clip, reporting in to Shell, getting confirmation of the position, circling over the clearing and having a look—a heart-saddening look—at the strip. It just wasn't what you would describe as an airstrip at all. My heart sank. I knew Roj needed to get out of there, because I know the way he works; he never spares himself. He'd been in there a couple of weeks almost and I knew he would be a wreck and needing badly to get clear of the place. So I was anxious to do my best, consistent with safety and our responsibility to MAF and the other folks that MAF serves.

"While I circled back I shook my head and said to myself, audibly: 'No, that just is no good; it's just impossible.' Nevertheless, I figured I owed Roj a better look, so I came by low a time or two, and one time I was about to cut the engine and yell down to Roj and tell him: 'I'm sorry; it's no soap.' But I went on by and took another look at it. He had it nicely marked with bandage material. He had 50 yards on the lead end toward the big house marked off, and then he had a line with the words 'WHEELS' on it. I knew I could touch down from where the 'WHEELS' sign was. Down at the far end he had marked off 250 yards. Then I got to thinking that I can't just say 'no' on a hunch; but I can, too. Sometimes a hunch saves a fellow's life, when a slide-rule says 'yes' and a hunch says 'no.' So I thought: 'Well, the airplane is light; about 250 yards more or less of strip; maybe I should try one approach.' The air certainly was quite steady and I thought that if I could get down there closer it might look different. So, I prepared to buzz the field, let down steeply over the trees, and down over the roof of Santiaku's house, going about a hundred miles an hour. When I got down in there, there was one tree sticking out along the edge of the strip, and I said to myself as though someone could hear: 'Roj, man, this thing does have wings sticking out,' and I pulled up and got to thinking the problem over. The surface looked all right; I trusted Roj on that; I know he's careful about making sure that there are no soft spots; he's been through two other strip inaugurations with me. That is to say, he's gone ahead to prepare and check the ground, so I felt confident.

"There wasn't much time left; I was well down in gas again; so, 'Here goes,' I said to myself, 'maybe I can get by that tree.' And then the thought came to me that I might not be able to get out of there later. I figured that between the two of us, with the Indians, we could fell enough trees in a couple of days to get *out* of there. The radio was working on the airplane; I could tell Marj where we were; I told Barb that Roj was okay. 'Okay,' I called in quickly, 'preparing to land at Santiaku's place.'

"I reeled the antenna in, slowed the plane down, and put it in the approach toward the trees. As I cleared the trees, I took it into a very steep sideslip, pulled the flaps into full position, and cleared Santiaku's house by about 15 to 20 feet. As I measured the situation, I wasn't measuring just the tree sticking out but the whole thing, seeing everything at once. As a matter of fact, I didn't even see that tree; at least, I wasn't conscious of it. In a situation like that a pilot's subconscious drives him pretty much. It's a kind of automatic pilot that takes over because you haven't time to think out individual problems. They had been thought out while I was circling above, thinking through objectively and I'd decided that I could go in there safely and, as an old-timer said, from there on 'the seat of your pants guides you.'

"I went on in there and I slipped that plane just as steep as she'd slip—a pretty solid forty-five miles an hour; I straightened out just over the 50-yard rough stretch, plunked the wheels down just beyond the 'WHEELS' sign and got stopped in a little over half of the 250 yards that was available.

"I thanked God first of all for my being on the ground safe and sound. Naturally, the first thing you do in a situation like that is to get the trailing antenna out and transmit the news of the successful arrival without accident or incident to Marj and other loved ones and colleagues who are listening on their radios prayerfully. But this time I didn't. It never came to mind; there were too many things happening there too fast.

"Roj came running up and said, 'Have you got any medicine?' 'Yes, I answered; 'it's in here,' and I tossed him the sack. I had it all bundled up ready to throw out of the plane. There wasn't any 'Hello, I'm glad to see you' or 'Dr. Livingstone, I presume' sort of stuff. Roj was haggard; he had a week's beard; a dirty tee-shirt, ripped full of holes; he was a really pitiful sight; emaciated. He was at the bundle, tooth and nail, taking that stuff out. Then he started shouting at the top of his lungs—voice almost breaking—to the Indians down the strip, barking orders. I've never seen Roj behave quite like that. I know that he can snap at people when things are tight, but in this case didn't know quite what to make of the whole situation, so I grabbed him kind of firmly by the arm and said: 'Slow down now, Roj; slow down; we've got time.' He looked up out of those eyes and said, 'We *haven't* got time; we *haven't* got time.' So I didn't argue with him. He handed me two bottles of penicillin and said: 'Here, shake these,' so I did. He was barking orders at the Indians and I thought to myself, 'My goodness, how on earth can these people think he's a friend when he talks to them like that?'

"The first thing I knew, everyone and his brother were getting shots. It was soon evident that just everybody was sick with grippe. Some of them looked as though they were ready to die right there while we were working with the medicines. I did what I could to help Roj. Santiaku was sitting on a log, stoop-shouldered, looking sick, painted up 'fit to kill,' doing his best to look like a chief, but very, very sick. Roj told me while he was 'shooting' that one of the chiefs had already died the week before. When he got there he had shot all the worst cases and they recovered and this was the next batch of light cases that were getting worse and worse and the people—well, you can imagine how they felt without any medical help.

"We had two little bottles of penicillin. How precious those bottles were, standing between life and death. When Roj threw down the first bottle, I said: 'Take it and try to see if there isn't another drop in it.' Mothers would shove their little bare-bottomed babies toward Roj. He'd give them a swipe with a cotton swab of alcohol. It was just a tiny bottle that Roj might so easily upset because his hand was shaking like a leaf. He'd holler out at the Indians: 'Now, don't move,' and everybody just obeyed his orders. He was the chief in that outfit, at the moment, the real master of the situation. There was no question about it."

Roj peered into the faces of the Indians as they came along. The graver cases got the medicine. He looked across the clearing, and there coming out of the forest was Tysha, a close Atshuara friend. The Indians had tried to save his life by carrying him out to an army base, but the river was too great an obstacle for him in his weak condition. He arrived in time to get the last drop of penicillin from Roj's needle. "Praise the Lord," said Roj, "it's unbelievable, but here he is, and this will probably save his life!"

Roj straightened up for the first time, looked at Nate, and smiled. The strain was off his shoulders. Nate looked at his watch—just a few minutes before their deadline for getting out of there. While Roj walked toward the plane, now at long last relaxed and at ease, Nate ran over and offered his hand to the bewildered chief. "He didn't know what to do with it, but I just grabbed his and started talking English. They'd understand as much of that as of Spanish. 'So long, glad to have known you fellows,' I said, and headed for the plane."

Roj was shaking his head, smiling. "Well, God is certainly in this thing."

Nate took off alone to satisfy himself that he could get out with the heavier load, and then came back in to pick up Roger. In the plane on the way to Wambimi, Roj told how the work on the strip had been hindered by sickness; how, because of the sickness, his Indian carrier had refused to bring the radio, and how he had worked on the strip himself for lack of anyone else to do it. At one point an Indian had shouted at him: "Watch out! There's a snake by your foot! Don't move!" Roj froze, and there, not two feet away from his foot, lay a bushmaster, coiled to strike. The Indian grabbed a stick. "Nothing doing—that's too short!" yelled Roj. With the words "God help me" on his lips, Roj slashed his machete at the snake's head, cutting it off cleanly.

"You can't imagine how I prayed that you wouldn't make it on Friday, as we had originally planned," said Roj. "Then Saturday I prayed you *would* get here, and began to wonder if you'd make it. It got to be four o'clock, and no plane. I was getting pretty discouraged. Finally, there it was. We heard it coming, all right, but no—it was turning away! I just died a thousand deaths out on that field. I was really shot. After working all day in the rain on Friday, straining every muscle to get it done, and then straining our ears all day Saturday, well . . . then half an hour later, we heard you again. Again, instead of growing louder, the sound faded away. The Indians tore down to the *chacra*, and saw the plane disappearing. This was it. I decided to call it a day, and gathered the Indians together for a meeting and a little Gospel teaching. We had just started when the Indians yelled that the plane was coming back. Some said, 'No, you're hearing it with your heart!' But soon we saw it. Man, you can't imagine what it does to a guy to see this little yellow job coming in over the trees!"

These two men, imbued with the Christian pioneering spirit of the first century, using the tools of the twentieth, had pushed back the boundaries of their faith one more step. Not only Roger and Nate, but also Jim, Pete, and Ed were missionary pioneers—always looking to the regions beyond immediate horizons. Just over the distant ridges were the Aucas. "One of these days we're going to spot those boys," Jim Elliot had said, "and from then on they'll be marked men!"

CHAPTER VIII
The Aucas

"For a number of years," Nate Saint once wrote, "the Aucas have constituted a hazard to explorers, an embarrassment to the Republic of Ecuador, and a challenge to missionaries of the Gospel."

Since his arrival in the Oriente, Nate had often flown over Auca territory, his trained eye trying to find houses or villages. It is no easy matter to find a people numbering perhaps five hundred to a thousand, in a dense jungle covering twelve thousand square miles. No census, of course, has ever been made; the area is merely estimated by the Quichuas—an area undoubtedly far larger than the Aucas themselves would claim, as the Quichuas (quite understandably) give them a wide berth. This part of the jungle lies about one hundred and fifty miles east of Quito. It is bordered by three rivers: on the west by the Arajuno, on the north by the Napo, on the south by the Villano. To the east it runs into the Peruvian border.

The history of the region goes back to the early days of the Spanish conquest of Ecuador. In 1541, Gonzalo Pizarro, brother of the famous Francisco Pizarro, who brought the Inca Empire to an end, crossed the Andes, explored their eastern slopes, and permitted one of his adventurous lieutenants to follow the Amazon to its mouth. In his astounding explorations he lost all but ninety-seven of his hundreds of soldiers. Some died of hardship but many were killed by hostile Indians. Some of these Indians were undoubtedly the ancestors of the Aucas. The conquistadors were followed in the seventeenth century by Jesuit missionaries, some of whom also were killed by hostile Indians. Little was done to settle or exploit the area from the seventeenth century to the middle of the nineteenth. Then the demand for rubber in the industrial parts of the world brought rubber hunters to the Amazonian basin, at that time the source of the best rubber in the world. Unscrupulous, treacherous, cruel, the rubber hunters wooed the Indians with presents only to raid their villages, plunder whatever of value they might find, carry off the able-bodied young men as slaves to work on haciendas, and murder the rest so that there would be no one left to drum up reprisals.

In 1874 a later Jesuit missionary made a trip down the Curaray intending to found a mission but instead spent his time—according to his own report—protecting the Indians from the rapacious rubber hunters. Another record called the rubber traders "civilized savages against unbaptized savages." Certainly from that time on, hatred spread throughout the Auca country, and a legacy of reprisal has been passed on from father to son. It was the behavior of the white man that closed off this area to colonization. There was a time when the country could have developed with the co-operation of the Aucas but that time is now past. In the early days of this century, haciendas were scattered throughout what is now a "closed" country.

The Aucas' growing distrust of the white man is illustrated in a story told in the Oriente of a hacienda owner, a Señor Santoval, who lived in the Aucas' domain shortly after the turn of the century. Señor Santoval had two captured Auca families working for him and managed to carry on a lively rubber trade with the Aucas still in the jungle. They would leave rubber for him at the edge of his property and in exchange he would leave machetes, knives, and clothing for them. For about ten years this peaceful trading continued with no violence on either side. The captured Aucas were such superior workmen that Santoval asked them to approach their tribesmen with offers of work on the hacienda. Through his intermediaries, the patron offered them fair pay, good living conditions, clothing, anything they felt they wanted. The offer was refused out of hand and the answer came back that the Aucas wanted nothing whatever of the white man's world, that they were independent and wished to remain so. Santoval died in 1917 and his death was the signal for an Auca attack on the hacienda. Almost all his Indian workers were killed; those that survived, including some of the captured Aucas, moved permanently out of range of Auca attacks.

The Shell Oil Company, prospecting for oil in the Oriente from 1940 to 1949, had to contend not only with the usual hazards and inconveniences of the jungle but with attacks from Aucas on their workmen. In 1942 three of their employees were killed in the company's camp at Arajuno. The incident is described in a letter written by a Shell Oil Company executive:

"We regret to have to inform you that a most unfortunate incident occurred on Wednesday, January 7th last, in our camp at Arajuno. A group of hostile Indians attacked a gang of our laborers working near our camp and our foreman and two other Ecuadorian laborers were killed with spears. This attack caused some panic among the laborers which was aggravated when the following morning these Indians made another appearance and seemed to be surrounding the camp. . . . We fear it will become more difficult than before to engage an adequate number of laborers for our camp at Arajuno."

One year later the company lost eight employees. In an attempt to win the confidence of the tribe and ward off further killings, a visit was made to an Auca house. Gifts of machetes, shirts, magazines, and empty bottles were left for the inhabitants, who proved to be absent when the white men arrived. The Aucas responded with a present of a vine-woven basket which they left on the trail. This encouraged the oil men, and one of them reported: "It seems that our hope of friendship is going the right way. I think that this will become a reality in the near future, so long as our personnel always follow the indicated line of conduct which could be put down as 'absolute respect of private property. . . .' A stray bullet might, in my opinion, con-stitute something like a declaration of war, which could be fatal to our party."

An attempt at dropping gifts from an airplane was also made by the Shell Oil people, but, as Nate later observed, "a two-thousand horsepower transport, roaring over the village at a low altitude, would seem sure to scare anyone, not to mention particularly a stone-age people with no knowledge whatsoever of science." In spite of all these overtures, the hopes of the Shell Oil Company were not realized and no one made any further serious attempts to win the Aucas.

It was becoming increasingly important for these young missionaries to know every available fact about the Aucas. They read the reports of the Shell Oil Company and talked to anyone who had ever had any contact with the Aucas. An invaluable source of information was Señor Carlos Sevilla, who owns and operates a hacienda about ten minutes' flight from Sandia. Don Carlos had lived in Auca territory for twenty-six years, before he was driven out by repeated attacks. He is a tall, spare Ecuadorian in his middle sixties who has probably had more experience with Aucas than any other living man. His body still bears six scars inflicted by Aucas during his last encounter with them.

His first narrow escape came in 1914 when seven Indians and one Columbian who were working for him were killed on the hacienda "El Capricho" on the Curaray. In 1919, while Sevilla was hunting for rubber, he left fifteen Indian families at a camp on the Tsupino River while he went upstream to get medicines. On his return, he was met by an Indian boy who was wounded in the arm, the sole survivor of an Auca attack on the camp. Hurriedly rounding up sixty

Quichuas, Sevilla set off to find the Aucas responsible for the massacre at his camp. He found an Auca house, and one woman peacefully working in the manioc patch. She was captured, but as Sevilla's men surrounded the house, she broke away from her guards, and ran screaming into the bush. This sounded the alarm, and those who had been in the house were able to escape while the guards rushed to recapture the woman. As Don Carlos repeats this story, so many years later, there is still a note of bitter disappointment in his voice.

He has been able to observe Auca strategy closely. It seems that attacks are always by surprise, and that the Aucas invariably outnumber their opponents. One method of surprising travelers is to wait at the bend of a river until the current forces a canoe close to the shore, and while the polers are frantically trying to pull the canoe back into the mainstream, the spears are hurled, accompanied by wild yells to confuse the victims. The advantage is all with the Aucas. Sevilla's advice to any adventurer in savage territory is that he travel with at least two canoes, so that one canoe could fire to protect the other should an attack come.

In 1925 Don Carlos and his Indians were attacked twice within four months. Sevilla and his men were traveling by canoe upstream on the Nushino when, at a narrow bend in the river, they found themselves the target of dozens of Auca lances. The canoe capsized, five Indians were slain immediately, and Sevilla and one other escaped. Fighting his way through the hail of spears, he succeeded in killing two of the attackers with their own weapons, but emerged severely wounded himself. Eight days later he reached his hacienda on the Ansuc River, his body rotting with infection, his wounds worm-eaten.

An attack in 1934 finally drove him out of the territory, but it has not discouraged his making plans for a possible re-entry.

"I don't think it is too late," says Sevilla. "True, we've lost our best chances, but perhaps if we build a strong, lance-proof house fairly close to the Auca houses, make a large clearing around it, keep constant watch, and never use a gun, they would ultimately accept our friendship."

But there are men in the Oriente, who roamed the region looking for rubber, gold, or oil in the days when this was "open country," who say that never, never will the Aucas allow the white man to live peacefully in their land. It is too late. By the flickering light of kerosene lamps on the verandas of haciendas, these old-timers sit evening after evening recalling their experiences and conjecturing about the Aucas' real motives. Are they natural born killers? Do they kill only to preserve their land from outsiders? Do they kill to rob? No one knows and there is no set pattern that shows any one single motive behind the killings.

It is known that a few killings have been followed by robbery. Articles which the Aucas considered useful, particularly the machete, have been stolen. Other things, whose use they do not understand, they leave behind. In some cases all possessions of the victims have been left intact. Surprisingly, Quichuas are allowed summer fishing privileges in the heart of the Auca domain; undisturbed, they take their canoes down the Napo or the Curaray for weeks at a time. Then for no apparent reason, the Aucas will attack. They may kill or wound a group of Quichua fishermen within Auca boundaries, or they move just beyond their frontiers and attack a Quichua family working in its *chacra*. One fact only seems firmly established: the white man is unwanted. When he sets foot within the area that the Aucas have marked off for themselves, he risks his life.

Killings, however, also occur within the tribe. Anger finds immediate expression in a killing. As it was with the Hatfields and McCoys of the Kentucky mountains, feuds flare up frequently, each death to be avenged by the surviving members of the family to form a chain-reaction of murder. Thus, the taking of life is not alien to the Aucas. From an early age on, young boys are trained in the accurate use of their nine-foot hardwood lances. Don Carlos tells of coming upon a deserted Auca hut, and finding there a life-sized human figure carved of balsa wood. The heart and facial features were clearly outlined with bright red achiote and the entire figure was torn with lance marks. This method, as modern as bayonet training for combat troops had been used to develop the deadly marksmanship for which the Aucas are famous.

Don Carlos has working for him on his hacienda an Auca woman who escaped some years ago from a tribal killing. There had been a typical family feud, in which both her parents and brothers and sisters were killed by a neighboring group. Dayuma, then in her mid-teens, had managed to escape by hiding out in the *chacra* until the invaders left. She then made her way to the nearest settlement of Quichuas, who took her to Don Carlos.

Like any refugee, Dayuma spent her first years among the Quichuas, adapting herself as quickly and totally as possible to their customs. One of her hardest adjustments was the food of her hosts. Aucas have no salt and it took her almost a year before she could enjoy seasoned food. Clothing was another major change. Aucas are entirely naked, except for vines that are tied tightly around wrists, ankles, and waist. Now Dayuma wears the customary shapeless cotton dress of the Quichua woman. In an effort to hide her Auca ancestry she combs her hair down to cover her disfigured ear lobes—ear lobes once adorned with round balsa wood plugs more than an inch in diameter. Watching her go about her work on the hacienda, feeding the animals, helping in the kitchen, there is little else to distinguish her from her Quichua fellow workers. The Aucas have the same straight black hair, the same tea-colored skin, and about the same height—a few inches over five feet.

Dayuma has been able to give many facts of ethnological interest. Although the Aucas drink chicha, made just as the Quichuas make it, they drink it unfermented; consequently Dayuma never saw drunkenness until she reached the outside world. Wife-beating was also unknown to her. Auca houses are long, oblong shaped, with mud-packed floors, and hammocks used as beds hanging from the roof. Living in each house may be anywhere from twenty to fifty members of a clan. The women work in the plantations of manioc and cotton. The men work on their lances, shaping the sharp points with stolen machetes. Every man in the household has his collection of nine or ten spears, which he takes with him on a foray for food or on a raiding expedition. Dayuma says that the Aucas can recognize a footprint—in much the same way that we would recognize a familiar face, they can identify the individual Indian who has passed by. She told Don Carlos that every step he had ever taken in Curaray country was known to her people. They also spent many hours spying on the Shell camp at Arajuno. At one time during the Shell occupancy, the people had considered approaching the white man. They had talked seriously among themselves of the possibility of sending in two men as a scouting party and, if they were not killed, the rest of the group would follow. In actual fact, just the opposite happened; the Aucas attacked and killed three Shell employees.

Pets are common among Aucas; they snare parrots, monkeys, and the wild boar when they are still young and keep them in small huts surrounding the large main house. Like other people the world over, they have their legends and fairy stories. At one time, so goes the Auca legend, "fire fell from heaven," spread out all over the world, and burned all the trees. The Aucas hid under the leaves of the sweet potato plant until the fire was over and then came out and repopulated the earth. They fear evil spirits, as do all jungle people. They like their children and amuse them with tales. Dayuma tells one of the tales whose hero is a turtle:

One day a baby turtle met a powerful jaguar on the road.

"Ha!" said the jaguar. "Your parents are far away and there is no one to protect you."

The little turtle in fear drew in his head.

"Put out your head," the jaguar commanded.

And the turtle, hearing the mighty voice, put out his head. Then, looking into the jaguar's savage mouth, he said, "What terrific teeth you have!"

The jaguar was flattered. He opened his mouth still wider to display all of his fine fierce teeth. So the little turtle, who was much quicker than he looked, jumped into the jaguar's mouth and bit his throat so hard that the jaguar forthwith died.

Then the little turtle left the jaguar and went to the neighboring Aucas and told them that he had killed a jaguar and left it lying in the path. The Indians went to see, and there was the dead jaguar. Happily they snatched out the teeth and claws to make ornaments for themselves and went off, entirely forgetting to thank the little turtle. So the little turtle simply returned to the jungle and grew up to be a big turtle!

Dayuma is constantly asked why the Aucas kill, and she can only answer that they are killers. "Never, never trust them," she repeats with emphasis; "they may appear friendly and then they will turn around and kill."

There are those, however, who have not and will not accept this verdict as final—those who cannot rest in peace while generations of Aucas remain beyond the frontiers of Christianity. Pete Fleming was one of those who could not be content while the Aucas remained in darkness. In his diary he wrote: "It is a grave and solemn problem; an unreachable people who murder and kill with extreme hatred. It comes to me strongly that God is leading me to do something about it, and a strong idea and impression comes into my mind that I ought to devote the majority of my time to collecting linguistic data on the tribe and making some intensive air surveys to look for Auca houses. . . . I know that this may be the most important decision of my life, but I have a quiet peace about it."

CHAPTER IX
September 1955

September 1955 was the month in which Operation Auca really started, the month in which the Lord began to weave five separate threads into a single glowing fabric for His own Glory. Five men with widely differing personalities had come to Ecuador from the eastern United States, the West Coast, and the Midwestern States. Representing three different "faith-missions," these men and their wives were one in their common belief in the Bible as the literal and supernatural and perfect word from God to man. Christ said "Go ye"; their answer was "Lord, send me."

The missionaries who were about to join forces in Operation Auca had made several moves. After the flood it had been decided to rebuild Shandia, keep it as the main station of this area, and build outstations. The technique of maintaining a number of outstations is particularly important in the Oriente because the Indians in this part of the world, as already pointed out, do not congregate in large villages, but are scattered in small groups throughout large areas of the jungle.

It was agreed that an outstation should be established in Puyu-pungu. Jim and Ed and Pete had visited this little settlement of

Quichuas on a survey trip down the Bobonaza River in August, 1953. There they had met Atanasio, the chief who had invited them to establish a school for his children. "Because of God, will you not stay?" he had asked. "We need you very much. I have—let's see—thirteen, fourteen, and another one, yes, *fifteen* children. No one has taught them. They want to learn to see paper. I have some orphans too in my house. Will you not come?"

Usually it is an uphill struggle to win the confidence of the people in a new area. Here, however, was not only an open door, but an outright invitation. The three men saw it as the answer to their prayer for enlarged borders. So plans were made. The McCullys moved to Shandia to begin their study of Quichua, and Pete, who was still single, was chosen to stay and help them learn the language and get established. Jim and I decided it was God's time for us to marry so that we could, together, open the station at Puyupungu.

Thus it was that Jim and I arrived there in November, 1953, with all our worldly goods in four canoes. After greeting us with much backslapping, handshaking, and laughter, the men carried the white man's incredible quantity of equipment up the high bank where Atanasio's two wives and throng of children waited expectantly.

The building of the house and airstrip did not take all of Jim's time. Together we began having meetings for the Indians, telling them in their own language the most wonderful story in the world, that of the Son of God who had come to earth and paid the price of man's sin with his own blood. The recognition of God's great love dawned slowly in the Indian mind. But one day we rejoiced as Atanasio said to Jim, "I am very old. Perhaps too old to understand well. But it seems to me your words are true. I will die in your words."

Meanwhile, the McCullys were making good progress learning the language in Shandia. Pete Fleming had built himself a little shack near their bamboo house, and took meals with them. He wrote in his

During a three-month period the missionaries made weekly flights over the Auca settlement that they called "Terminal City," dropping a line with gifts (such as this kettle). Occasionally they pulled up Auca gifts tied to the line. Nate Saint displays a feathered headdress.

OVERLEAF: One of the palm-thatched Auca houses, photographed during a gift-drop. About sixty feet long, it can house from twenty to fifty people. Surrounding smaller shelters are for Auca pet animals.

A friendly beachhead in hostile Auca territory: After months of preparation, the missionaries landed on a Curaray River sandbar that they named "Palm Beach." On Tuesday, January 3, 1956, Nate Saint made five flights from Arajuno—ferrying in Ed McCully, Jim Elliot, Roger Youderian, as well as supplies. While Nate was flying, the others built a shelter thirty feet up an ironwood tree (*RIGHT*). On the last flight that day, Nate flew over "Terminal City" and shouted in the Auca language: "Come tomorrow to the Curaray."

On Wednesday the missionaries began the period of waiting for a visit from the Aucas. They fished, read, and studied their notebooks of Auca phrases.

LEFT: Jim, Roj, and Nate return to Palm Beach after chopping down trees that might endanger the plane on landings and take-offs. *BELOW:* Jim holds up a catfish. *RIGHT:* "Except for forty-seven billion insects of every sort this place is a little paradise," wrote Nate in his diary. Here, with *Time* magazine, he takes what he called his "hydraulic siesta" to escape the insects.

On Thursday the waiting continued. During the day Nate Saint took the plane up several times, circled above Palm Beach, and gunned the engine to help pinpoint their location for the Aucas. *ABOVE:* Two missionaries rest in the shade of the beach house. *RIGHT:* During the period of waiting, the men felt that they were being watched by unseen eyes, but they got no sight of "neighbors." Jim Elliot, Auca notebook in hand, stands in the shallow river and shouts words of welcome into the jungle in the hope that Aucas might be lurking there.

Arms outstretched, Ed McCully demonstrates both by gesture and by word to any hidden observers that he and the other emissaries from the hated outside world are waiting in friendship.

RIGHT: The missionaries' efforts were rewarded at 11:15 Friday morning, when three Aucas stepped out of the jungle and met their first white friends. This is the man of the trio, nicknamed "George" on the spot. He wears the Auca earmark, a piece of balsa wood through the lobes, and a skein of red wool—a gift from Roger.

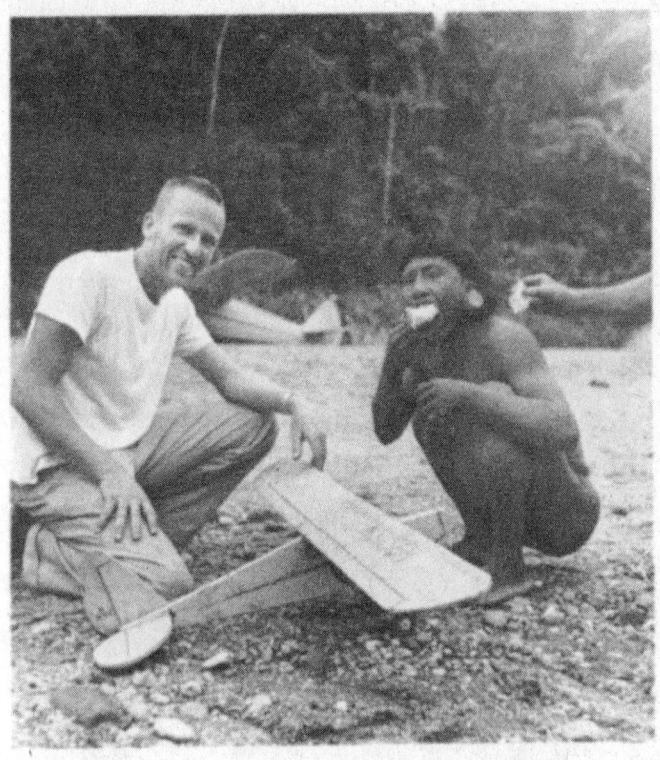

LEFT: Phrase book in hand, Pete Fleming points out the different parts of the model plane to "George," who is sitting in characteristic Auca fashion. Later, the missionaries tried to explain to him the need for the Aucas to cut down trees and build a permanent airstrip near their village. This area would not be imperiled, as is Palm Beach, by floodwaters.

ABOVE: "George" enjoys his first hamburger while Roger rubs him with insect repellent. "George's" biggest thrill came from his plane ride with Nate over his Auca village. From the moment he climbed into the plane, he shouted out the side—aping the missionaries, who, during the giftdrops, called to the Aucas below.

BELOW: The older of the two women in the Auca party stayed longer than her companions. She sat by the fire during the evening, chattering volubly to Roger, undisturbed by the fact that he could not follow her conversation. That night she settled down beside the fire, but evidently left early in the morning; when the men got up, her fire was still burning. Nate Saint, who made still pictures on the beach, also made a short film in color of his experiences. An Auca woman, Dayuma, who escaped from her tribe several years ago, and now lives on a hacienda outside Auca territory, has seen this film. She believes that the older woman is her mother's younger sister. She does not recognize the other two members of the Auca trio.

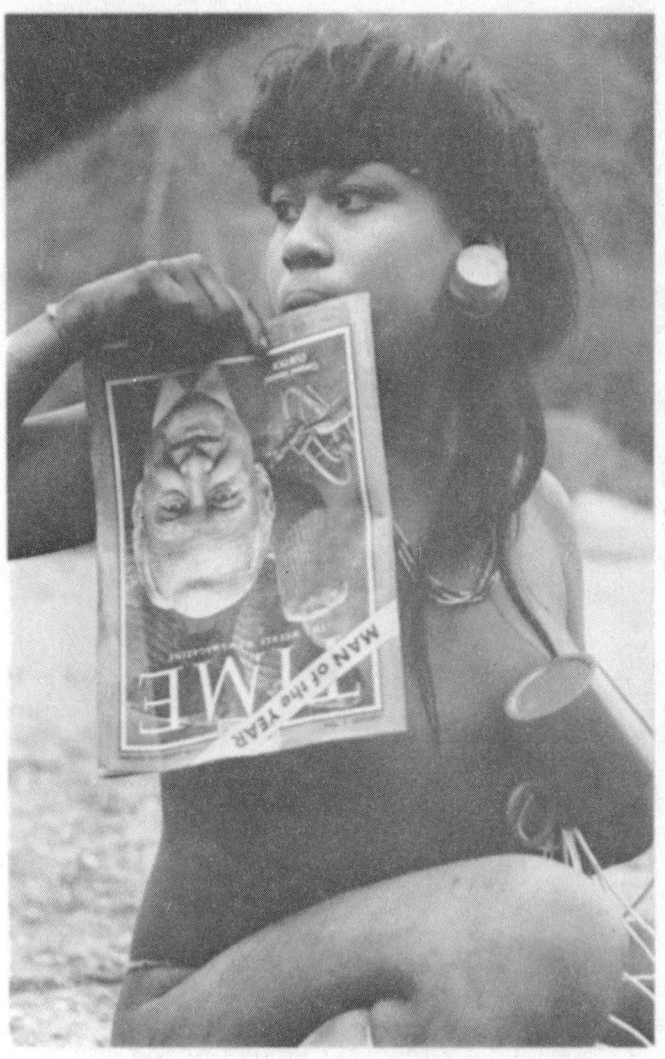

The youngest of the visiting Aucas was promptly dubbed "Delilah" by the missionaries. At the end of the day she stalked down the beach. "George" called to her, but, failing to stop her, followed her into the forest.

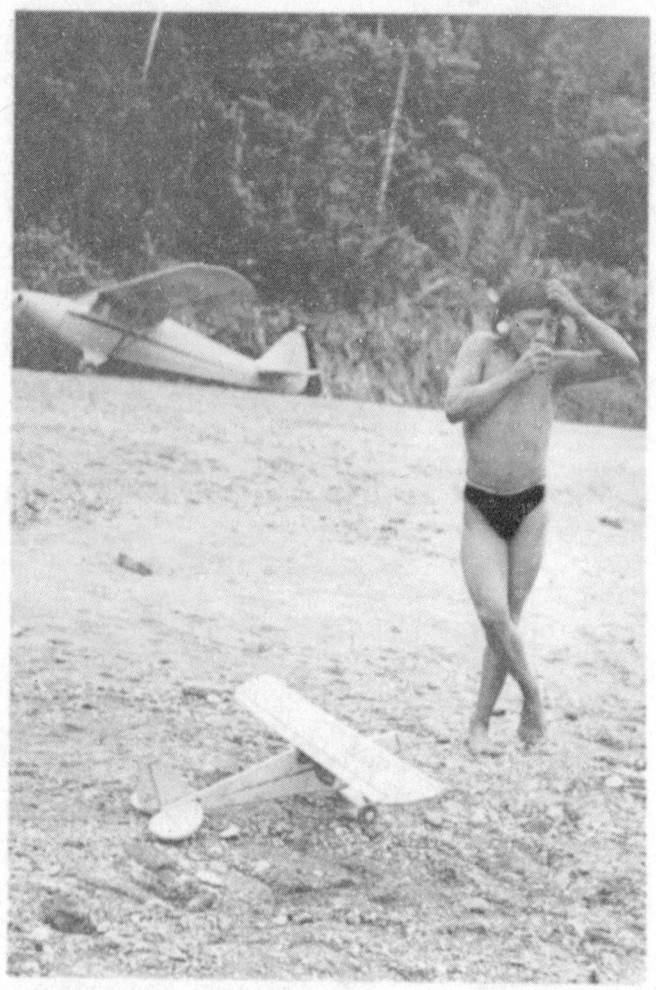

"George" stands beside the model plane that the missionaries had made the insignia of Operation Auca. He now has the model with him in his Auca settlement, and when pilots of the Missionary Aviation Fellowship fly over the Indian houses, he rushes out and waves the little plane. In the background is Nate Saint's Piper Cruiser.

diary: "It is surprising what joy and pleasure I had in building my little two-room house. I really got a kick out of it, and though it took only four or five days, I could hardly wait to move in. It is *very* comfortable and it is *pure luxury* to have a place to myself, a bed, a desk, and chair where I will not be under observation. Best of all, it aids in leading a disciplined life, things are in a convenient place, and privacy for prayer is now possible. I have begun again to add to my file system on the New Testament, a thing I haven't done since I left the U.S. I am happy inside myself to be getting things done in an orderly way again. There is no question that it is the way I was meant to live, with regular bedtime, evenings free for study, and a full hour's devotional time in the morning."

As Pete watched the McCullys become oriented in the work, he began thinking more specifically about his own future. And about his fiancée Olive Ainslie, a slim and beautiful girl, with dark eyebrows in striking contrast to lighter hair and blue eyes. They had become engaged in an exchange of letters while he was in the jungle. With typical candor this quiet, studious man wondered if there were any conflict between his coming marriage and his "call" to the Aucas?

"Last night Nate and I talked a long time about the Auca problem," he wrote. "Strangely enough, I do not feel my coming marriage will prohibit me from being eligible to help in efforts to reach them. I feel that if pushed to it, Olive would rather have me die after we had lived together than to indefinitely postpone our wedding on the possibility that something fatal might happen. Our life has become one, and I do not feel that God will separate us in our discernment of the will of God."

In June, 1954, Pete felt free to return to the United States to marry Olive. After Pete's departure Jim and I moved back to Shandia with Ed and Marilou McCully. Puyupungu having been established as an outstation, we arranged for future visitation and teaching sessions. Shandia, with a school, medical clinic, and small store, was considered our permanent base of operations.

We all agreed that Jim and I could take the responsibilities of the

Shandia station, so Ed and Marilou began to consider a move to an area of their own—another place where the Gospel had not been carried. The McCullys knew of Arajuno, the abandoned Shell Oil Company base on the very edge of Auca territory. In survey flights over the area, Ed had estimated the Quichua Indian population to be somewhere around one hundred. Why not take advantage of the excellent airstrip which the company had built, and move in there for a while to preach to these Indians? The runway would need only a day's work at the most to clear it of grass, and the gravel base would be as good as new. Arajuno, one of several Shell Company projects aimed at finding oil in the area, had been fabulously expensive. A small city had been hacked out of the forest; roads had been built; a hotel and tennis courts, bakery, and even a narrow-gauge railroad had been included in the project. Now, abandoned since 1949, the buildings had been claimed by the rot and ruin of the jungle. However, some useful materials might be salvaged. The idea of opening a station at Arajuno seemed a good one.

Ed began visiting Arajuno each weekend, flying over with Nate on Friday. Ed visited the Indians' homes and conducted meetings for them on Saturday and Sunday. The welcome he received encouraged him to build a simple house, using the foundations of one of the abandoned Shell Oil buildings and boards salvaged from round about. Finally when Ed decided to stay on full time at Arajuno, he moved Marilou and the two children to their "new" quarters. Marilou soon had an attractive home fixed up—bright curtains at the screened windows, a "sofa" made of a pile of salvaged bricks covered with a mattress and a sheet of plastic, pictures on the bamboo walls, and colorful Ecuadorian rugs on the cement slab floor. Nate Saint spent several nights rigging up a burglar-alarm system and an electric fence, for the McCullys and their co-workers on other stations were fully aware of the dangers of living near the Aucas. The Arajuno River forms the western boundary of the Auca territory and the new mission station was on the Auca side of the river. It was the very site where the Shell Oil employees had been killed some years before. Such sporadic raids, with the Aucas darting from the jungle to kill swiftly and disappear again, had made the Aucas fearful and fascinating to their Quichua neighbors.

The Quichuas never allowed the McCullys to forget the possibility of a visit from the Aucas. The Quichuas refused to remain after four o'clock on that side of the Arajuno River. "This is the Auca part," they would say. Every so often rumors would spread around that Auca footprints had been found near the house, or that the grass was pressed down, indicating that Aucas had been lying there, spying on the foreigners.

The electric fence was set up a good thirty yards from the house, beyond accurate spear-throwing range, and Ed and Marilou always kept a pistol or gun handy. "Even though we don't think they're around," Ed said, "it gives you a good feeling to know that the fence is buzzing. With our lights on in the house at night we'd make a good target!"

Thus it was that the Lord had placed Ed and Marilou in the strategic spot that was to become the base of Operation Auca.

Meanwhile, Pete had returned from the United States to Quito with his bride, Olive. They spent a year in the mountains while she learned Spanish and he translated Scriptures into Quichua, spoke at Indian gatherings, and refreshed his own knowledge of Spanish. In the fall of 1955, Pete and Olive came to the Oriente to begin Indian work together at Puyupungu, where they settled in the little thatched house which Jim and I had built. Pete began again to teach the Indians there, slowly and carefully, reviewing the things they had learned before, leading them into new truths.

Olive's initiation into jungle life included a spectacular display by the active volcano Sangay, visible from the living room at Puyupungu. "At night," Pete wrote, "it looks like a huge bonfire out of which shoot flares in a long graceful arc landing a couple of thousand feet down the mountainside. With the binoculars we could see individual balls of fire burst and spray out all over. It was a real show. Clouds of steam coming from the lava on the snow would momentarily blot out the pyrotechnic display, only to have it clear and start over again."

Their hearts were sometimes saddened by the drunken behavior of many of the Indians at a fiesta. The results of such fiestas can be imagined—husbands beating their wives; pitiful naked children left to find their own place to sleep at night while parents stagger about until dead drunk. On one occasion a drunken mother rolled on her two-week-old baby, smothering it. An Indian will sometimes attempt to find his way home through the dark forest, usually ending up asleep on the muddy trail, waking hours later to find huge scavenger beetles digging under his legs in an attempt to bury him.

But there were signs, too, that the Gospel message was getting through to these sons of the jungle. Pete's journal records: "Today the angels are rejoicing over Puyupungu, and so are we. How faithful God is. This morning a number of Indians decided for Christ. I felt led to speak on baptism since I had noted several misunderstandings while I listened to Indians talk. So after speaking from the story of Philip and the eunuch, I tried to explain simply and clearly the difference between faith and baptism. After an early fight with squalling babies the attention was excellent and I felt the Spirit moving in hearts, so asked for a show of hands after carefully explaining what a decision for Christ would involve. A number of hands showed— Tito, Benito, Pascual, and others. A number more began to put up their hands when Alejo broke out from the back telling them that it would mean giving up drinking and living immorally. Some of the hands went down at that. I closed in prayer, inviting those who were really repentant to go into the back room of the school where I could deal more carefully with them. Twelve came. We encouraged and exhorted them and arranged for a believers' meeting on Friday afternoon. Several others are very close. What joy! *This* is what we came here for.

"At twenty-six years how good God has been and how full and blessed His ways. How continually I thank God for bringing me here, almost overcoming the impossible and pushing me out. I felt 'thrust out' and how grateful I am for God's impelling."

In September 1955, "God's impelling" moved five pioneering missionary families to crystallize their plans of months and years into common action. Truly they were being "thrust out" to carry the Word of God to the Aucas. The McCullys, in the station at Arajuno, provided the vanguard. Jim and I were in Shandia. The Flemings were in Puyupungu. Roger Youderian and his family had returned from their outstation at Wambimi and were again helping the Drowns at Macuma. Nate Saint with his little yellow plane and Marj at the radio remained at Shell Mera, their permanent base at the hub of these outlying jungle stations.

CHAPTER X
Operation Auca Begins

On the evening of the second day of October, 1955, Nate Saint fed some yellow tissue into his old typewriter and began:

"This will be an attempt to note developments that have led to the recent decision to launch efforts toward contacting the Auca tribe. These notes, of course, will record only personal points of view of the situation and will not touch past efforts of other missionaries.

"Last night Ed McCully, Jim Elliot, Johnny Keenan, and I were on the living room floor on elbows and knees poring over a map of the eastern jungles of Ecuador. We had just decided that it was the Lord's time to try to contact the savage Auca tribe located somewhere east of Ed's Quichua Indian mission station at Arajuno.

"Later, in the kitchen over a midnight cup of cocoa, we decided that our efforts should be carried forward as secretly as practicable so as to avoid arousing other non-missionary groups to competitive efforts. Their efforts would undoubtedly employ a heavily-armed invasion party going in overland. This we fear might set back for decades the missionary effort among these stone-age people.

"This afternoon, in meditation on the situation, it seemed to me a shame that the secrecy required might deny our prayer-supporting colleagues at home the blessing of a fresh running account, reported at first-hand, of our efforts and of the Lord's good hand upon them. Therefore I have taken it upon myself to set down the *status quo* and hope to add to it as we progress in the days ahead.

"A number of sporadic efforts have been made to change the status of these killers of the forests. Armed attacks and counterattacks on the part of whites only thinned out the tribe and fanned the furor of hatred already present. Fear of firearms did not diminish the Aucas' desire for revenge even though it had to be carried out from ambush with hardwood lances.

"The story of the exploration attempted by Rolf Blomberg, a Swedish explorer, and guided by a missionary in 1947, has been written in detail. The party was approaching the Aucas' location on balsa rafts when they were ambushed at a point where the current pushed the rafts close to the riverbank. An Indian porter in the party opened fire immediately and then dove into the river, following the missionary who was swimming underwater. This experience makes us wary of combining our efforts with those who have no love or special regard for these people."

When Ed McCully moved his family to Arajuno he asked Nate for an aerial survey of the Auca territory, and together they looked up and down the Nushino River valley, where the Aucas were known to have been some seven years before. They found nothing more than had Pete and Jim in their survey two years earlier—only the vast ocean of dark green treetops that stretches off into a smudgy horizon. The effect of an ocean is heightened by the choppy, wavelike hills that break up the terrain. The coffee-with-cream-colored rivers snaking through the trees serve as a reminder that it is landscape, not seascape. Only the trained eye, however, would be able to spot human habitation in this wilderness—perhaps a ragged scarf of smoke rising above the green, or the infinitesimal spot which indicates an Indian *chacra*.

Nate's diary continues: "The actual search did not get under way until the morning of September 19, when I was letting down for

Arajuno on the regular weekly vegetable-run. It was around 8:30 A.M., as I recall, and the atmosphere was unusually clear. Visibility was about seventy-five miles and all the little river valleys, which are usually camouflaged by the more common light-haze foliage combinations, were clearly discernible in the distance.

"When I climbed out of the plane and greeted Ed, I asked him how he'd like to go looking for his 'neighbors.' He was all for it, so we set to work raiding Marilou's larder for canned goods and scrounged around for other special emergency equipment and took off about half an hour later.

"We followed the Nushino east, but flying the north side this time. We were able to scan a six- or eight-mile sweth. About fifty miles east of Ed's place, out over the middle of nowhere, we turned due north toward Coca on the Rio Napo. About five minutes later we spied some spots that looked as if they might have been planted manioc patches years ago. It's hard to be sure from a bird's point of view, even after you've been studying the woods for some time. We circled and then went on north until the Napo was getting close, without seeing anything more. The left turn toward home was inevitable. We didn't have gas enough to press on much farther and we had covered what we had outlined for this particular trip. However, it was hard to give up. It takes so long to get that far out, and it is so difficult to find such ideal weather. I'd been eying a blemish, barely discernible in the jungle, maybe five miles away. Ed couldn't make it out, but we decided to fly that way for just a couple of minutes, and if we didn't turn up something more concrete we'd beat it for home.

"The blemish grew into a well-defined pockmark, and then into a good-sized clearing covered with well-cleaned manioc. *This was it.* We'd been cruising very slowly and our fuel consumption was getting low, but we could still hang around for fifteen minutes without cutting into the reserve. So we hung around. All told, we must have seen about fifteen clearings and a few houses. It was an exciting old time . . . a time we'd waited for.

"We never did let down for a close look. In the first place, we had to watch fuel consumption; in the second, we didn't want anyone to get frightened on our first visit. We'd be back again with more thoughts on the best manner to approach these people.

"On the way back Ed observed that he thought there must be other clearings closer to his place. He felt it would be a long hike for Aucas from this settlement to show up at his place or in its environs. I didn't think so. To me it seemed logical that they should all be way out there in the wilderness since there had been a raid at their old location on the Nushino. We decided to keep thinking about the whole thing and to compare notes later. We also decided to keep the 'find' in the family until we were sure it was okay to spill it.

"The news was exciting to Marj and to Ruth and Johnny Keenan. As we reflected, it seemed providential that we had investigated that tiny spot that turned into the first Auca clearing we had ever laid eyes on.

"A couple of weeks later (September 29) I was to take Jim Elliot and Pete Fleming over to Villano where they were to spend several days preaching among a group of Quichuas who had never heard the Gospel. Our route was to be via Arajuno, so we decided that since we'd be flying over what was Auca territory, and since it would take two trips to move in the men and their equipment and two Indian guides—which would mean that I would cross the area four times—we would keep our eyes open and fly slightly different routes each time.

"On the first trip over with Jim and the equipment we didn't see a sign of life. The return trip also yielded nothing. Then Pete and the two guides and I started out. Having decided to go far enough east to see an area that hadn't been covered by the previous two crossings, we zigzagged slowly, favoring the more hospitable-looking jungle valleys.

"About fifteen minutes from Arajuno we spotted some clearings. Pete and I spoke only in English, but there was no hiding our excitement. Our Indian guides spotted the clearings also. They were sharpies and immediately said 'Aucas.' It was their first time up in a plane, yet they knew just where they were and could name the rivers. We flew down a little river and spotted a half-dozen big houses with smaller ones around them. That was it. There they were as plain as the nose on your face *and only fifteen minutes from Ed's place at Arajuno by plane.*

"As we approached Villano we talked over the problem of keeping the guides quiet. We decided that we would have to impress on them the danger to them personally if word of the location of the Aucas got around and if, as a result, there were attacks on the Aucas by the Quichuas or others, followed by Auca reprisal raids.

"I landed from the inhabited end of the Villano strip, coming in fast so as to appear to have to use most of the strip. That took us away from the waiting crowd and gave Pete time to admonish the guides as per our agreement. They agreed to keep the secret . . . (probably as secret as a full-sized toy elephant under a Christmas tree).

"Everyone who was in on our plan was again thrilled by the news. To some of us the most significant thing was not the information gained but the fact that after so much fruitless searching we had located the first group of Aucas and then in a couple of weeks had stumbled over the other group. It seemed to mean that now was the Lord's time to do something about them. Again we agreed to pray about the matter and compare notes further, after the whole episode had a chance to sink in.

"Several days later when Johnny Keenan was moving Jim and Pete and their guides from Villano back to Arajuno, he hit bad weather and finally had to come on back to Shell Mera to land and spend the night. That was the night that the map was on the living-room floor surrounded by four men who were now laboring under the conviction that the Lord was leading us to do something about the Aucas.

"That night and into the wee hours of the morning we circum-navigated the problem a dozen different times. It is most fascinating to try to imagine how those people would respond to different approaches."

One of the problems that the missionaries grappled with that night was that of language. The need to convince the Aucas that here were friendly white men, could best be effected by communicating with them in their own language. This was of the essence. As the men talked over this problem, Jim Elliot came up with the answer. He remembered having seen Dayuma on Señor Carlos Sevilla's hacienda, which lay only four hours' walk from Shandia. He offered to go and talk to her to pick up phrases that could be useful in case contact were made.

A few days later, Jim trekked over. He found Dayuma cooperative, although he was very careful not to divulge to her the reason for his desire to be taught some simple Auca phrases. Among Quichuas gossip spreads as quickly as anywhere else. Fortunately, Dayuma—accustomed to the strange ways of strange people—assumed he was only casually interested in learning the language.

"Biti miti punimupa," which means "I like you; I want to be your friend," Jim wrote carefully in his notebook. This was followed by *"Biti winki pungi amupa"*—"I want to approach you," or, more colloquially, "Let's get together."

"How do you say, 'What is your name?'" Jim asked in Quichua.

"Awum irimi," Dayuma answered in Auca.

And so Jim built a practical vocabulary list.

Thus, one of the obstacles that lay in the path of the missionaries was partly overcome. A presentation of gifts seemed the obvious next step. Perhaps a carefully-planned, regular program of gift-drops, made over a period of time, would show the Indians that the intentions of these white men were friendly, and the repetition would gradually convince them.

CHAPTER XI
A Line from Plane to Ground

The men decided to begin the gift-drops to the savage Aucas at the earliest possible moment, employing the spiraling-line technique that Nate Saint had pioneered in Atshuara country. There, the accuracy of delivery had been of paramount importance. In the new venture, the technique would have the additional value of making it clear to the Aucas that the visitors in the plane had the power to give or retain the gift right up until the moment of delivery. From captive Aucas it had been learned that the Indians thought that the gifts from the Shell plane fell out of its "stomach" as a result of its being wounded or scared by the lances they had thrown.

Nate typed out his continuing record of the start of Operation Auca:

"That night on the living-room floor it was decided that we would make our aerial visits regularly, leaving something different each week in order to work on their curiosity. We calculated that under the circumstances, sooner or later the hostile spirit would melt.

"The following day Johnny flew Jim and Ed back to Arajuno. At Shell Mera I began tests with the line to see what kind of simple, dependable mechanism we could use to release our gifts when they touched the ground. Johnny and I flew together on most of the tests and Marj and Ruth hooked on the test weights and watched their release on the runway. We marked off a target on the runway and tried to hit it.

"Finally we were ready for a dress rehearsal. The test went off fine, except that when we flew over the strip to drop the line, it fouled the strut and we had to tie a knife on a stick so that we could try to cut it loose. There was no danger except that it could have come loose by itself while we were not over the field. And that is just what happened. I saw the line drape itself in some tall trees just beyond the end of the runway. However, by the time we landed and got in there to hunt for it, it was too dark, so that it had to remain there till morning.

"That night I was so keyed up I couldn't sleep much. On the other hand, I realized that the whole thing was in the Lord's hands. I had no way of knowing how long it would take the next morning to get the line out of the trees, but I told Marj that if I could be ready to take off by 9 A.M. we would go through with it; if not, we'd cancel until the following day.

"Next morning I rigged a 'fishing line' with a weight that I could toss over the lost line high in the trees. With that and a lot of trudging around through brush I finally got all the line and by 9 A.M. we were ready for take-off.

"October 6, 1955. The first gift was a small aluminum kettle with a lid. Inside we put about twenty brightly colored buttons—obviously not for their nonexistent clothes! But buttons do make good ornaments. Also we included a little sack with a few pounds of rock salt. We understand that they do not have any salt of their own. If only they could discover what the stuff was good for we felt sure we'd win friends. To these things we attached some fifteen brightly colored ribbon streamers about a yard long. All was ready.

"Out at Arajuno all was readiness and happy anticipation. I was very anxious lest by some fault of mine we might miss on this first attempt.

"We loaded in our emergency equipment, rigged our special

gear, made a 'dry-run' test of getting the rig overboard, and took off for points east. We could hardly believe that we were to have the privilege of making the initial effort. Fifteen minutes' flying brought us over the first clearings. It was Ed's first look at his 'neighbors,' and he was plenty keyed up about it.

"We decided to try to find the downstream edge of their domain so that if we had a forced landing we could travel downstream away from their territory. About fifteen minutes more of looking around assured us that we were over the house that interested us.

"We were about 3,000 feet above the ground, and could not see anyone below; yet every indication showed that the house was occupied. The large house was thatched, with round ends, Jivaro style, and around it were several smaller squarish houses with thatched roofs, square on the ends. Well-beaten paths linked the smaller houses to the large central one. The main house was about forty yards from the edge of the stream and had a nice playa [sandbar] in front of it, perhaps seventy-five yards long and twenty-five yards wide at the widest place. A path showed that they used the playa frequently. It would be our target.

"We slowed the plane to fifty-five miles per hour and held the gifts over the side—the door having been removed at Arajuno—and hooked up the automatic-release mechanism. Slowly we lowered the gift packet until it was well clear of the plane. Then we allowed the airspeed to come up to sixty-five and began the heart-racking job of reeling out the line. I say heart-racking because if there is a bad knot anywhere in the bundle of cord, the whole effort is lost for that time. But all went well and we began circling at about sixty-five miles per hour.

"Since our altimeter reads only the altitude above sea level, we had no way of knowing how high we were above the ground. No sign of life below. We continued circling until the gift was drifting in a small, lazy circle below us, ribbons fluttering nicely. If no one was watching, it made it more important that we put the gift in an obvious place. The gift still seemed pretty high, so we started spiraling down, noting a considerable wind drift from the north, necessitating correction every time around in order to keep us over the target.

"Finally the gift appeared to be pretty close to the trees below. Time for the attempt. The wind was making it difficult and the hills on either side of the stream were covered with tall trees. A couple of times it seemed that we snatched our charge upward just in the nick of time to keep it out of trees bordering the sandbar. Once I believe the ribbons dragged across a tree and hung up momentarily. At any rate, that gave us our working elevation. We made about six attempts at this elevation, gradually drifting the prize against the wind until it was over the bar. Then we rolled the turn steeper and held our breath while it lowered toward the earth. It wouldn't be ideal for it to hit the water, and it was heading close . . . close . . . closer . . . plunk! It hit about two or three feet from the water, directly in line with the path to the house. They couldn't miss it, since they probably got their water for cooking right at that spot.

"Now another problem. I thought I saw our gift move just a little as we began a slow climb, still circling. That raised the question as to whether it was released or dragging on the line. But finally we were sure the line was free . . . and there was our messenger of good will, love, and faith, 2,000 feet below on the sandbar. In a sense we had delivered the first Gospel-message-by-sign-language to a people who were a quarter of a mile away vertically, fifty miles horizontally, and continents and wide seas away psychologically.

"How much do these people know? What do they think of what little they have seen of the outside world? We know they used to watch airplanes of the Shell Oil Company land and take off at Arajuno, for the Shell workers saw the spots where they hid in the bush to watch these monstrous messengers of another world.

"The trip back to Arajuno was short and happy. Back home again everybody who was in on the secret wanted to know if we had seen any Aucas. They were a little skeptical about anyone's finding our gift when we confessed we hadn't seen a soul. Nevertheless, a start had been made.

"Friday, October 14, 1955. I haven't brought the narrative up to the moment but rather than let the hottest stuff cool off while I catch up, I'm going to go ahead with what just happened today.

"This morning the weather was good, so we took off around 8 A.M. On the way out we could see some early-morning fog still lingering in the river valleys to the east so we were in no great hurry. We landed at Arajuno and began to prepare for the 'drop,' which was to be a new machete. We understand that these people have killed for machetes. That is, they have killed people working in the fields in order to steal their machetes or axes. It is easy to imagine the importance of such items among a stone-age people. We wrapped the blade in canvas so that no one would get cut and then tied on a number of colored ribbon streamers. After rigging the automatic touch-release gadget, we climbed in the plane for a dress rehearsal. Going over all our plans and precautions again, it seemed that we were ready, so we had a word of prayer for the success of the trip and took off.

"It is always a bit of a strain on me to reel out the line in the air. But I slowed the plane down and we carefully lowered our second 'messenger of good will' over the side. By the time the line was all out we were almost at our destination. We used a little less line this time than last.

"Our plan was to check the sand bar where we left the gift last week. There were some low clouds but we found the house and the sandbar. The gift was gone. The binoculars removed any doubt. Either they had 'accepted' it or a flood had taken it away. We saw no one, but it was evident that the site was well occupied. The plan was to fly upstream to the next house this time and leave the gift there. We figured that if we specialized on one house, the others might get jealous or become suspicious that the occupant of that house was in league with us, or was in some way a traitor to their cause. When we got to the target house, we found it directly under a cloud so we inferred that the Lord would have us go on to the next.

"As we approached the house we had decided on, we spotted

three or four canoes pulled up to the streambank in front of the house. That was interesting because one report has it they don't have canoes . . . but there they were. That meant, too, that somebody must be around nearby.

"As we started to circle about 2,500 feet above the house it became apparent that we were going to be inside the cloud about ten percent of the time, but all other conditions seemed so favorable that we decided to go ahead. The high-riding machete was behaving nicely. Ed was glued to the binoculars. All of a sudden he let out a yell and all but crawled out the open door to get a better look. We were seeing our first Auca! He was running around but not hiding. Pretty soon there were three of them out in front of their big leaf-covered house. Now we felt sure that they had received our gift of last week and that the idea had caught on in a hurry. If it was half the sport for them that it was for us, their excitement was understandable.

"After about four circles we had compensated for the wind, et cetera, and started letting the gift down. I was no longer worried about their getting it because we felt sure they were already watching the dangling prize. We let on down. At first it looked as if it would hit the house, but it drifted toward the stream. . . . Splash! Then, quicker than you could bat an eye, another splash; an Auca had dived after the treasure. Minutes later there must have been a half dozen or eight of the men on the bank examining the prize. Our hearts were grateful. We had not hoped to see this for perhaps months. Of course, we wonder what they were thinking.

"Several things seemed evident: They got our first gift. They aren't afraid of us in this type of approach. They are as animated, in one way or another, about this thing as we are."

Back at Arajuno, Ed learned another interesting bit of news. His local Indians reported the tracks of Aucas who had apparently hidden in the brush near Ed's house to observe what was going on there. Although there was no way of verifying this conjecture, it was credible. A Quichua woman, Joaquina, who had been captured by the Aucas and later escaped, had once told Dr. Tidmarsh that it was the

Aucas' practice to sit on a certain hill overlooking the camp at Arajuno to observe what went on. It seemed that they had an intricate espionage system, which perhaps at this very moment was operating near the McCully's house.

The men planned to make a wooden model of the plane—with ribbons dangling from it—to hang outside Ed's house in order to identify Ed with the operation.

Eight days after writing the previous report, Nate Saint typed a heading on a fresh sheet of tissue:

"Report on the third visit to the 'neighbors.' " He continued:

"We refer to the Aucas as 'neighbors' and to their area as the 'neighborhood' to avoid the use of the name on the radio, or in the hearing of those who aren't supposed to be interested.

"We couldn't go out on 'visitation' on Thursday as we had planned because the Army called on us for a flight down the Curaray River in the interior looking for the body of a soldier who had drowned. We did not see any sign of the missing man but we did see a lot of Ecuador that lies beyond habitation. We understand that beyond the area we checked, out toward the Napo, some vestiges of civilization reappear. However, we flew for forty-five minutes, following every curve in the river without seeing a single sign of human life . . . saw a little wild life: several tapir, some giant turtles, and an abundance of birds of paradise . . . beautiful things gliding over the woods below.

"Next day, Ed and I got away from Arajuno at about eleven o'clock while Marilou kept all the Indians in school so they wouldn't ask too many difficult questions.

"First we flew down the Curaray looking for possible camp sites or temporary landing strip sites. (This was forty or fifty miles above the start of the area searched yesterday for the missing soldier.) We saw some interesting possibilities, but nothing ideal for an airstrip.

"However, up on the horizon along the ridges we saw something that looked like smoke. It seemed to be about the place where the Aucas are, so we decided to have a look. Maybe the boys had a smudge going so we'd be sure to find them with our gift bag. The smoke turned out to be the remnant of a low cloud, but we found ourselves over the Auca neighborhood at a lower altitude than we'd ever been before, and took the occasion to circle each of the four main houses and take some pictures. We saw Indians all over, some running down the stream bed from the manioc patch toward home, others coming from other directions. They didn't seem at all afraid. We shouted Auca phrases until we were hoarse.

"After we circled the house where we had received such an open reception last week, and flew on toward the next house, the Indians apparently thought the show was scheduled there for this week, and all took off down the stream bed to try to be in on it. At any rate, when we decided to repeat at the same house to reward their confidence, we came back over and found the place deserted except for what appeared to be two women. But soon the menfolk came charging back up the stream bed. There must have been big excitement down there.

"This week our gift was to be another aluminum pot containing a bunch of trinkets and beads, well ribboned. We also tied on a little ten-inch Indian basket (empty) in hopes they might put something in it and send it back up. But somehow or other, after we got the whole thing clear of the plane, the automatic release failed and we lost the kettle to the jungle below, perhaps 300 yards distant from a smaller manioc patch. It seems likely that they might find it, but not too probable since everyone was over at the big clearing waiting for the show to begin. We were already getting a little tired from all the photographing and shouting to them, but we felt we mustn't leave without giving them something, so we tied on a new machete from our emergency kit, left on the little basket, and lowered the whole works without any release mechanism.

"One of the more tiring elements on this trip was the rough air.

We were constantly bouncing around and had a snappy drift from the northeast, so that our machete drifted badly. Several times when it was lowering near them they would scramble helter-skelter in that direction. It is really great sport. We don't know whether or not they have any system for determining who gets the prize. But as long as the supply holds up they should all keep encouraged.

"Finally after a couple of near misses, we set the packet within ten feet of the front door of their house. They had it immediately and took it out on the riverbank. Here the wind fouled up the works because every time around I had to roll completely out of the turn to compensate for drift and thus stay over the house. And every time I'd roll out of the turn, the pull on the line got really hard. They must have had the line for several minutes. We could not tell whether they were putting anything in the basket or not. They may have put in something too heavy to pick up, or they may have tied the line to something. At any rate we finally saw one fellow run diagonally into the river and stop abruptly and do something, suggesting that he was unsnagging the line. I felt the line loosen and we were free. We shouted at each other about the thrill of holding a line, the other end of which an Auca held.

"Our next decision was to fly past them low enough so that they could see us. That meant pulling in the entire line, a tough job, but after ten minutes of hard work we had it all in. Then down we circled. As we got lower, the crowd, formerly eight or ten, thinned out until there were only two or three in sight. We had another little bundle of ribbon to throw out as we went by. We tossed the ribbon from about 200 feet and a brown-skinned man had it like the spider takes a fly. We shouted. From the man's gestures and from past experience in similar operations among other Indians, I feel sure that the man shouted back to us, flailing his arms. He was the only one in sight and when we circled around the other side of the house he ran in one side of the house and out the other.

"I felt a keen disappointment as I thought how frightened they must have been when we swooped low. However, as we circled slowly higher and higher, they seemed to regain confidence and slowly reappeared. Finally everyone seemed to be present. How we hope that they regained their 'party' spirit and laughed off their fright.

"Going away, we flew directly toward the Curaray, since we feel more and more that that will be the site of the first contact if the Lord is pleased to continue blessing our efforts."

CHAPTER XII
The Savages Respond

From all appearances, the Aucas understood the white man's attempt to introduce himself. They seemed to recognize the regularity of the flights, and in successive weeks appeared in large numbers, more eager than ever to receive the gifts. Had they any idea of reciprocating? What were their real reactions?

For the fourth flight, Nate rigged up the plane with a battery-powered loudspeaker. As they approached the clearings, Jim called out the Auca words, "I like you! I am your friend! I like you!" Then they dropped another machete, wrapped and decorated as usual. Jim's diary describes the reaction:

"A group raced back into the trees behind the house, and one lone man walked to the beach. He cupped his hands and seemed to shout, then flashed the new machete over his head. We dropped a small aluminum pot, with ribbons. It contained a yellow shirt and beads. The Aucas below us converged on it 'like women at a bargain counter,' as Nate put it, and one was soon flailing the shirt. As we approached the house, two canoes some distance below it going downstream turned and came back upstream hurriedly. At one time I noticed people come running up through the water onto the beach, and another time a single one with a white cloth.

"We returned via the Curaray, looking for possible landing beaches. Hopes not good. Guide us, Lord God."

Back at Arajuno, the three pioneers had a council of war, deciding that the next full moon would witness the first attempt at a contact on the ground with these remote people who had won their hearts. Nate wrote that night: "May God continue to put His good hand on the project and may we drop it when not fully assured of His direction. At present we feel unanimously that God is in it. May the praise be His, and may it be that some Auca, clothed in the righteousness of Jesus Christ, will be with us as we lift our voices in praise before His throne. Amen."

On the next trip their reception was even more favorable. McCully manned the mike to call out, "We like you! We like you! We have come to pay a visit." The Aucas danced about eagerly, grabbing the machete the men had thrown, and stripped its canvas so that it shone in the sun. While circling low Ed leaned far out the door and held out both hands. The Indians, about three of them, responded by reaching out their hands too.

Ed's observations on this trip were:

"No fear manifest today, even when the plane was down low. No running inside or away. Most stood under the banana trees, possibly because of the sun. The plane gets close but somehow one longs to get closer. No sign of malice or anger. No lances seen. If there were a ladder down from the plane to them it would seem a good and safe thing to go among them."

By this time each man on the team had had time to form a judgment. "The team has a spectrum that ranges from impatience to conservatism," wrote Nate. Pete, who constantly conferred with the other three, did not feel that the next full moon was the right time for the first attempt at contact. It was too soon to assume that a long-standing hatred of white men had been overcome. The language problem was a big one—and it lay within their power to gain more knowledge of it, by working with Dayuma, the escaped Auca woman from whom Jim had gathered his material. Ed's reaction was that the next move should not necessarily be an effort at contact, but rather the establishment of a usable airstrip down the Curaray, perhaps within five miles of the "neighborhood." Meanwhile Jim was "chewing the bit." If a friendly contact were made, Jim and I were prepared to leave the work in Shandia for a time, and go in and live among the Aucas. Nate felt that the men should follow the already-established course of making regular contacts and that nothing should be done suddenly, but that each advance be allowed to "soak in" before pressing another.

On November 12, Nate Saint returned to his self-imposed task of keeping the record of Operation Auca. He wrote:

"This was the sixth week in succession that we have visited the 'neighbors.' It was a beautiful Saturday morning. There wasn't much cargo to go along, nor much fog in the river valleys, so I got out to Ed's place at about 8:30 A.M. He was waiting at the airstrip when I arrived.

"We took off with the public-address system and reel aboard. Ed had a machete and a small aluminum pot and a large aluminum pot set up with ribbons. Again we flew down the Curaray at low altitude so as to familiarize ourselves with the sandbars and various possible landing locations along the river. With familiarity, the sandbars look increasingly useful for our purposes. When we got to the point where we were closest to the 'neighbors' we decided that rather than turn in to them, we would fly on down the big river to see if perhaps there might not be some ideal landing spot farther down. We found none. Then we decided that since we were down that far we'd go a little farther and turn back up the little branch river along which the Aucas live.

"We flew perhaps eight to ten minutes up the small river before we stumbled onto a house . . . one that we hadn't seen before. It had the coarser-leaf type of roof which slanted all the way to the ground, a gable roof. The ends of the house were also of leaf and slanted perhaps ten to fifteen degrees out from the vertical. We saw no one by whom we could judge the size of the house. It appeared to be smaller than the others, but if in reality it is smaller, then the doors in the ends were such as to require one to stoop quite low to enter. Outside the house were two distinct plantings—two patches. The taller growth was darker green and covered perhaps an acre. It did not appear to be manioc, being taller and thicker in the foliage cover. But, the interesting thing was that the plot was surrounded by a well-made fence comprised of upright posts perhaps six feet apart, interwoven with what could have been opened-up bamboo basket-weave style, so that apparently an animal larger than a cat might not be able to pass through the fence.

"After circling three times to have a good look, we headed upstream to the next house, which was the one we had previously supposed to be the most easterly of this group. This house is also the one at which we did the first 'line' drop of the little pailful of buttons. Here for the first time now on this trip we saw people, about six, I would guess. One went out on the sandbar where we had left the kettle before and waited patiently. When we waved and yelled, he waved but not with the enthusiasm that is always displayed at the other place. We supposed that he was an older fellow. His body appeared to be smeared with something opaque such as clay. There were no clothes in evidence. We made a run and dropped him a machete, free-fall. It landed right on the sandbar and was carried off with relatively little ceremony or enthusiasm. Nevertheless, there seemed to be no demonstration of hostility whatsoever; nor fear. We went on, after shouting with the public-address system that we were friends.

"At the next house we ran across a few of the 'neighbors' on the sandbar. We flew quite low, shouting and waving to them without using the public-address system. Then we dropped them the little pot. It hit the playa near them and was enthusiastically received. They jumped around quite excitedly.

"Also at this house (let's number them from the east, making this one No. 3) we noticed two items especially. First, at either side of the doorway were boards perhaps twenty-five inches wide and about five feet high, decorated with bold, bright red decorations. I suppose they are doors of some sort. The other item of note was that the owners had made a woven-leaf end for their house; heretofore it has been open where it faced on the river.

"From there we went on to house No. 4, which is the one we've visited most often and at which we've been received with the most evident enthusiasm. There was a good crowd on hand to welcome us. And to our surprise, out behind their house where there had been a stand of trees and undergrowth, there was now a clean clearing about seventy-five to ninety yards in diameter. Some of the stumps were still there, but aside from that it was as clean as a basketball court. From the reaction of the people below I would guess that they couldn't decide whether to expect the drop on their new clearing, or whether we would drop it down by the house as has been the custom."

Ed's diary picks up the account of this day's operation:

"We went in low and threw an axhead, wrapped in canvas. It lit just on the west side of the clearing in the bushes. They pounced on it immediately. Then we yelled. 'We will give you a pot,' and went up higher. Tied on the pot, and reeled it out. This was a definite leading of God, for we had almost decided to throw the pot free instead of bothering with the line. Nate made a perfect drop. I held the line and could feel their holding on to it. They cut the pot off—*and tied something on!* Nate spotted it and praised the Lord. When we got back to Arajuno we found that it was a *llaitu* or headband of woven feathers. A real answer to prayer; another sign to proceed, an encouragement that friendly relations are possible and that they will hear the Gospel!"

On November 26 Nate Saint recorded later developments:

"Last week, since Ed was not back from Quito in time for the usual run, Jim Elliot took it on with me. I picked him up in Shandia after doing some shuttling between Pano and Tena and Pano and Shandia. We stopped by Arajuno and picked up the 'gear.' There were two Indians near the plane and despite our caution they apparently managed to find out what was in the supply and said to Jim, 'Why do you crazy fellows give all that good stuff to Aucas?' Jim ignored the question; but it meant quite surely that the secret was more or less out, even though they could not know any of the details.

"We flew, as I recall, quite directly to the 'neighborhood' and started visiting around. At No. 4 house two men had climbed up on top of what we had previously thought of as a sun shelter—a high bamboo roof or platform perhaps six feet off the ground. We circled low several times and decided to go ahead with a previously-discussed plan aimed at getting them to cut down the trees at the far side of the clearing as a sort of approach or 'go-around' which would permit us to fly low enough for them to see us so as to be able to recognize us later on the ground. The plan was to drop our gifts into the trees we wanted down.

"First we dropped an axhead. Unfortunately it landed at the foot of the trees in question. Next time around we tossed out four plastic combs with streamers of bandage material tied on them. Happily a couple of them at least got hung up in the trees.

"Next we went to No. 3. Everyone was out in great style. One man had one of our gift shirts on. (The rest were in more typical uniform.) We circled and waved and then went on down to the old man's house He was out with his two women. We didn't feel that he warranted too good a gift, so we tossed him a pair of 'store-bought' trousers. After circling back to make sure he got them okay, we went on back to No. 3. We tossed the people there a machete with a pair of shorts attached.

"From here we climbed on up over No. 4 to get ready to let down the kettle for the last act of the day.

"I neglected to mention earlier that in rummaging in the emergency kit Ed had made up, we found a roll of tissue. We thought it might help to get those tall trees down if we were to drape the tissue along the treetops. Such a drop might seem to be utilizing their curiosity to an unfair advantage but on the other hand they were amply repaid for any trouble that they went to. When we tossed the roll, however, it reeled off about six feet and then the wind tore off that length. This process was repeated until there was a curious white dotted line floating down into the trees.

"The wind was rather strong today and I had trouble staying over the clearing as we let the kettle down. It required some six or eight attempts before the kettle landed in the little river at the edge of the clearing. They were at it in an instant. But in that same instant I had to roll out of the turn upwind to keep from getting too far from the clearing. That put quite a pull on the line at the moment they were trying to work with it. In about thirty seconds they let it go. It appeared to have a gift on it . . . something small, perhaps, like the combs [received earlier with the headband].

"As we left the area I called in and reported that we were on our way back. Marj answered that the Drown baby was sick and that I should make the best possible time so as to be able to fly into Macuma if necessary. Therefore, I flew at seventy miles per hour and somewhere along the line we lost the gift. About halfway back I noticed that it was missing. It was a keen disappointment."

In Jim's account of this day's operation, he said: "I saw a thing that thrilled me—it seemed an old man who stood beside the house waved with both his arms as if to signal us to come down! *Aucas*, waving to me to come! God send me soon to the Aucas!"

At the end of his record of the eighth visit, Nate wrote: "One of the problems we face now is getting another man to bring our manpower up to strength. The Lord is abundantly able!"

Although five men would eventually make up "Operation Auca," only three—Nate, Jim, and Ed—were definitely committed at this time. Pete, who had been as vitally interested as these three, was, however, not clear whether God's leading was for him to go or to stay.

It was now that Nate thought of Roger Youderian. They had worked together opening up the Atshuara country, building two other utstation airstrips, and Nate was sure of Roger's capabilities.

He saw him as a soldier of Christ, "a man capable of great effort, trained and disciplined," he wrote of him. "He knows the importance of unswerving conformity to the will of his Captain. Obedience is not a momentary option; it is a diecast decision made beforehand. He was a disciplined paratrooper. He gave Uncle Sam his best in that battle and now he is determined that the Lord Jesus Christ shall not get less than his best. Everything that made him a good soldier has been consecrated to Christ, his new Captain!"

Ed and Jim hardly knew Roger; working with different Indians in another part of the Oriente, they had had little occasion for more than a passing acquaintance. But they trusted Nate's judgment implicitly.

As it happened, Roger was in Shell Mera at this time. He had come out from Macuma to help build a mission-sponsored hospital there. So one day, as Roger was nailing down sheets of aluminum on the roof, Nate came to him, told him of Operation Auca, and asked him to go along as the badly-needed fourth man. Nate did not want to leave his plane on the beach at night where it might be open to damage. Neither was he anxious to leave the two men alone overnight. Would Roj go?

Roger agreed immediately. But all unknown to the others, he was, at that time, passing through a deeply personal spiritual struggle and he began to wonder if he should join the others in the physical venture when not with them completely in spirit.

Only he and Barbara were aware of the struggle he was going through. He questioned whether, after all, he was accomplishing anything whatever in the mission field. He had broken the language barrier, to be sure, but why had there not been an immediate show of fruit for his labors?

A missionary plods through the first year or two, thinking that things will be different when he speaks the language. He is baffled to find, frequently, that they are not. He is stripped of all that may be called "romance." Life has fallen more or less into a pattern. Day follows day in unbroken succession; there are no crises, no mass conversions, sometimes not even one or two to whom he can point and say: "There is a transformed life. If I had not come, he would never have known Christ." There will be those among the Indians who say that they accept Christ, but what of the forsaking of heathen custom and turning from sin to a life of holiness? The missionary watches, and longs, and his heart sickens.

The forces of evil, unchallenged for so long, are now set in array against the missionary.

Roger Youderian was finding out the power of these forces. He wrote in his diary: "About ready to call it quits. Seems to me there is no future in the Jivaria for us, and the wisest thing for us to do will be to pull stakes. Will wait until I've had a chance to talk it over with Barb and see what she has to say. We might pass Christmas here, finish the hospital in Shell, and head home. The reason: Failure to measure up as a missionary and get next to the people. As far as my heart and aspirations are concerned, the issue is settled. It's a bit difficult to discern just what is the cause of my failure and the forces behind it. Since March, when we left Wambimi, there has been no message from the Lord for us. I just picked up my Bible to share with the same Lord who made me a new creature in England eleven years ago. There was no word of encouragement from Him. He had kept us safe wonderfully, and met our needs, but the issue is far greater than that. There is no ministry for me among the Jivaros or the Spanish, and I'm not going to try to fool myself. I wouldn't support a missionary such as I know myself to be, and I'm not going to ask anyone else to. Three years is long enough to learn a lesson and learn it well. Some people are slow to catch on. It will be tough on Barb and the children, but I've always been convinced that honesty and sincerity pays. The milk is spilled—I'm not going to cry over it. The cause of Christ in the Jivaria will not suffer for our having been there, but I must be honest and confess that it has not been *helped*. I don't think it will come as much of a surprise to many and will only be an 'I told you so.'

"There is no spiritual pressure in the issue, and in fact very little of emotion or stress; perhaps none.

"I realize that many along the way will say that we gave up too easy. Perhaps. But I believe that God's way is to face the issue and let our *yea* be *yea* and *nay* be *nay*. I'm *amen* for the cause of Christ but believe that the part I ch——, no I cannot say the part I chose; I believe that the Lord chose the Jivaria for us but I just didn't measure up to it. You will say that when the Lord calls, He supplies. You can have my boots anytime you want them. It isn't there. I'm not good at pretending.

"I do not put any blame on personalities or circumstances involved; the failure is mine, and my failure to achieve the personal experience of Christ that could meet the needs here. It didn't pan out. It is not because of wife and family. Macuma station is ample for a home for them and all we need has been offered.

"The issue is personal, and personal it shall remain. What is the answer? I do not know. And I'm discouraged about finding any satisfactory solution. Have been battling and thinking the issue for many months. There is no answer. It is a combination of situations and talents that has me buffaloed. This is the first time in my life that I have turned my back, but they say there is a first time for everything.

"We are a happy family. He has kept us well and given us sound bodies and, we trust, sound minds. Whatever He has for us is fine but I'm afraid that anything along missionary lines has been scared out of me. If I couldn't make the grade here in Macuma I'm not foolish enough to expect a change of setting would change *me*. This is my personal 'Waterloo' as a missionary.

"It seems strange to try and sit back and view it in an impersonal way. Of this much I'm sure: it will draw me to read His word more, be more tolerant of others, and less venturesome in my activities.

"Some will wonder why we don't seek a place in the Spanish or Quichua work. Frankly, I'm not interested. And, especially after this experience, I'm not begging for any more headaches. Only a fool makes the same mistake twice. One mess seems to me ought to be enough.

"Here I sit at 11 A.M. Wednesday listening to the services. I told them from the window that I would not come. First they sang 'Wonderful Words of Life,' and then 'Oh Say but I'm Glad.' I've found an English hymn book to see if there might be some consolation in a hymn. There is none. It is beyond me. My, what a world of time I've wasted. The ruts are worn deep and it won't be easy to change habits and give up the lost ground or let it be gained by the Lord. But surely it will be worth the battle. My mind was made only to love Him; my body, also, which includes my tongue in all its activities. How slow some of us are to learn.

"I will be led and taught of the Holy Spirit. God desires full development, use, and activity of our faculties. The Holy Spirit can and will guide me in direct proportion to the time and effort I will expend to know and do the will of God. I must read the Bible to know God's will. At every point I will obey and do.

"A week spent in Shell Mera, prior to this period, when I reiterated many times a day 'Thy will be done' helped much to fortify me for this struggle."

Roger had not yet emerged from his "dark night of the soul" when Nate approached him. The days which followed found him in a desperate struggle to know the will of God. He had no doubt of his own desire—he would go if that were all that mattered. But to go without the smile of God—that would be impossible. "If Thy presence go not with us, carry us not up hence." Roger recognized something of what this decision might mean for him, and the hours spent on his knees with God witnessed agony of soul. But God, "who causes us to triumph," brought him out of his slough of despond.

"He was cleansed through the Spirit for the task that lay ahead of him," said Barbara afterward, "and went with a happy, expectant mind and his heart full of joy."

On December 19 he wrote in his diary: "I will die to self. I will begin to ask God to put me in a service of constant circumstances where to live Christ I must die to self. I will be alive unto God. That I may learn to love Him with my heart, mind, soul, and body."

Just before he left Macuma to join the four in Arajuno, he wrote:

> "There is a seeking of honest love
> Drawn from a soul storm-tossed,
> A seeking for the gain of Christ,
> To bless the blinded, the beaten, the lost.

> "Those who sought found Heavenly Love
> And were filled with joy divine,
> They walk today with Christ above
> . . . ."

The last line eluded him, and as he put down his pencil, he said, "Barb, I'll finish it when I get home."

CHAPTER XIII
The Search for "Palm Beach"

Although plans for meeting the Aucas on the ground occupied more and more time, the regular weekly visits to "Terminal City," the name the men had given to the Auca village, were continued without a break. On December 3 Nate recorded the ninth visit:

"We left Arajuno at about 8:45 with good weather. Before taking off, Ed and I shot some pictures that we hope will be suitable for enlargement up to almost life-size so that the 'neighbors' will recognize us when they first see us on the ground. We took close-ups of our faces, together with the combs and headdress they had given us.

"When we got over the first house, No. 4, we noted that a couple of pretty big trees were chopped down where we had tossed the gifts into the trees for that purpose. There are not many trees left now between the two clearings. If we can get them to cut down the rest, we will be able to make low passes.

"Once this morning we swooped down so low that the two men who were up on the platform 'directing traffic' ducked down. When we swooped down again the two were content to view the proceedings from the ground. The platform appeared to be perhaps eight feet off the ground. Both the platform-men had on shirts, period: shirts we had given them, of course. In these runs we dropped an axhead, a plastic cup, and a cheap knife. We tried again to put these in the trees that still separate the two clearings. There were perhaps a half dozen other people around No. 4.

"From there we went to No. 3. As we made a low pass we nearly fell out of the airplane, for there on the grass roof of the house was a model plane! We wondered if they made it after observing the model plane at Ed's place. In any case it indicates good will, and a craftsmanship hitherto unsuspected among such primitives.

"We noticed another platform, larger and higher than the other and made of chonta. I'd guess it is fifteen feet off the ground. On top was a man complete with his uniform (shirt). He waved responsively as we waved to him. We made a couple of passes and tossed out a machete so that it fell just beyond the 'director.' We noted that the east wall of leaves was off the house, so that we could see inside . . . fire sites, et cetera. It was a very friendly-looking deal, but it's possible that they are going to put in a chonta wall to replace the leaves. Yes, I just checked the photo of No. 3 taken a while back, and it shows leaf-wall all the way around except at the river end which was open. It is easy to see how the availability of even so simple a tool as the machete can profoundly alter a culture.

"Next we decided to have a close look at a fresh clearing that has been made on the ridge-crest just above No. 3. No one was there. We discussed briefly the possible benefits of trying to lure them up and decided to try. First time around we tossed out an aluminum kettle. It was a poor shot and fell into the forest, fortunately on the slope facing the No. 3 house. It was then that we noticed that the undergrowth on the slope was in the process of being cleared out. That means that they will be tipping over the trees on that edge of the clearing which will enable us to fly within twenty feet of them in perfect safety. As a further lure Ed decided we should toss out a cheap, plastic-handled knife. (All these gifts are generously trailed by ribbon and bandage material.) In view of the miss with the kettle I said to Ed as we approached, 'Let's put this one right on top of the house,' referring to the sketchy shelter that must serve as a sun-shade while they work on the new clearing project. And that's exactly where it landed . . . right on the roof.

" 'Let's go see how the old man liked his new pants,' I suggested. 'Okay' . . . so we went. He is about two minutes away from No. 3. He was waiting for us in pants and tee-shirt. His two women were out, too. One 'wore' a baby and the other nothing. The area around their house was nicely cleaned up, grass cut down to roots, et cetera. The old man evidenced the usual reserve and lack of enthusiasm. We dropped him a machete. One of the women had to go get it. His gestures are willing but slow. We flew by within 200 feet of them about three times, and headed back up river to No. 3.

"Back at No. 3 area we checked the hilltop clearing again. From a quarter-mile away I could see that someone was there. We were thrilled by this quick result since we had thought it might take weeks to coax them up. The figures proved to be two women, young; I would say about sixteen and twenty, maybe. They had got the knife and we passed within fifty feet of them taking pictures. We made about four passes and for the first time looked full into an Auca face. She was good looking with hair cropped to bangs in front. The 'controller' of No. 3 was still on the platform. We waved good-by to him and headed on toward No. 4.

"Back at No. 4 the boys were all waiting for the last act, the 'bucket drop.' We climbed up to 3,000 feet and slowed down to forty-five miles per hour with power off. In this slow, power-off glide the kettle gets clear of the plane very nicely. It took only about three times around to set the kettle in the middle of the big clearing behind the house. They ran back and forth in a group, curiously to us. I was afraid that I was piling loose cord in after the kettle . . . however it seemed to have too much tension on it for that. Finally, after a minute and a half, they turned it loose and up it came with a gift . . . bright red and good-sized.

"We flew back to Arajuno at fifty-five to sixty miles per hour so as not to lose the gift if we could help it. We had no trouble setting the gift down on the runway and then we dropped the cord. On the ground we ran to the spot. We found another feathered crown— a new one, freshly made, and attached to it a little hank of hand-spun cotton string. It was all attached to our drop-line with a square knot."

That night Ed noted in his diary: "It is time we were getting closer to them on the ground." To Jim he wrote: "I've been giving the trip some thought, and I feel this way: we should set a definite limit on the number of days we will wait on the Curaray for them, and if they don't show, we should be ready to go in to them. For myself, I am definitely ready to go in and feel that it would be reasonably safe . . . if we can ever use that term in our initial ground contact with these people! We should go in (1) wearing the headdresses, (2) carrying small airplanes such as I have hanging here, (3) carrying gifts wrapped as we have been wrapping them, (4) shouting '*biti miti punimupa*' (I like you) or other phrases that we are making familiar from the plane. God being with us—and up to this point we have every confidence that He is—I think this would put us in. The whole project is moving faster than we had originally dared to hope, and while I'm not for getting ahead of God, I feel that we shouldn't lag."

On December 10, Nate's journal continues with an account of the next visit:

"In spite of our evasive maneuver Ed's Indians tell him that they were down the Curaray last week and saw us go by. They say (what a sense of humor!) that they stripped off their clothes when they heard us coming and got sticks like lances so that we would think they were 'neighbors.' They probably thought that we would drop them gifts.

"During the week, in talks with the members of the team it was decided that January 2 would be the tentative date for the entry attempt. We were thinking in terms of going down with Indians, setting up a house and then having the Indians retire while the team would wait for a contact. Then with the plane we would try to get the 'neighbors' to come over and pay a visit. We know how to say 'come to my house' and also 'Curaray' in their tongue. And I feel confident that by repeated circling right over the ridge from them we can use curiosity to bring them over to the big river.

"Roughly, the strategy calls for the carrying of arms only by missionary personnel, and that out of sight. We presume that the first shot fired signals the failure of the entire project and the scuttling of any hope in the near future. Therefore utmost care will be taken and the guns will be used only to frighten the savages in case of need of self-defense.

"There were two views or two possibilities under consideration: (1) Set up a little house at Palm Beach [the name agreed upon to designate the river beach chosen for landing the plane] and then retire until the 'neighbors' would have had time to visit the site, and go back later; or, (2) Set up and attempt to make contact on that first trip. Since the events of this morning further affect this decision, I'll leave further discussion of it till later.

"This morning we took off from 'Centerville' [Arajuno] at about 9:15, armed with gift-wrapped machetes, axes and small knives, and plastic items.

"We also had three pairs of one-pound paper packages of paint pigment powder in three bright colors. These were for measuring playa sites that might serve for Palm Beach. Yesterday we ran tests here at Shell and found that when flying at sixty-five miles per hour we could drop little bags of flour at seven-second intervals and pretty consistently mark off from 190 to 210 yards. This measure was taken in view of the impossibility of satisfactorily estimating the length of sandbars where there is nothing that would serve as a basis of comparison.

"We took a route down the Nushino, inasmuch as some of the Indians from Ed's station were down on the Curaray River fishing again this week. We gradually eased over to the south and picked up the Curaray in the area where we hoped to find a good site for Palm Beach. It wasn't long before we located a possibility. Most of the larger playas are on bends and therefore of no value without having approaches cut first. The river is so serpentine that there are few possibilities of a sandbar along a straight stretch. We dragged [flew low over] the first. It seemed reasonable. The only drawback was that this beach would require take-offs with the prevailing wind . . . a serious difficulty. Nevertheless, after dragging it a time or two we 'bombed' it with pigment and found that it had about 200 yards usable. Another difficulty was a big dead tree lying on the sand which forced the landing area very close to the river-bank foilage.

"The next one we found was about a mile or less downstream. It looked better—better approaches, especially into the prevailing wind. The approach would be steep but possible. The playa is low to the water so that a flood would easily cover it, but it is pebbly and firm-looking. We 'bombed' it and found a conservative 200 yards usable. I should not be surprised if a measure would show it to be more like 230 yards usable. Also it is such that an overshot landing would only put us into shallow water. We dragged it once, keeping good airspeed until more familiar with the pull-out area. In the pull-out the trees along the banks overhang enough that it is a little squeaky, but by tipping over two trees after we land, we can take care of that problem.

"It began to look as if this would be our 'Palm Beach.' We decided to shoot a simulated landing on it. Down close to it I could see the surface well and I put the wheels down lightly twice as we accelerated again for the pull-up. The surface was smooth as a gravel runway and seemed hard. It is really ideal, except for vulnerability to flooding.

"This finding brings into focus the possibility of landing the team right there with a prefabricated tree house and aluminum for a roof. It would mean that no Indians need to be in on the deal at all, and barring flood it would mean that I'd be able to fly them all out following a contact or whenever they should be ready to come.

"The picture would be something like this: (1) On a Friday morning, Lord willing, free-fall supplies and equipment onto the Palm Beach site from very low (just off the runway) so as to be sure they would not be in the landing area. (2) We land with Jim and Roger, keeping the plane very light. (3) We land with Ed and aluminum. (4) We land with Pete and more supplies (if Pete should feel led to go).

"On arrival, Jim and Roj would go to work tipping over the two or three medium-to-small trees in the approach. Then they would pick out a suitable tree for mounting the prefab tree house and start clearing around it. When the others are with them, all would go downstream to the first bend and tip over at least one of the two trees on opposite banks which make the pass rather narrow. (This is not an absolute must, but would be highly desirable.) During this part of the operation someone should always have a hand on a weapon inside a bag so that it could be fired on a moment's notice and thus upset the equilibrium of any possible lancer.

"Next, back to the sandbar, with two men widening the clearing at the foot of the tree while two work on getting the tree house up in place and the aluminum roof on. Once the house is all set, the men would rotate on the clearing, perhaps with one fellow still concentrating on getting food supplies, stove, water, et cetera, up onto the platform. One man, resting from the clearing crew, could sit on the platform and cover the men on the ground, always keeping arms strictly out of sight. By evening, there ought to be a fair-sized clearing at the base of the tree, connected by clearing to the playa. The plane returns to Arajuno after checking radio set-up in the tree house, et cetera.

"Next day the plane begins the invitation of the 'neighbors' to the Palm Beach site, both by calling phrases as well as by coaxing, circling in that direction from where they are and then landing at Palm Beach and repeating every hour or so until we're sure they've caught on. Another detail will be the installation of a good-sized model plane on the site.

"Maybe five days would be committed to the effort. If unsuccessful we would withdraw, either by air or by sending a crew of Indians down river in canoes. Supplies in the tree house should be sufficient for two weeks to cover possible loss of the playa by flood or siege, the two rougher possibilities to be faced.

"The practicability of a raft composed of air mattresses and bamboo should be reckoned with as a downstream exit to an Army base on the Curaray in case the Indians should refuse to go to the rescue.

"Back to the narrative: We checked course and distance from the Palm Beach possibility to Terminal City—135 degrees and three minutes at ninety miles per hour. That makes about four and one-half miles from the beach on the Curaray to the Auca village.

"While letting down we headed east to the old man's house. The old boy wasn't there but a young man was waving something like bark cloth and clearly offering it for trade. In the course of four passes we dropped (I think) a small knife, plastic cup, and possibly some article of clothing . . . not sure of the latter.

"Next we moved up to the clearing on the hill above the airplane house, or No. 3. There were two women there. We dropped a small knife. The head man was down by the house on his platform directing traffic. He had on a red and black checkered shirt we dropped last week. We signaled and shouted to him, indicating that we wanted him to come up to the hilltop. While we circled some more he disappeared from the platform and two younger boys took up his post. Next we made a low pass to drop an axhead beyond the platform. We must have scared the younger fellows because one of them had a lance in his hand as we circled back. That was an unkind gesture and we swooped down low again to see if they would show any hostility. Someone must have given them the word because the lance had disappeared and all seemed well. Now we spotted the boss-man in the checkered shirt up on the hill. We couldn't afford to slight him so we made two passes and on the second dropped him a pair of pants which he caught in mid-air. (These fellows will be dressed like dudes before we get to see them on the ground.)

"Next, up to No. 4 and the main act. The big shots, four of them, were clad in white tee-shirts. Youngsters and women were in the older uniform. The trees that we had tried to get them to cut down by tossing stuff into them, were now cut down. Also the walls (chonta) were off the house. (I failed to mention that they were also off No. 3.)

And beside the house they had built a new and higher platform like No. 3's.

"We made a couple of low passes, calling to them, 'I like you, I like you,' et cetera. On the last low pass we tossed them a machete. While passing low we saw one of the four Big Wheels holding up a package, roundish and brown. We figured this was our trade item. We pulled up and climbed slowly. Ed was feeling pretty rough. It has been an unusually strenuous workout and Ed had had to attend to a sick baby across the river from his place earlier in the morning. He hadn't been feeling too sharp then. I was also feeling as though I'd been dragged through a keyhole but it was worth it. At 3,000 feet I throttled all the way back, pulled flaps, and settled into the quiet of a forty-five-mile-per-hour glide while Ed got the gift overboard on the line. This week we gave them a couple of little bundles of string, a few smaller items, and four six-by-nine-inch portraits of the team members, tinted and bearing the insignia of the operation, a drawing of the little yellow airplane. These were glue-mounted on Masonite board.

"When this stuff got down over by the trees, they got it and quickly took it out to the center of the clearing. They went into a 100 percent huddle over the contents of the white cloth mail sack that carried the mentioned items, except for the fellow who was busy fastening on their gift to us. I saw the gift leave him, drifting lazily. I rolled out of the turn and added power. Within three or four seconds the package was swished skyward from them and the last man joined the huddle over the pictures. What wouldn't we have given to see those boys studying out our pictures and see their reactions!

"We headed home at sixty-five miles per hour with the prize dangling at the end of the line. At Arajuno we set it down at the edge of the strip, cut the line and landed. On the ground, I bashed my way through the brush at the edge of the strip while Ed lost his breakfast. This is the first time I've beat him to the prize. (His legs are at least a foot longer than mine.) When I got to the bark-cloth bag, it was moving. Since we had given them a chicken last week I figured it would be a bird, but as I started to peek in a hole the thought of a snake crossed my mind. However, it was a nice parrot in a basket covered with bark. It was well tied and was complete with a partially-nibbled banana inside for the trip!

"I had lunch with Ed and Marilou and talked of the possibilities opened to us by the finding of a beach we could land on. We praise God for this—another indication of His leading and care. We believe that in a short time we shall have the privilege of meeting these fellows with the story of the Grace of God."

CHAPTER XIV
An Auca on the Path

Friday a.m.!" Nate tapped out this opening on a borrowed typewriter in Arajuno, and continued: "This morning in Shell Mera as I was dressing in the bedroom adjoining the office-radio room, I heard Marj checking a message just received from Marilou McCully, who was holding down Arajuno alone while Ed helped in a conference ministry at Puyupungu. Marilou said she had rather sound reason to believe that Aucas were in the neighborhood.

"Two things flashed through my mind: first, the opportunity to make contact with them, then the danger that a shot by one of the local Indians would ruin all the efforts made up till now—and the consequent closing of the door that seems to be opening to us.

"While Marj got the message relayed to Ed down at Puyupungu, I was rolling the plane out of the hangar. Too much was at stake to hesitate. Also, the weather was threatening to sour to the north. The mission house at Puyupungu is about five minutes from the airstrip. I got to the airstrip about one minute before Ed. We returned to Shell Mera immediately. Then while Johnny gassed the plane, Marj and Ruth got some cargo and vegetables ready. Ed loaded, and I got some equipment together for the special nature of the expedition. I found that the little blank pistol I had just bought in Quito felt very nice in my pocket. It must be because I feel that it would surely break up an attack, yet I can feel confident of not accidentally hurting anyone with it. It also shoots tear gas cartridges, but as Ed notes, if there is an attack on and I get close enough to use tear gas . . . well.

"The weather held okay until we got over the Arajuno headwater valleys. There, low ceilings pushed us down into the valley and within five minutes of Arajuno the clouds were on the mesas that line the half-mile-wide valley. I kept a weather eye on the valley behind, got a final look at the clear area beyond the edge of the overcast and weighed the alternatives. In case of trouble, I could spiral up to 5,000 and head southwest into the clear area five minutes away. I yawed the plane to check the turn-and-bank indicator, without which this maneuver would be impossible. It was okay. Light rain—heavier in patches—made us circle a time or two to get a good look ahead. We slipped across the ridge and down the other valley. In about another minute (these are the long kind of minutes that seem to last about five minutes each) we had the strip under us. We kind of figured the Aucas might have wanted to take a look at the plane on the ground, and, not having found it at Arajuno, they might have headed for home. We then circled several times to let the 'neighbors' know we'd come to welcome them. We landed around 8:30. As the bad weather moved southwest it became apparent that if we had delayed five or ten minutes we would have been too late.

"Walking from the strip to the house we wondered if we were being watched. Ed went ahead with both hands full. If they are looking for large steaks on long bone, they passed it up this time. I had one hand in my pocket nonchalantly flipping the safety on and off on my blank pistol, all the while wondering how far things should go before allowing a shot to signal the end of the whole operation. Again we felt the need of God's guidance and intervention in a special way.

"As we neared the house we heard a Christmas carol in Quichua. Ed explained that Marilou was rehearsing the local Indians for a Christmas program. When we got in the house, Ed took over for a few minutes and gave the locals a pep talk on 'How to win friends and influence people,' also exhorting the Indians regarding our Christian obligations to reach the Aucas with the Gospel. It would seem that at this point the measure of missionary zeal among these new converts would depend pretty much on who saw whom first and under what circumstances.

"The rehearsal for the Christmas program proceeded rather anemically a few minutes longer and was then dismissed. Ed politely asked the Indians to hit the road for home. But they hung around. Finally, Ed offered them candy if they'd go. They agreed. He gave the two leaders some special candy for extra bravery.

"When we were finally alone, Ed ambled into the living room like the friendly local patrolman and said to Marilou, 'Now get ahold of yourself, lady. Everything's going to be okay. All we want are the facts.' (The capacity of these guys to toss something like this into a serious situation is a great asset. It kind of double-clutches you into second gear when you've been pulling too hard in high.)

"It seems that at 5:40 A.M., Fermin, the Indian who has been sleeping in the schoolhouse to help guard while Ed is away, went down the path toward the *chacra* to take care of the exigencies of nature. When about as far as the pole that holds the model plane aloft, he spotted a man at the end of the path . . . naked, with lance, and with hair tied up in a bun on the back of his head. As they saw each other the Auca ran into the forest. At 5:40 and ten seconds past, Fermin was calling at Marilou's window. Fortunately his gun (in the schoolroom) was not loaded and he needed powder and shot. Of course Marilou would not give him any. He was sure she had gone mad and proceeded to try to convince her with sound advice on how to take care of Aucas. He was genuinely pale and excited. It looked like the real thing.

"First Marilou took the empty gun from the poor fellow. Then, although she is seven months pregnant, Marilou took a machete for a gift and headed down the path calling '*biti miti punimupa*' . . . I like you . . . I like you. In between her calls she could hear Fermin calling after her in Quichua . . . 'You're crazy . . . you're crazy . . . they'll kill you first.' When she was two-thirds the way to the spot where the savage had been seen, Fermin and Carmela, the Indian girl who lives with Marilou to help in the house, both came running and caught up just in time for them all three to see a fresh wet footprint on a dry board across a little ditch. The print was headed toward the house. Across the path they found grass recently stepped on, leading to the forest. Marilou then tossed the machete on the fresh path, called out some more, and returned to the house. Half an hour later when the local witch doctor arrived for school, he accompanied Marilou to the spot. Finding no further indication of visitors, Marilou picked up the machete and they came back to the house. Carmela expressed a common feeling when she said she would have suspected that Fermin imagined seeing an Auca until she saw the footprint. When Marilou asked her if she was afraid she said she was only a little afraid, and that she was sure God would take care of them. Then Marilou heard Fermin call in to Carmela and ask if the Señora was scared. Carmela answered that as far as she could tell, she wasn't; to which Fermin answered that she would be when night came and he wasn't there to protect them. Marilou then asked him if he was going to stay that night. 'I will stay,' he said, 'if I have a loaded gun. Without a gun we will all be killed.'

"We talked things over while Ed prepared a machete and a pot the way we do when we deliver them at the 'neighborhood.' At 10:30 (still raining lightly) we paraded down the airstrip decked out in the feather headdresses they have given us on the line and calling in Auca phrases while waving the gifts over our heads. We must have looked like a couple of Don Quixotes in the role of Santa Claus delivering goodies to the trees.

"At 2:30 P.M., we made another safari down to the far end of the airstrip making our most unusual offer. Then we decided that evening would be the most probable time to contact them here so we'd fly down to the 'neighborhood,' count heads, and do tomorrow's drop today. We got ready and off, arriving over Palm Beach at 3:30. Spent about ten minutes there rechecking the beach. Dye and bandage material still on the sand, although nearby playas seem to have been under water at some time since last week's visit. We rolled the wheels of the plane on the beach about seventy-five yards and then poured on the coal. The approach is really difficult, but the pull-out is good except for one narrow place, but that is a good way downstream. The whole site had a friendly look to us this time. We checked trees along the beach that might be suitable for the tree house and then took the three-minute trip over to the 'neighborhood.'

"We found our friends scattered, with no waiting traffic manager, making us think that maybe indeed we had gotten them on a seven-day week by the regularity of previous visits. We made a couple of low passes over the old man's house, taking movies in slow motion. One person showed up holding the same piece of material as last week. We dropped nothing. At the airplane house we found about four people around the house and platform and three up on the cleared hill. The fellow on the hilltop had on the red swimming trunks [an earlier gift]. We dropped him a small knife with appropriate ribbons and hurried on to the main house, since by now we were convinced that men were clearly missing, making it probable that the visit at Arajuno was indeed real.

"We made a couple of low passes taking movies and then pulled up and let out a pot on the line. The contents of the pot this week were little packages of food wrapped in banana leaves, beef, chocolate, manioc, cookies, candy, and some beads. They received these gifts and helped themselves to about twenty to fifty yards of line and tied on a gift. It was larger and heavier than any so far. We made tracks for Arajuno with it. We let it down, cut the line, landed, and hit out through the brush, trusting that any intelligent snake would know enough to get out of our way. (There's anti-venin in the plane.) The gift was a large black bird, apparently their chicken, in a basket cage reinforced with netting and a piece of bark cloth. We still haven't decided what to do with the bird. Also in the cage there was a spinner's distaff loaded with cotton yarn, a well-received gift.

"Evening and night in Arajuno . . ."

CHAPTER XV
Why Did the Men Go?

The time was ripening fast. The men and the other wives and I spent long hours discussing this project of which we had dreamed for so many months and years. Olive Fleming remembered what she had read in Pete's diary of his willingness to give his life for the Aucas. I reminded Jim of what we both knew it might mean if he went. "Well, if that's the way God wants it to be," was his calm reply. "I'm ready to die for the salvation of the Aucas." While still a student in college Jim had written: "He is no fool who gives what he cannot keep to gain what he cannot lose."

Marilou McCully said: "I hope no one feels any pressure is being put on Ed to go. This is a thing for each couple to face by themselves."

Two gift flights remained before the actual ground operation was to begin. On December 23, when the Elliots and Flemings had gone to Arajuno to spend Christmas with the McCullys, Nate flew Jim over the Auca settlement. Seeing the same old man they had noticed before standing in a clearing, they swooped down past him at no more than fifty feet.

"Wow!" said Jim, "That guy's scared stiff!"

Nate agreed. "It's as though they had steeled themselves against doing anything that would express either fear or hostility," he wrote later. "Possibly afraid that they might scare away the chicken that lays the golden eggs. But their eyes don't lie—they're full of terror. Understandable, though. The expression is that of a six-year-old in the front row when the circus clown points a big gun right in his face. He's sure it's all in fun, but . . . oh, brother!

"At the main house the 'chief traffic director' was in full uniform—shirt and pants—everyone else more typically dressed, or undressed. Jim counted thirteen on hand. On our first swoop past, one of them held up what was apparently to be our gift. We dropped them a carrying net containing white cloth, a flashlight, a pair of pants, and other trinkets. What wouldn't we give to see them trying to make sense out of that flashlight!

"Jim announced the take-off of their gift on the line, and I rolled out of the turn to hold it up. It is the heaviest yet. We cruised at sixty-five back to Arajuno, and let the bark-cloth bundle down hard. It hit in some bushes about twenty yards from Ed's house. Contents:

"Cooked fish
Two or three little packets of peanuts
A couple of pieces of cooked manioc
A cooked plantain
Two squirrels, very apparently killed by the hard fall
One parrot, alive but a bit nervous
Two bananas in with the parrot
Two pieces of pottery, clay, busted to bits in the fall
A piece of cooked meat and a smoked monkey tail

"This is by far the most all-out effort at a fair-trade arrangement on the part of the neighbors. We are all delighted. Jim and Ed sampled the meat, and we all ate some of the peanuts. Then, meaning no ill to the kind folks who mailed all those goodies to us, we sat down and ate the meal that Marilou had prepared."

Even though Pete had not yet made his final decision, he and Olive with three other couples who would be directly involved in the project were together on the 23rd for discussion. (Roger and Barbara Youderian still were on their station in the southern jungle.) The wives were particularly concerned to know exactly what provisions were to be made for safety. It was decided that arms would be carried, concealed, and that if the situation appeared to be getting delicate, they would be shown, simply to let the Aucas know that the white man held the upper hand. If this were not enough, shots would be fired with the intention only of scaring them.

Roger had drawn up a plan of operation. Jim was assigned to the task of prefabricating a house to put up in a tree. This would ensure safety at night, especially if a gasoline pressure lamp were kept burning to illumine the area at the foot of the tree. Ed was responsible for collecting items for trade with the Aucas. Roj would make up the first-aid kit, Nate saw to the communications and transportation, Jim took charge of arms and ammunition, and when later on Pete decided that he would go too, he was to be responsible for helping Nate on the flights to and from Arajuno, for flights over the Auca houses when he would shout over the loudspeaker, and for keeping supplies on the beach. Roj prepared a set of code signs to be drawn in the sand on the beach in case of emergency, and drew maps for each man with the code names he had made up for the strategic points.

The language material which Jim and I had gathered in previous weeks was organized and memorized by each member of the party. Marj's place was to be at the radio in Shell Mera, standing by at all times when the plane was flying, and keeping set schedules of contact with the men on the ground. It was decided that Barbara would stay in Arajuno, helping Marilou with the preparation of food which Nate was to fly daily to Palm Beach.

The appearance of the Auca at Arajuno, the fact that the Quichuas were guessing a little too shrewdly for comfort, the great encouragement in the drop flights—indeed, even the weather itself—seemed to be catapulting them toward their D-day with now-

or-never exigency. Within a month the rainy season would start, flooding the rivers and making landings impossible. The ideal time for establishment of their beachhead in Auca territory would be early January during the full of the moon.

They set the date for Tuesday, January 3, 1956.

Christmas at Arajuno was made as much like Christmas at home as Marilou's genius could make it. She even had a little Christmas tree, made of bamboo and decorated with lights and tinsel. Ed and Jim, who already had "reserved seats" for the trip to Palm Beach, were keyed up. Pete was still waiting on God in prayer before making his final decision to go.

The other wives and I talked together one night about the possibility of becoming widows. What would we do? God gave us peace of heart, and confidence that whatever might happen, His Word would hold. We knew that "when He putteth forth His sheep, He goeth before them." God's leading was unmistakable up to this point. Each of us knew when we married our husbands that there would never be any question about who came first—God and His work held first place in each life. It was the condition of true discipleship; it became devastatingly meaningful now.

It was a time for soul-searching, a time for counting the possible cost. Was it the thrill of adventure that drew our husbands on? No. Their letters and journals make it abundantly clear that these men did not go out as some men go out to shoot a lion or climb a mountain. Their compulsion was from a different source. Each had made a personal transaction with God, recognizing that he belonged to God, first of all by creation, and secondly by redemption through the death of His Son, Jesus Christ. This double claim on his life settled once and for all the question of allegiance. It was not a matter of striving to follow the example of a great Teacher. To conform to the perfect life of Jesus was impossible for a human being. To these men, Jesus Christ was God, and had actually taken upon Himself human form, in order that He might die, and, by His death, provide not only escape from the punishment which their sin merited, but also a *new kind of life*, eternal both in length and in quality. This meant simply that Christ was to be obeyed, and more than that, that He would provide the power to obey. The point of decision had been reached. God's command "Go ye, and preach the gospel to every creature" was the categorical imperative. The question of personal safety was wholly irrelevant.

On Sunday afternoon, December 18, Nate Saint sat at his typewriter to tell the world why they were going—just in case. In speaking these words he spoke for all: "As we weigh the future and seek the will of God, does it seem right that we should hazard our lives for just a few savages? As we ask ourselves this question, we realize that it is not the call of the needy thousands, rather it is the simple intimation of the prophetic Word that there shall be some from every tribe in His presence in the last day and in our hearts we feel that it is pleasing to Him that we should interest ourselves in making an opening into the Auca prison for Christ.

"As we have a high old time this Christmas, may we who know Christ hear the cry of the damned as they hurtle headlong into the Christless night without ever a chance. May we be moved with compassion as our Lord was. May we shed tears of repentance for these we have failed to bring out of darkness. Beyond the smiling scenes of Bethlehem may we see the crushing agony of Golgotha. May God give us a new vision of His will concerning the lost and our responsibility.

"Would that we could comprehend the lot of these stone-age people who live in mortal fear of ambush on the jungle trail . . . those to whom the bark of a gun means sudden, mysterious death . . . those who think all men in all the world are killers like themselves. If God would grant us the vision, the word sacrifice would disappear from our lips and thoughts; we would hate the things that seem now so dear to us; our lives would suddenly be too short, we would despise time-robbing distractions and charge the enemy with all our energies in the name of Christ. May God help us to judge ourselves by the eternities that separate the Aucas from a comprehension of Christmas and Him, who, though He was rich, yet for our sakes became poor so that we might, through His poverty, be made rich.

"Lord, God, speak to my own heart and give me to know Thy Holy will and the joy of walking in it. Amen."

CHAPTER XVI
"We Go Not Forth Alone"

New Year's Day, 1956, saw Ed and his family, and Pete and Olive Fleming, in Shandia with Jim and me, while Roger and Barbara Youderian stayed in the McCully house in Arajuno, to be on hand in case the "neighbors" came calling. Nate was completing his preparations for the very serious task of transporting the missionaries and their equipment to the beachhead. Monday morning, January 2, was a clear day for flying. By this time Pete had decided to go, so Nate had planned to get Pete and Olive and the McCullys back to Arajuno from Shandia that day, and to shuttle Jim over on Tuesday. But on the morning radio contact he said: "Think you better get ready to go to Arajuno today, Jim. We need time tonight for plans, and ought to take advantage of the good weather."

Jim began throwing his things into an Indian carrying-net while the McCullys and Flemings were flown over to Arajuno. Everything he could think of that might help or amuse the Aucas, should they pay the men a visit, Jim put into the bag: harmonica, snakebite kit, flashlight, View-Master with picture reels, yo-yo, and, above all, the precious notebook of Auca language material, with the carefully arranged morphology file. I helped Jim get his things together, wondering all the while, "Will this be the last time I'll help him pack? Will this be the last lunch he'll eat in Shandia?"

When the little plane returned, circling over the airstrip, preparing to land to pick up Jim, his baggage, and the last few pieces of the prefabricated tree house he had made, we went together out the front door. Jim did not look back. At the strip he kissed me good-by, and the plane was off.

That night in Arajuno the five men made a tentative schedule of timing for the next day's landing on Palm Beach in order to see whether the whole setup on the beach could be ready by evening. No detail was omitted; lists of equipment for each flight were made, and copies distributed among members. After supper and schedule conference, the stuff was laid out. The place began to look like a full-scale beachhead as each man checked and completed his equipment lists.

When they turned in, sleep did not come easily for Nate, on whom rested the greatest burden of responsibility. He was spending the night at Arajuno in order to save time in the morning. His diary tells of that night:

"I drowsed off quite soon, but was checking the luminous face of my watch dial at 12:30, again at 2:00, and from then on I was on horizontal listening-post guard duty. I prayed, tried repeating verses from memory, and even counting. My entire share in this business seemed to hinge on that first take-off and landing. Then, too, I had told the fellows that I would only take one in alone on the first trip. That meant a lonely vigil for someone. Roj was ruled out, because he spoke only Jivaro. Ed had already beat Jim by pulling straws, but Jim held out, claiming to be lighter. When I said a difference of fifteen pounds would be decisive, they dragged out the bathroom scales. Ed was only seven pounds heavier than Jim. 'Why, you cotton picker!' said Jim. 'You've lost weight.' "

Nate continued in his diary: "If I should misjudge, Ed and I would really be in a fix. If the plane were damaged it would mean vulnerability in a flood, possibly even dismantling it and making a strip on higher ground—all this in a forest inhabited by Aucas! We had faced it in the light of past tests and decided to go ahead. As I slept, or tried, it was still a rough decision. But there was no doubt in my mind that we should forge ahead. The stakes warranted it.

"The last time I 'punched in' was 4 A.M. From four until movement in the house woke me at 5:45, I slept."

The morning of January 3 dawned clear. Somehow Nate found time later to record the events of that day—the day of the first landing in Auca territory:

"Roj and I got right out to the plane. We'd been losing fluid out of the right brake. With a ten-cc syringe and No. 22 hypodermic needle we sucked brake fluid out of the left master cylinder and injected it into the right. No soap. Not enough. We'd lost too much when I fixed the brake fitting the night before.

"The others were hauling boards and equipment and aluminum to the strip and arranging all in order of priority.

"At the 7 A.M. radio contact we asked Marj to ask Johnny to bring us brake fluid as quickly as possible. Also, Olive had had a rough night (sick) and planned to go back to Shell with Johnny. This delay gave us a peaceful breakfast and time for prayer together."

At the close of their prayers the five men sang one of their favorite hymns, "We Rest on Thee," to the stirring tune of "Finlandia." Jim and Ed had sung this hymn since college days and knew the verses by heart. On the last verse their voices rang out with deep conviction.

"We rest on Thee, our Shield and our Defender,
Thine is the battle, Thine shall be the praise
When passing through the gates of pearly splendor
Victors, we rest with Thee through endless days."

Nate's terse account continues: "It was a beautiful day. Chiggers kept us scratching, but spirits were all high. Johnny hove in sight at 7:40. We decided he should stand by till we'd see how the first landing turned out. Ed and I got airborne at about 8:02 A.M. Curiously enough we had started the tentative schedule on paper at 8 A.M.—and when we got up over the first ridge we could see by the river fog over the Curaray that we never could have made it earlier. The fog got uncomfortably thicker under us but the holes allowed us to keep in touch with the river. The sun was shining and we figured it better to wait, if necessary, for the right holes rather than turn back and make a later attempt.

"As we got within two minutes of the site, the fog thinned so that we could safely slip down under it and make an approach. We went in, simulating a real landing, checked the full length for sticks and other hazards and pulled up.

"I had planned three runs before landing, but the thing was exactly as we had seen it several times before. As we came in the second time we slipped down between the trees in a steep side slip. It felt good as we made the last turn and came to the sand, so I set it down. The right wheel hit within six feet of the water and the left ten feet later. As the weight settled on the wheels I felt it was soft sand—too late to back out now. I hugged the stick back and waited. One softer spot and we'd have been on our nose—maybe our back. It never came.

"We jumped out, rejoicing in the deliverance. The relief at being past that hurdle without damage dampened my sensitivity to the glaring possibility that I might not be able to take off. It was great just to be there.

"We ran up and down the sand hunting the best course for a take-off attempt and removing sticks that could puncture a tire. Then Ed took the movie camera to the far end while I taxied back toward a take-off position.

"About thirty yards from the end I felt the right wheel sink, and my heart sank with it. I cut the engine and Ed came on the double. He lifted the low wing and I hoisted the tail around. Then using the engine, and with Ed listing the wing, we got out of the softer stuff and cut the engine. Again we searched for harder spots. Finally we pushed the airplane backward into some bushes right at the edge of the beach. It meant losing thirty yards of the total 200 available—a critical loss in view of the generally soft consistency of the whole area. However, the plane had been lightened and we were now working only 1,000 feet above sea level, where we would get more lift out of the wing.

"As I got back into the plane, Ed went again to the far end of the beach. It shook me a little to think what Ed might record with that movie camera. After a final check I let 'er go. The sand really grabbed the wheels, but the acceleration still seemed satisfactory, so I hung on and was airborne in about 130 yards (about forty or fifty before being over the water) at about thirty miles per hour. I held it down close to the water to gain speed and then pulled up steeply out of that hardwood canyon; circled back, saluted Ed, and beat a trail for Arajuno—not quite sure yet what I should do next. At least I knew now what I was in for.

"At Arajuno everyone was glad to see the plane back, but my story dampened the festive spirit appreciably. We scrapped the scheduled list for flight No. 2 and took, instead, Jim and Roj and such basic equipment as was absolutely essential—like the walkie-talkie and a little more food. The men gave me more ballast aft. If anything went wrong—if we nosed over in the landing—there would be four of us at least. Johnny continues to stand by now. He suggested softening the tires to keep them up in the sand. It never occurred to me, but having taken them down to about twelve pounds each, I felt much better.

"We took off three minutes behind schedule. The fog was almost gone. We circled once, checked safety harness and slipped down between the trees. The soft tires stayed on top of the sand much better and the sun was drying things out.

"The meeting of the three musketeers was jubilant. They set to work clearing debris from the playa while I got the plane into position for take-off just as I had done last time—same deal: cut over the water, and then up and out.

"Trip No. 3 took in their radio and some tools and the first-priority boards for the tree house. Running about ten minutes behind schedule, I believe.

"The three fellows on the beach located a good tree, close to the open sand and slanted very slightly, in which they started to nail up the ladder and tree house. They hadn't figured on its being an ironwood tree, but that is what it proved to be—a wood which lives up to its name. Next flights brought in personal items, a larger radio, more food, and the last boards and aluminum."

Later Nate recorded: "Now twenty-five minutes behind schedule because I was spending time in unscheduled committee meetings on the beach."

Working with safety belts, plagued by myriads of sweat bees and tiny gnats, the men managed to nail up the two platforms on which they were to sleep, with an aluminum roof overhead. With Nate's fifth flight completed, he headed for Terminal City, where he called out to the Aucas over the public-address system: "Come tomorrow to the Curaray." The Indians "showed puzzlement at hearing this message." Nate swung briefly back to Palm Beach and called to the fellows that he had given the message to the Aucas. Then he flew to Arajuno to sleep.

Next morning, Wednesday, January 4, Jim wrote me a letter. "Just worked up a sweat on the hand crank of the radio. Nobody's reading us but we read all the morning contacts clearly. We had a good night with a coffee-and-sandwich break at 2 A.M. Didn't set a watch last night, as we really feel cozy and secure thirty-five feet off the ground in our little bunks. The beach is good for landings, but too soft for take-offs. We have these three alternatives: (1) wait for the sun to harden it up and sit until a stiff breeze makes a take-off possible; (2) go make a strip in Terminal City; (3) walk out. We saw puma [jungle lion] tracks on the sand and heard them last night. It is a beautiful jungle, open and full of palms. Much hotter than Shandia. Sweat with just a net over me last night. Our hopes are up, but no signs of the 'neighbors' yet. Perhaps today is the day the Aucas will be reached. It was a fight getting this hut up, but it is sure worth it to be up off the ground. We're going down now. Pistols, gifts, novelties, and prayer in our hearts. All for now . . ."

Ed wrote to Marilou:

Dearest Baby:

It is 1:00 P.M. and we've just finished dinner and Nate is taking off to see if he can spot the boys. We are waiting for them to show up. Meals are fine and plentiful. I'll send some dirty clothes back with Nate this evening. Bugs are bad. Here's a list of things we need:

1. Two air mattresses—we are sending plastic ones back.
2. The pricker for gasoline pressure stove.
3. Three shigras [Indian carrying-nets] to hang up in our tree house to put stuff in.
4. 1 empty milk can to put candy in.
5. Alcohol for pressure stove.
6. My sun glasses.
7. Insect repellant.
8. More milk and lemonade.
9. Old scraps of meat for fish bait.

I love you very much. Give my love to the boys.

Ed
Thanks for everything.

10. Sun helmet, if around.

On Wednesday morning Nate and Pete took off from Arajuno, flew over Terminal City, and noticed a definite "thinning out of the crowd" there. This encouraged them to think "the boys" were on their way to Palm Beach. Landing on the sandstrip at Palm Beach, they found Ed, Roj, and Jim pacing the beach, holding out gifts and shouting welcome phrases to the trees. Nate set to work checking the radio and found the transmitter had not functioned because of a loose connection in the microphone. He was relieved to re-establish contact with Marj in Shell Mera. Roj and Nate built a beach house, then went swimming while Ed and Jim "sacked out" in the tree house.

The afternoon drowsed by, and as the tropical sun began to slide down behind the great forest trees, Nate once more elbowed the little plane out of the river valley, and he and Pete headed for Arajuno to spend another night. "Thank God for the unusually evident blessing we have seen yesterday and today," Nate wrote in his diary. "Thank God for a good team, and forbid that any man should fail to praise HIM."

Again on Thursday, January 5, Nate, with a driving sense of urgency, was writing of events as they happened. His account of the day's events, in the last week, was scrawled in pencil in a schoolboy's notebook (there was no typewriter on Palm Beach):

"All's quiet at Palm Beach. However, we feel sure we are being watched. On the way in this morning, Pete and I flew over Terminal City; two women and two children at Old Man's house. Airplane house is deserted. Probably women and children have gone up to big house. Big house showed five or six women, several children and possibly one old man.

"While letting down for Palm Beach we checked about a mile of playas below camp site. Saw several tracks, probably of tapir and other smaller stuff. On way up to camp site we were down in riverbed thinking to salute the fellows and pull up and around to land when, just one bend below camp, we sighted footprints. We pulled up and doubled back for another look. They were unmistakable. We buzzed on up past camp, saluted, pulled up and around checking the two playas above camp (no soap) and landed. News of the footprints livened up the party considerably.

"Everyone had had a good night's sleep in the tree house. At 9 P.M. strong wind swayed trees and made such sounds that woke up the three men. But all three were soon asleep again. They had a lighted lantern up there to keep the target well lit. At 5 A.M. they shined the flashlight down on the playa to check a gift machete left the night before. It was gone! For the next fifteen minutes the jungles rang with Auca phrases—perhaps with a Midwestern accent. They then shined the light for a closer look. A big leaf had fallen on the knife so as to hide it. Tough!

"As Pete and I pulled in here Jim was out in the river fishing almost in Auca uniform. Modesty seems a small consideration after seeing the dress of our 'neighbors.' If our dress is any criterion, we're giving them everything. Pete's long-sleeved shirt, pants, and straw hat make him look like a beachcomber. Flies keep the rest of us pretty well clad in tee-shirts, pants, and tennis shoes. Jim sits in the smoke from the fire when not fishing or standing in the middle of the river 'preaching' out of his notebook of phrases.

"Except for forty-seven billion flying insects of every sort, this place is a little paradise. With the help of smoke and repellant we are all enjoying the experience immensely. A little while ago Jim pulled in a fifteen-inch catfish. It is roasting over the fire now. Ed and Roj are up at the bend clearing a bad group of trees out of the approach. It's pretty close dropping down through there—will be much better now.

"Pete is stirring. Getting interested in lunch. Just emptied a plastic bag of prepared raw vegetables into a pressure cooker already partly filled with meat chunks. He's gone up to the tree house now for salt.

"The 'armor' Roj made (breast and tummy plate) out of a gas drum worked very well for a stove. While getting steam up on the stew we tossed termite nests on the fire to chase the gnats like the Indians do. By the time the three musketeers got back the stew was done and everyone was ready to test it. It went down easily, flushed along by generous quantities of lukewarm lemonade.

"Ever since Pete and I landed and reported the human footprints among the tapir and others, we were the objects of boisterous ridicule. However, curiosity brought on the acid test, and Jim and Roj started downstream, wading and running the beaches to check up at close range. We agreed that if they didn't show up in an hour, we'd look for them from the air. Fifty minutes later we saw them coming. I waded out to meet them and get the word—'Tapir,' they called. Then at closer range—'Aucas—at least thirty of them.' Characters! Sure enough, there were footprints—an adult, a youngster, perhaps twelve years old, and a little tot, but the prints were maybe a week old. The mud they were stamped in was cracked from drying. Sixty miles per hour or no, we had sure enough distinguished the prints from the many animal tracks.

"Among other tracks there were alligator, puma, tapir, et cetera. We also saw some good-sized ducks. Someone said, 'Too bad they're out of season.' (We banned firing guns for fear of frightening the Indians.)

"When someone noted with humor that although in Ecuador, we weren't speaking any Spanish, the response was, 'No one else around here does either.'

"We had all discovered the benefits of lolling in the shallow water nine-tenths submerged, and since I had just finished with the 2 P.M. contact, I shed my clothes and raced the gnats to the water, taking the sun helmet along. The fellows thought it a regal sight— nothing but a helmet and two bare feet sticking out of the water, so they dug out a couple of cameras. We enhanced some of the shots by adding *Time* magazine to the 'hydraulic siesta.'

"Jim then started reading us a novel. We roared over even remotely funny suggestions and finally skipped to the end to see who married whom and set it aside in favor of some readings from *Time* magazine. One indulgent description really rolled us—'He looked like a tenement Tom starting his ninth life in the garbage can circuit.'

"At 3 P.M. I went aloft and circled up to 6,000 feet, where I could see the Auca clearing and Palm Beach at the same time. And then I glided down slowly, pausing now and then to circle tightly at full throttle so that anyone could hear me and judge the direction from the sound. As I approached to land I thought I saw fresh human tracks just two bends upstream from camp. They were among old tapir tracks—couldn't arouse any enthusiasm over it at camp. I was about fresh out of enthusiasm too—for everything.

"By 4:30 everyone felt that the Aucas had not yet found our loc tion. Yet everyone was determined to 'sweat it out' till they shou locate us and show themselves. One thing sure is that if *we* a fagged just waiting on the beach—the Aucas are really going to los their zip by the time they locate us after tramping two or three da through the jungle. Pete and I were ready to take off for Arajuno a 4:45. The air was dead. We left all unnecessary weight behind. As w started slogging down through the soft sand on the take-off run w weren't doing at all well. At about the half-way point I cut the throttl and we stopped in about thirty yards. It looked like Pete might help guard the tree house for the night, but we plowed back to take-off position for one more try. Roj talked us into shutting the engine off and pushing the plane by hand just as far back as we possibly could. The tail wheel was just a few feet from the water! Then Jim went down to the wind sock to give signals and with Ed and Roj pushing the wing struts we started out. This time we made it okay and made a bee-line for Terminal City. We circled the main house twice, repeating the words 'Curaray Apa' (River).

"Engine skipped a beat over Terminal City (sparkplug trouble). A man was on the platform kneeling toward the direction of the camp site and pointing with both hands. This really gave us a boost. We hurried back and glided down over camp shouting the news. They signaled okay and we hit for home. At Arajuno we circled a couple of times, shouting a welcome to 'anyone' who might be in the bush, then landed. After landing, Pete and I walked the airstrip with a gift machete—no soap.

"We find we have a friendlier feeling for these fellows all the time. We must not let that lead us to carelessness. It is no small thing to try to bridge between twentieth century and the stone age. God help us to take care.

"Everyone is in bed and asleep here now. So it is left to me to go down the path and shut off the diesel. My little blank revolver is a welcome companion on such a venture. But safety is of the Lord. May we see 'them' soon. Nite."

CHAPTER XVII
Success on Friday

About eleven o'clock Friday morning, January 6, Nate and Pete sat in the small cooking shelter they had built on the sand. Ed was at the upper end of the beach, Roj in the center, Jim at the lower end, continuing their verbal bombardments of the jungle. At 11:15 their hearts jumped when a clear masculine voice boomed out from across the river answering Ed's call. Immediately three Aucas stepped out into the open. They were a young man and two women—one about thirty years of age, the other a girl of about sixteen—naked except for strings tied about the waist, wrists, and thighs, and large wooden plugs in distended ear lobes. The missionaries, temporarily struck dumb by the surprise appearance, finally managed to shout simultaneously, in Auca: *"Puinani! . . .* Welcome!"

The Auca man replied with a verbal flood, pointing frequently to the girl. His language was unintelligible, but his gestures were plain. "He's offering her for trade," exclaimed Pete, "or maybe as a gift."

When it seemed that the Aucas wanted someone to come across, Jim peeled to his shorts and began wading over to them. The others cautioned him to go slow. Jim hesitated and the Aucas were slightly hesitant, but as Jim gradually approached, the girl edged toward the water and stepped off a log. The man and the other woman followed shortly. Jim seized their hands and led them across.

With broad smiles, many "*puinanis*" and much reference to their phrase books, the five conveyed the idea that their visitors had "come well" and need not be afraid. The Aucas' uneasiness fell from them, and they began jabbering happily to themselves and to the men, "seemingly with little idea that we didn't understand them."

Roj brought out some paring knives, which they accepted with cries of delight. Nate presented them with a machete and model airplane. The others, suddenly remembering the guns in the cook shack and tree house, went back to hide the weapons beneath their duffel. They dug out cameras and shot dozens of photos, while the women looked through a copy of *Time* magazine, and the man was being doused with insecticide to demonstrate civilization's way of dealing with the swarming pests. The group spontaneously began referring to him as "George."

Presently the girl—the men called her "Delilah"—drifted over toward the Piper, rubbing her body against the fabric, and imitating with her hands the plane's movement. She seemed "dreamy," wrote Pete, "while the man was natural and self-possessed, completely unafraid. They showed neither fear nor comprehension of the cameras."

Pete continued: "Soon the fellow began to show interest in the plane and we guessed from his talk that he was willing to fly over the village to call his comrades. We put a shirt on him (it's cold up high), and he climbed into the plane with no sign of any emotion except eagerness to do his part. He acted out how he was going to call and repeated the words. Nate taxied down the strip and took off while 'George' shouted all the way. After circling and shouting briefly Nate landed again, thinking to give the fellow a rest before making the flight to his village. Nothing doing! He was ready to go right then."

Up they went again, this time to circle Terminal City. What must have been the thoughts of that primitive man as he peered down at the treetops and at the green sea below him, and suddenly recognized a familiar clearing, with familiar figures in it? "George" chortled with delight, and leaned out to wave and yell at his fellow villagers. "The woman at the Old Man's house," wrote Nate, "—her jaw dropped on seeing 'George' . . . expression of delight on the face of the young man on the platform."

Back on the sand strip, "George" leaped out, clapping his hands. The five men immediately gave thanks to God, with heads up to try to show their visitors that they were addressing their Heavenly Father. As Ezekiel said, "The Word was in my bones as a living fire," and for these men the drive to deliver to the Aucas the message of redemption through the blood of Jesus was blocked only by the language barrier. If only they might suddenly leap over the barrier and convey to the Indians one hint of the love of God!

The missionaries demonstrated for their guests such modern marvels as rubberbands, balloons, and a yo-yo; served them lemonade and hamburgers with mustard, which they evidently enjoyed. Then they tried to get across the idea that an invitation to visit the Auca village would not be scorned. For this notion "George" displayed no enthusiasm.

"Why is it he's so reluctant whenever we broach the subject?" one of the five demanded.

Another replied: "Maybe he lacks the authority to invite us on his own."

"At 4:15," Nate wrote, "we decide to fly again. 'George' decides to go along. We say 'no.' He puts his machete and envelope of valuables in the plane and looks at Pete as though he had already said it was okay and climbs in. On the way over we finally get Marj on the radio. Great rejoicing.

"Back on Palm Beach we held a strategy meeting; talking of going over to Auca houses if a delegation of, say, six Aucas arrive and seem happy to escort us. After that, every effort would be bent toward building an airstrip in their valley. The fellows tried to explain to 'George' how an airstrip should be cleared in his village."

At first he did not understand their word for trees. When he finally got it, he corrected their pronunciation. They stuck sticks in the sand to represent trees; then, with one of the model planes, Nate showed "George" how the airplane would crash and tumble among the trees. With the model lying on its back among the sticks in the sand, the fellows all shook their heads and moaned in evident distress. The scene was then re-enacted, only this time the fellows took machetes and cut down all the trees (sticks) and smoothed the sand carefully. The model airplane approached for a smooth landing, accompanied by great rejoicing.

As the day wore on, "Delilah" showed signs of impatience. Once when Jim Elliot left the group to climb up to the tree house, she leaped up and followed. When he then turned and rejoined the others, she acted downcast.

Later, as Nate and Pete got ready to return to Arajuno, "George" seemed to understand that he could not accompany them. Before the airplane took off the fellows carefully gathered all of the exposed film and everything that had been written to fly it out for safekeeping. If something unforeseen should happen, they did not want the record lost.

When the Aucas indicated that they might spend the night on the beach, the three musketeers hospitably offered them the small shack they had been using for cooking, motioning that it was theirs to occupy if they wished. "Delilah," however, had other ideas. She wheeled and walked off down the beach. "George" called to her, but she kept going. He followed her into the forest. The older woman stayed by the fire "talking a blue streak with Roj." She stayed on the beach most of the night. The next morning when Jim came down to start the fire, he found her gone, but the embers from her fire were still red.

The events of the next day, Saturday, January 7, were anticlimactic. The men waited hopefully, expecting the Aucas to arrive momentarily with an invitation to their village. But no one came. Around noon Jim looked at his watch.

"Okay, boys," he said. "I give them five minutes. If they don't show up, I'm going over!" Wisdom prevented him from carrying out his threat, but he did go back into the forest on a rudimentary trail he had discovered behind the tree house, hoping to find some trace of them. He found the forest floor remarkably open, and abounding in animal trails, but no human footprints.

Nate and Pete then flew over Terminal City and were disheartened to find some signs of fear. On the first trip all of the women and children ran to hide. A few men in sight seemed relieved to hear Nate call "Come, come, come!" He threw them a blanket and a pair of shorts to reassure them.

On the second flight "George" appeared with a group of men. One old man pointed toward Palm Beach, and "seemed friendly but not exuberant." The third trip showed that fear had vanished. Nate reported: "I got some good smiles from 'George' and another young man who, one can imagine, probably aspires to ride in the plane."

Ed wrote a note to Marilou that afternoon:

Dearest Baby:

It's 4:30 and no sign of our visitors yet but we believe they'll arrive, if not tonight, then early tomorrow. Thanks for the clothes and food again. We are certainly eating well. This has been a well-fed operation from start to end.

We feel now that we ought to press going over there and get the airstrip in as fast as possible—but we'll have to wait and see how God leads us, and them, too. Looks like Pete will be there to help you tomorrow morning. Give Stevie and Mikey my love and tell them I'll see them soon, and Carmela too. All for now. All of my love,

Ed.

Tossing on his bunk that night at Arajuno Nate wondered if everything possible had been done to interest the visitors and encourage them to return with their friends. Why had they been so casual? They seemed almost *bored* at times as he looked back on it. Jim's explanation had reassured him:

"That's Indian. If you landed him on the moon, he'd be satisfied in five minutes."

As they climbed into the Piper on Sunday morning, Pete called: "So long, girls. Pray. I believe today's the day."

At Palm Beach the fellows enjoyed the ice cream and warm blueberry muffins, fresh from the oven, Marilou had sent along. All then agreed on a visit to Terminal City. This time Nate went alone. Circling over Terminal City, he found only a handful of women and children. This sent his spirits soaring. Undoubtedly the men were at last on their way to the Curaray! And, sure enough, on the flight back he spotted a group of men "en route" to Palm Beach. As he touched his wheels down he shouted to the four, "This is it, guys! They're on the way!"

A contact with Marj in Shell Mera had been arranged for twelve thirty. Breathlessly and still using their code words, Nate told of spotting a "commission of ten" on the way from Terminal City, adding, "Looks like they'll be here for the early afternoon service. Pray for us. This *is* the day! Will contact you next at four thirty."

CHAPTER XVIII
Silence

At four thirty sharp Marj Saint eagerly switched on the radio receiver in Shell Mera. This was the moment when the big news would come. Had the men been invited to follow the Aucas to their houses? What further developments would Nate be able to report?

She looked at her watch again. Yes, it was at least four-thirty. No sound from Palm Beach. She and Olive hunched close to the radio. The atmosphere was not giving any interference. Perhaps Nate's watch had run a little slow.

In Arajuno, Marilou and Barbara had their radio on, too. Silence. They waited a few minutes, then called Shell Mera.

"Arajuno calling Shell Mera. Arajuno standing by for Shell Mera. Any word from Palm Beach, Marj? Over."

"Shell Mera standing by. No, no word as yet. We'll be standing by."

Not a crackle broke the silence.

Were the men so preoccupied with entertaining their visitors that they had forgotten the planned contact? Five minutes . . . ten minutes . . . No, it was inconceivable that all five would forget. It was the first time since Nate had started jungle flying in 1948 that he and Marj had been out of contact even for an hour.

But—perhaps their radio was not functioning. It happened occasionally. The women clung to each little hope, refusing to entertain the thought of anything's really having gone wrong. Their suspense was the sharper because most of their missionary friends on the network were unaware that Operation Auca was in progress. In Arajuno, Barbara and little Beth Youderian had primped up a bit, since it had been planned that Roj would come to Arajuno that night, while Pete took a turn sleeping in the tree house. Surely the little plane would come winging over the treetops before sundown. They walked up and down the airstrip, waiting. . . .

Just after sundown Art Johnston, one of the doctors with Hospital Vozandes, affiliated with the missionary radio station HCJB in Quito, came into the radio room in Shell Mera. The radio was still on, but Marj sat with her head down on the desk.

"Is something the matter, Marj?"

She told him the situation briefly, but asked that he not divulge it yet. If nothing serious had actually happened, it would be disastrous to publicize what was taking place. There was little sleep that night for any of the wives.

By seven o'clock on the morning of Monday, January 9, 1956, Johnny Keenan, Nate's colleague in the MAF, was in the air flying toward the sand strip which Nate had earlier pointed out to him. As he flew, Marj called me in Shandia: "We haven't heard from the fellows since yesterday noon. Would you stand by at ten o'clock for Johnny's report?"

It was the first I knew that anything was amiss. A verse God had impressed on my mind when I first arrived in Ecuador came back suddenly and sharply: "When thou passest through the waters, I will be with thee, and through the rivers, they shall not overflow thee. . . ." I went upstairs to continue teaching the Indian girls' literacy class, praying silently, "Lord, let not the waters overflow."

At about nine thirty Johnny's report came through. Marj relayed it to me in Shandia:

"Johnny has found the plane on the beach. All the fabric is stripped off. There is no sign of the fellows."

In Shell Mera, a pilot of the Summer Institute of Linguistics, Larry

Montgomery (who is also a reserve officer in the USAF), lost no time in contacting Lieutenant General William K. Harrison, commander in chief of the Caribbean command, which included the United States Air Rescue Service in Panama. Radio station HCJB was also informed and news flashed around the world: "FIVE MEN MISSING IN AUCA TERRITORY." By noon, all possible forces which might contribute to their rescue, including the prayers of thousands of people in all parts of the world, were set in motion.

Barbara and Marilou were flown from Arajuno to Shell Mera. They felt confident that there would be some survivors, and so left a note on the door of the house in Arajuno, stating where medicine and food could be found. What if one of them should stagger home wounded, or if all of them arrived back after a grueling trip in the jungle? Marilou decided that she must return, to be there to help them. Late Monday afternoon she was flown home again, where she was to remain three more days. On Monday evening it was decided that a ground search party should be organized, on the assumption that one or more of the men still lived, and Frank Drown, Roger Youderian's colleague, a man with twelve years of jungle experience among the Jivaros, was unanimously elected to lead the party. Dr. Art Johnston offered to go along in his capacity as physician. Thirteen Ecuadorian soldiers promptly volunteered.

The news "put me in a cold sweat," said Frank, "but I asked my wife, Marie, if she minded if I went." "Of course you must go," was her reply, and Frank accepted without hesitation.

On Tuesday morning I was flown out of Shandia with Nate's sister Rachel, who had been with me while the men went on the Auca trip. Frank was brought out from Macuma, and many of the missionary men arrived in Shell Mera from Quito, some as volunteers to go on the ground party. Word was received via short wave that a helicopter was on its way from Panama, which lifted the spirits in Shell Mera. That night the pilot of an Ecuadorian airline came to the house to tell the wives that he had flown over the scene at about six o'clock in the evening, and saw, a short distance upstream, a large fire, "without any smoke," which would indicate perhaps a gasoline fire or a signal fire. Nate always carried signal flares in his emergency kit. This was a ray of hope for the five wives to sleep on that night.

On Wednesday Johnny Keenan took off again in MAF's second Piper Cruiser, a twin to Nate's plane, on his fourth flight over Palm Beach to see if there were any signs of life. Marj, who had hardly left the radio since Sunday afternoon, stood by for his reports. Barbara, Olive, and I were upstairs. Suddenly, Marj called: "Betty! Barbara! Olive!"

I raced down the stairs. Marj was standing with her head against the radio, her eyes closed. After a while she spoke: "They found one body."

A quarter mile downriver from the little denuded plane Johnny had sighted a body, floating facedown in the water, dressed in khaki pants and white tee shirt, the usual uniform of the men. Barbara felt it was not Roger; he had been wearing blue jeans.

Some of the land party went over to Arajuno to prepare the air-strip for the big planes which would be arriving soon from Panama. Late on Wednesday afternoon the roar of the planes was heard, and far on the western horizon where the volcano Sangay stands, a smoking pyramid, the great planes were silhouetted. As they drew near and circled the strip, the red, white, and blue of the United States Air Force became visible.

During the day the remaining volunteers who made up the ground party were transported to Arajuno where Indians, soldiers, and others of the missionaries were milling around the airstrip, waiting to start. In spite of the strain she was under, Marilou remained her efficient self; she had a meal ready for all the men before they headed down-river. There was some difficulty in securing Quichua carriers; they had long lived too close for comfort to the Aucas and did not want to get any closer. However, their loyalty to the men who had worked among them overcame their hesitancy, and about ten-thirty the party was ready to move off on foot, guns handy, eyes sharp.

Dee Short, a missionary from western Ecuador, who happened to be in Quito when news of the disaster arrived, had come to

Arajuno. As the party left, Marilou turned to him and said with finality: "There is no hope. All the men are dead." Probably most of the ground party would have agreed with her, but, nonetheless, every time they rounded a bend of the river they looked expectantly for one or more of the missing men.

Back in Shell Mera the radio crackled again. Marj answered: "Shell Mera standing by."

Johnny Keenan reported. "Another body sighted, about 200 feet below Palm Beach."

And once again, God, who had promised grace to help in time of need, was true to His word. None of us wives knew which two these bodies might prove to be but we did know "in Whom we had believed." His grace was sufficient.

At about four o'clock in the afternoon the ground party reached Oglan, an Indian settlement situated at the place where the Oglan River meets the Curaray. Here camp was set up for the night. Frank Drown organized the group, appointing one man to hire canoes, one in charge of cargo, one to plan seating in the canoes, one as mess chief, two for safety precautions. That night they slept on beds of banana leaves. Watches were kept all night.

Before the party set off on Thursday morning, the missionaries offered up prayer, committing themselves into the hands of God; and the Ecuadorian soldiers, of a different faith, prayed with them. The party moved cautiously down the Curaray; the river was at its lowest, making navigation difficult, and special care was exercised in rounding the many bends, for it was feared Aucas might be lying in wait.

At about ten o'clock Johnny Keenan again flew over the ground party in the Piper, and Frank Drown was able to make contact with him by means of a two-way radio which the Air Rescue Service had supplied. Johnny told them of two canoes of Quichuas, proceeding upriver in the direction of the ground party; he feared that in their excitement some one of the men in the party might shoot at the first sight of an Indian on the river. Soon the two canoes of Quichuas appeared. They were a small group of Indians from McCully's station at

Arajuno. On their own initiative they had boldly pressed into Auca territory ahead of anyone else, and had gone all the way to Palm Beach. The ground party was saddened when one of the Indians, a believer who had come to know Christ since Ed had gone to Arajuno, told them of having found Ed's body on the beach at the edge of the water. He had Ed's watch with him.

Now the missionaries knew who one of their fallen colleagues was, but a chance remained that at least three others had survived. They pressed on.

In the big house at Shell Mera, children played, babies were fed and bathed, the members of the Rescue Service came and went, Marj maintained contact on the short wave, meals were somehow cooked and served, visitors greeted and informed of the latest word, and prayer went up to God continually. The mechanics were making the final adjustment on the blades of the Army helicopter which had been dismantled and shipped from Panama in an Air Force cargo plane.

My diary recounts the events of Thursday afternoon, as the helicopter was dispatched to Palm Beach:

"2:00. Johnny's Piper and helicopter headed for Arajuno. Also Navy R-4D, Captain McGee and Major Nurnberg in helicopter.

RIGHT: First evidence foreshadowing the tragedy of Operation Auca: the mutilated missionary plane sighted by Pilot Johnny Keenan Monday morning. He radioed a terse report to Marj Saint, who was keeping vigil beside her shortwave receiver at Shell Mera. She flashed word to the other wives at their jungle stations: "Johnny has found the plane on the beach. All of the fabric is stripped off. There is no sign of the fellows." Fellow missionaries and American and Ecuadorian military men quickly organized a rescue party. On Wednesday it set off from Arajuno for Palm Beach. Many of its members still had hope in their hearts that at every bend of the river they would meet at least one of the five missionaries coming out on foot.

OVERLEAF: When members of the rescue party reached Palm Beach they discovered four bodies. Here, the men are towing the body of one of the missionaries, found in the river, to the common grave. A broken Auca lance protrudes from the right hip.

The ground party conducted a brief burial service. While it was in progress, a violent tropical storm broke around them, drenching everyone and terrifying the Indian guides (who are convinced that the Auca witch doctor conjures up a storm every time his people plan a murderous attack). In the darkness of the storm (*LEFT*) the group offers up a prayer of praise and dedication, led by Frank Drown.

ABOVE: Soldiers stand guard over the little company, shielding themselves from the rain with a sheet of aluminum roofing.

Immediately after the burial, the ground party left Palm Beach and headed out through Auca territory. At first the engine of the helicopter coughed and sputtered and everyone feared that it might have to be left behind. Finally, however, the craft rose into the air. *RIGHT:* To ease the load in the canoes traveling upstream, and to shortcut the tortuous bends of the river, the ground party crisscrossed the Curaray——alternating by foot and canoe.

OVERLEAF: Members of the ground party on the long trek home, their guns at the ready as they pass through Auca territory.

While still on the march, members of the ground party read a newspaper account of the massacre. The helicopter brought them a Quito newspaper. Wet from jungle rains, it was hung up to dry.

RIGHT: The men pray before a meal in Auca territory.

OVERLEAF: Camping overnight on the way home, the ground party maintains a sharp watch. When the Indian guides insisted that animal cries from the surrounding jungle were Auca signals, Major Nurnberg fired his carbine as a warning. The sounds ceased.

By midday Saturday the ground party had pushed its way out of Auca territory. The rest of the trip was just weary footslogging. Saturday night was spent about six hours' march from Arajuno. By three o'clock Sunday afternoon the men started straggling into Arajuno. The Indians arrived carrying the Auca lances that had been found on the beach, and also the struts of the Piper plane. These were brought back for use as spare parts for the MAF's second plane.

OVERLEAF: Eyes haunted by tragedy: Dee Short, a member of the ground party, photographed on his return to Arajuno.

The end of the record of Operation Auca: These sheets, torn from Nate Saint's pocket diary and laid out to dry, were found on his body and were brought back to Marj by the ground party.

ABOVE: In Arajuno the widows discuss Major Nurnberg's report of the massacre. *Left to right:* Betty Elliot, Olive Fleming, Marilou McCully, Barbara Youderian, and Marj Saint.

TOP RIGHT: Marilou listens to an account by Fermin, an Arajuno Christian, as he demonstrates the position of Ed's body.

BOTTOM RIGHT: Marj listens to Major Nurnberg's story.

FAR RIGHT: Olive and Barbara pause while helping Marilou pack.

TOP LEFT: On Saturday the widows are flown over Palm Beach in one of the Rescue Service planes and given a brief glimpse of their husbands' common grave under the tree house.

LOWER LEFT: Despite the overwhelming stress of these days, Marj continues her radio contact work, keeping in touch with the Air Rescue Service planes as they fly over the Curaray.

RIGHT: On her way back to the United States for the birth of her third child, Marilou says good-by to the Quichua community of Arajuno.

OVERLEAF: The Quichua death wail arises around Betty Elliot as she leaves Shandia by plane. She had come to Shandia to tell the Indians personally what had happened.

The work of caring for the children continued all week. *ABOVE:* Betty holds ten-month-old daughter Valerie, and Marj feeds young Philip, while Kathy Saint looks on.

LEFT: On the back porch of the house at Shell Mera, Marj Saint copes with the laundry problem created by the presence of four babies in the house.

RIGHT: One week after the martyrdom of the five missionaries, a memorial service is held in the Bible Institute at Shell Mera.

OVERLEAF: Around the kitchen table in Shell Mera, the widows listen as Dr. Art Johnston tells of the discovery of their husbands' bodies.

A living reminder of the once-friendly contacts with the Aucas:

Stevie Saint with a gift-parrot received from the tribe.

Among the objects brought back from Palm Beach were Auca lances. This one, pulled from Nate Saint's body, had a Gospel tract wrapped around it. The tract had been dropped to the Aucas, probably as a gift-wrapping. Members of the ground party speculated that Nate, as the pilot of the missionary plane, had been singled out by the Aucas to be killed by this particular lance.

Surviving fragments of Operation Auca: Nate Saint's Spanish New Testament, wedding ring, camera, watch, and diary-notebook.

OVERLEAF: Out of Nate Saint's camera, found at the bottom of the river, came these last pictures of "Delilah" and the older woman.

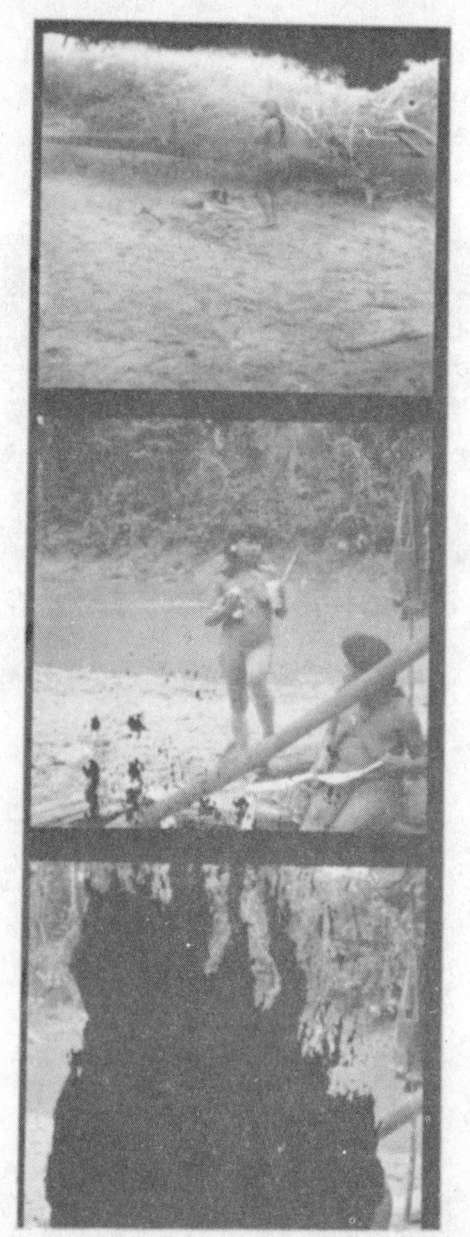

"3:00. The aircraft are stacking up over the site of the incident now. I feel sick at my stomach.

"3:20. 'Blessed is she that believed. . . .' The aircraft are circling the site.

"3:30. 'Yea, in the way of Thy judgment, O Lord, have we waited for Thee. The desire of our soul is to Thy name.'

"4:00. Still circling. 'Hope thou in God, for I shall yet praise Him. . . .'"

As the wives hoped and prayed and waited the procession of flying machines moved slowly down toward Palm Beach, the airplanes circling to keep pace with the slower helicopter skimming along at treetop level and following the bends of the river. The airplanes chose different altitudes to avoid danger of collision as pilots circled with eyes on the jungle below. Johnny Keenan in the little yellow Piper was lowest. A few hundred feet above were the U.S. Navy R-4D (the Navy version of the familiar DC-3), and higher, the big amphibian of the Air Rescue Service. Close by, Colonel Izurieta in a plane of the Ecuadorian Air Force flew in wider circles ready to help should decisions be needed. The teamwork of the United States Army, Air Force, and Navy and of the government and military services of Ecuador was heartwarming to the wives.

Air Force Major Nurnberg, riding in the Army helicopter, landed briefly to talk with the ground party, still some distance up the river from Palm Beach. Ed McCully's name was mentioned guardedly on the radio. Those hearing guessed that somehow Ed's body had been identified. Was his one of the two bodies that had been seen from the air? Had three perhaps escaped into the jungle? Or been taken captive?

After a few moments the helicopter moved on. Finally, rounding a bend, it came at last to Palm Beach and landed. Nurnberg, carbine at the ready, jumped out and looked around. Anxious minutes went by. Back in the "chopper" he radioed: "No one here." Hope flickered brighter in those who heard.

The helicopter was off again and started slowly down the river.

Crossing to the other side it stopped, hovering, the force of its down-washing disturbing the muddy surface of the water. Minutes later it moved on, only to stop again two hundred yards farther on. A third and a fourth time Nurnberg and McGee hung motionless ten feet above the water, rotor blades beating dangerously close to overhanging jungle trees. Hearts sank in the aircraft above as those watching guessed the meaning of those stops.

The aircraft returned to Arajuno. Once on the ground, Nurnberg, his face showing strain, confirmed suspicions. Speaking in low tones to the tight circle of military men, he explained that McCully's body, identified by the small party of Quichuas the day before, was now gone from the beach, no doubt washed away by the rain and higher water in the night. He leafed through his notebook for a moment. A few Indians stood silent in the tall grass nearby, listening and watching. "We found four in the river," Nurnberg said, finally. "I don't think identification will be possible from what I have here—" indicating his notebook. "One of them may be McCully."

He did not have to say what was in every mind. There might be one who got away, possibly wounded, still in the jungle.

How to inform the wives was the question uppermost in military minds. Should Marilou be told? She was right there at Arajuno in the house.

"We'd better wait," Nurnberg said. "DeWitt is running this show. Let's get back to Shell and talk it over." Captain DeWitt in the big Air Force amphibian was overhead, not wanting to risk a landing on the small strip at Arajuno. All returned to Shell and the military men gathered in the cabin of the amphibian. The wives would have to be told. But how?

Someone else had wisely decided to tell Marilou that four bodies had been found. Later in the afternoon Johnny flew her out to Shell to be with the other four wives.

In the end it was the wives who persuaded DeWitt and Nurnberg that there was no need to soften the blow. We wanted to know everything in detail. We gathered in Marj's bedroom away from the children Major Nurnberg opened his notebook and in tense sentences described what he had found. It was immediately evident that identification could not be positive. One body was caught under the branches of a fallen tree; only a large foot with a gray sock appeared at the surface of the muddy water. In reading his notes of another, Nurnberg said: "This one had on a red belt of some woven material." Four of us turned our eyes toward the fifth, Olive Fleming.

"That was Pete," Olive said simply.

As the major concluded, it was still not known whether Ed's body was one of those in the river. There was still the hope that one might have got away.

The military men, to whom the breaking of such news to loved ones was no new thing, left the bedroom silently. Their news had been met with serenity. No tears could rise from depth of trust which supported the wives.

Barbara Youderian wrote in her diary:

"Tonight the Captain told us of his finding four bodies in the river. One had tee-shirt and blue-jeans. Roj was the only one who wore them. . . . God gave me this verse two days ago, Psalm 48:14, 'For this God is our God for ever and ever; He will be our Guide even unto death.' As I came face to face with the news of Roj's death, my heart filled with praise. He was worthy of his home-going. Help me, Lord, to be both mummy and daddy. 'To know wisdom and instruction . . .' To-night Beth prayed for daddy in Heaven, and asked me if daddy would come down from Heaven to get a letter she wanted to write him. I said, 'He can't come down. He's with Jesus.' She said, 'But Jesus can help him come down, and God will take his hand so he won't slip.'

"I wrote a letter to the mission family, trying to explain the peace I have. I want to be free of self-pity. It is a tool of Satan to rot away a life. I am sure that this is the perfect will of God. Many will say, 'Why did Roj get mixed up in this, when his work was with Jivaros?' Because Roj came to do the will of Him that sent him. The Lord has closed our hearts to grief and hysteria, and filled in with His perfect peace."

That Thursday night the ground party pitched camp at "El Capricho," the former hacienda where there had been some Auca killings. Throwing up some little leaf shacks, a guard was set up of two missionaries, two soldiers, and two Indians. The missionaries, when not on guard duty with the others, tried to decide the best course of action, knowing, through contact with the helicopter, that four of their colleagues were dead. It was a long night, and Frank Drown felt an old fear that had haunted him all his life of touching the body of a friend: "Here I was, getting nearer and nearer to seeing the bodies of five fellows who were as dear to me as my own brothers."

Starting out again at six in the morning on Friday, January 13, the party was on the last lap of its mission, with a date to meet the helicopter at Palm Beach at ten. The men had to hurry to get there and everyone was jittery from the strain of the trip and the thought of the job that lay ahead. At this point the course of the Curaray is a series of short, sharp bends and twists and offers an ideal ambush for an Auca attack.

At last the beach was reached. Quichuas were sent up first, as they were best able to spot evidence of recent Auca visits. There was none. The rest of the party followed. "I remember," says Frank Drown, "that the first thing that struck me as we hit the beach was the smell from a pot of beans that had been overturned and were spread all over. I don't think that I'll ever forget that terrible, rotten smell."

There was no sign as yet of the helicopter. The ground party set to work, everyone having been assigned different duties: the Ecuadorian soldiers spread out in a semicircle in the jungle behind the beach to act as cover, two Indians set to digging a common grave under the tree house, others waded into the river looking for the men's possessions. Dee Short and Frank Drown crawled up into the tree house to try to find a clue to what had happened. Some of the men began to dismantle the plane, others looked for bodies. It was not until the helicopter arrived at twelve fifteen and hovered over the bodies where they lay in the muddy waters of the Curaray, that the ground crew was able to find them. Frank Drown told of the scene:

"First Nurnberg pointed out one body downstream and Fuller jumped into the water and pulled the body across. Then Nurnberg showed us Nate Saint's body, and we got in a canoe and went downstream, and saw an arm coming out of the water, so I tried to attach a string to the arm and I just could not bring myself to do it. I'd reach out and try and then pull back, and have to try again until finally the man who was in the canoe with me did it. Now we were three canoes with three bodies attached to them, going upstream. We laid all four face down in a row on the beach. We never did get the fifth, which was Ed McCully's body. Then I got over my feeling of hating to touch the bodies, because a body is only a house and these fellows had left their house and, after the soul leaves, the body isn't much after all. The thing that is beautiful to us is the soul, not the body."

Identification of the four bodies was finally positive from wedding rings and watches, change purse, notebooks. Ed was not one of the four, so it was finally definite: all five were dead. In the providence of God the missing body was the one identified by the Quichuas the day before. Not only had they brought back his watch, but also they had taken off one of his shoes (a tremendous shoe—size thirteen and one-half) and thrown it up on the beach. The day before, Nurnberg had picked it up and brought it back to Shell Mera.

While the bodies were drawn ashore a violent tropical storm was gathering. At that moment the helicopter came in low and fast. Cornell Capa, a photographer-correspondent on assignment for *Life* magazine, jumped out, camera in hand, and ran across the beach. Then the full fury of the storm struck and the missionaries felt as if the powers of darkness had been let loose.

Later Capa wrote an account of his landing and of subsequent events:

"We floated above the jungle about two hundred feet over the treetops. The Naval Mission plane circling overhead did not let us out of their sight. Suddenly the sun disappeared and we headed into a tropical storm. The pilot looked grim and wasted not a minute landing on Palm Beach.

"The atmosphere on the beach was fantastic. Everybody's hand was on the trigger, looking toward the jungle. I did not have to ask why. The rain was coming down in buckets; my handkerchief served no more to clean my water-soaked lenses. Suddenly I saw a struggling group of men carrying the last of the missionaries to his common grave. He was on an improvised stretcher, made out of the aluminum sheets that had covered the tree house where the men had lived.

"It was a terrible sight. The light was eerie. The pallbearers struggled against a muddy bank that led to the grave. I just made it in time to see the lifeless legs disappearing into the hole. Grim, weary missionaries looked for the last time at their friends, whom they could no more identify. One said: 'It's better this way. I feel less miserable.' They lingered for a moment, offering up a few words of prayer. At the end, Major Nurnberg, facing the jungle with carbine in hand, turned back toward the small knot of men about the grave and called: 'Let's get out of here!'

"The rain let up a bit, the helicopter was ready to leave and the time was near for decision. I could either go back with the pilot or stay with the ground party starting the overnight homeward trek. It was an easy decision. To leave now would be cheating. I gave my exposed film to the pilot. The struggle of the living to stay alive had just begun.

"At last, they were off. The canoes were overloaded and at the slightest movement water poured through the side. This was to be no fun at all, I thought quietly to myself. Major Nurnberg was in front with his carbine and I could see from the back of his head that he had a mean look in his eyes. Nurnberg leaned back on Dee Short (a red-headed, very long-legged missionary, in a very small boat), who in turned leaned on me, and I leaned on the dismounted wheel of the ill-fated plane which we had salvaged. My back ached. Like a mother hen, I tried to protect my film pouches and to hide my cameras from the rain. It was futile.

"Soon my rangefinder clouded up. I had to guess the focus. A little later my viewfinder fogged up as well. Now I only aimed the camera and prayed—like a missionary—that it was pointed in the right direction.

"In and out of the canoe . . . marching with water squelching out of my boots. Anxious eyes everywhere. I unbuttoned my .45 holster. Fortunately, no sign of Aucas. This lasted for about two hours; then it was time to bed down for the night.

"Major Nurnberg, Missionary Drown and the Ecuadorian under-officer picked an open site for the camp. Their aim was to give us a chance to spot the Aucas before they had a chance to throw their spears. Guards were posted all around the perimeter and changed every two hours. We had a meal, cooked by one of the missionaries. Shelters were erected from the metal sheets we carried, and palm leaves formed the side walls and the floor. It was a temporary paradise.

"Missionary Don Johnson, sitting in the darkness of the house, buried his face in his hands, and offered a prayer. He thanked the Lord for helping them to reach and bury their friends. Then, with great feeling, he evoked the modest and loved characters of the departed men. In the darkness of the night, with the firelight flickering on his face, and the sound of jungle birds and pumas' groans punctuating the air, this clearly spoken 'conversation' with God was of great emotional impact. Don was not expressing sorrow for the departed so much as testifying to his faith in the Lord's will. When he finished only the crackling of the campfire filled the air.

"But there was to be no sleep. All through the night we were in a wakeful readiness.

"The rushing waters of the River Curaray were always in the background. There was the sound of an occasional tree falling to set off the trigger fingers of the nervous guards. And at intervals came the beams from their flashlights as the guards made their rounds. Slowly dawn came and our nervousness increased for this was the hour, we had been told, when the Aucas liked to attack. Our Indian guides stirred, particularly when they heard the continuing sounds of a puma. The Aucas are well known for their clever imitation of the jungle animals, and the guides were sure that in the shadows of the early morning light our 'neighbors' were everywhere. Major Nurnberg crawled forward and with a sudden burst of fire silenced the 'puma.'

"Breakfast was oatmeal and coffee. Then we collected our gear and the march was on. Dried socks became wet again. Tired feet dragged. The searching eyes and ready fingers of Nurnberg and Drown brought up the rear. Sudden excitement: the 'chopper' appeared overhead, always watched by its 'Big Brother,' the Navy's R-4D. Suddenly the Twentieth Century descended in the wilderness of the jungle. The helicopter had come for me. . . . As I took off I was sorry to leave my friends, but, no, not sorry to leave."

On Saturday morning Captain DeWitt of the Rescue Service asked us five widows if we would "care to fly over Palm Beach to see your husbands' grave?"

We replied that if this were not asking too much, we would be grateful. The Navy R-4D took us out over the jungle, where the Curaray lay like a brown snake in the undulating green. Pressing our faces close to the windows as we knelt on the floor of the plane, we could see the slice of white sand where the Piper stood. Olive Fleming recalled the verses that God had impressed on her mind that morning: 'For we know that if our earthly house of this tabernacle were dissolved, we have a building of God, an house not made with hands, eternal in the heavens.' *He who has prepared us for this very thing is God* . . . 'Therefore we are always confident, knowing that, whilst we are at home in the body, we are absent from the Lord.' "

As the plane veered away, Marj Saint said: "That is the most beautiful little cemetery in the world."

Marilou McCully with Michael.

Betty Elliot with Valerie.

Olive Fleming.

Barbara Youderian with Jerry.

Marj Saint with Philip.

ABOVE: Betty Elliot, accompanied by the women and children of the Shandia community, walks down the path leading to the schoolhouse. Behind her stands the home that Jim built.

RIGHT: Betty comforts Eugenia, a Quichua friend. Betty is staying in Shandia to continue the work that Jim had begun three years earlier.

Young Venancio, a Quichua convert at Shandia, preaches there on the Sunday following Jim's death. He had been among the first of the Shandia Indians to make overtures of friendship to Jim and Pete, and is now assistant teacher at the Shandia school.

Dayuma, the escaped Auca woman who taught Jim Elliot his vocabulary for Operation Auca, is helping Rachel Saint prepare a list of key tribal words and phrases. This list will be used by future missionaries who will seek to take the Gospel to this savage tribe.

CHAPTER XIX
"Yet Have We Not Forgotten Thee"

Two days later we widows—already we were adjusting ourselves to the use of the word—sat together at the kitchen table in Shell Mera. Dr. Art Johnston was describing the finding of the bodies. He had just returned with the weary, straggling ground party. When he hesitated, we urged him to give us all the facts.

It was evident that death had been caused by lance wounds. But how had ten Aucas managed to overwhelm five strong men who were armed with guns? Over and over we asked ourselves this question. The only possible answer was an ambush. Somehow, the Aucas must have succeeded in convincing the men of their peaceful intentions. Nate had assured Marj that they would never allow Aucas with spears in their hands to approach them. Perhaps the "commission of ten" that Nate mentioned on the radio had been a decoy party. Certainly if this party had carried spears, Nate would have reported this and the men would have not looked forward so eagerly to their arrival. This group may have walked peacefully onto the beach while a second party, carrying spears, moved up under cover of the jungle foliage to carry out a surprise attack. It seems likely that the missionaries and the unarmed Aucas had been mingling together, as they had on the previous Friday, with friendly words and gestures. And then, at a secret signal . . .

There was evidence of a struggle on the beach—marks of Ed's leather heels in the sand; one bullet hole through the windshield of the plane. However, no blood was found. If any Aucas had suffered, it was not apparent. Had the men tried to avoid shooting by backing into the river? A lance was found thrust into the sand in the river bottom near the body of Jim Elliot. The fact that all of the bodies were in the water might indicate that they had tried desperately to show the Aucas that they would shoot only as a last resort.

The condition of the Piper showed real malice. Possibly some Auca had punctured the fabric of the plane with a spear, and, finding it vulnerable, had begun to peel it off. Others helped, and soon they had denuded it completely, tossing the strips into the water nearby. But someone intended to put this man-carrying bird out of commission once and for all. Some of the framework was bent, and a part of the landing gear, made of tubular steel, was battered in as if by a very heavy object. The propeller and instrument panel, however, were intact. Perhaps to touch the "soul" of the creature was taboo, but they had torn the stuffing from the seats, as if to disembowel the flying beast.

Why, after the overtures of friendship on Friday, had the Aucas turned with such sudden and destructive anger on their white visitors on Sunday? The answer can only be guessed. Among the most qualified to venture a guess is Frank Drown, whose work with the Jivaros had given him shrewd insight into Indian thinking. He says: "An Indian, when he first hears or sees something new, will accept it. Perhaps he accepts merely from normal curiosity, but he does accept. But after he has had time to think about the novelty he begins to feel threatened, and that is the time when he may attack. A group of Indians will sit back and discuss a new contrivance or a new way of doing things with some eagerness; but the witch doctors, who are the real conservatives, can be counted on for rejection. They have a lot of authority and, when they work on their fellow tribesmen to reject an innovation, the people seldom go contrary to their advice. As in any culture, the younger men may be looking for a new way of life, but the older ones hang on to their traditions and maintain the status quo. Furthermore, most Indians are basically and understandably skeptical of anything the white man offers him. And don't forget that, after all, this was the first time within memory that the Aucas have had an encounter with the white man which was completely friendly. We can only hope they are pondering that fact right now."

In the kitchen we sat quietly as the reports were finished, fingering the watches and wedding rings that had been brought back, trying for the hundredth time to picture the scene. Which of the men watched the others fall? Which of them had time to think of his wife and children? Had one been covering the others in the tree house, and come down in an attempt to save them? Had they suffered long? The answers to these questions remained a mystery. This much we knew: "Whosoever shall lose his life for my sake and the Gospel's, the same shall save it." There was no question as to the present state of our loved ones. They were "with Christ."

And, once more, ancient words from the Book of Books came to mind: "All this has come upon us, yet have we not forgotten thee. . . . Our heart is not turned back, neither have our steps declined from Thy way, though Thou hast sore broken us in the place of dragons, and covered us with the shadow of death."

The quiet trust of the mothers helped the children to know that this was not a tragedy. This was what God had planned. "I know my daddy is with Jesus, but I miss him, and I wish he would just come down and play with me once in a while," said three-year-old Stevie McCully. Several weeks later, back in the States, Stevie's little brother, Matthew, was born. One day the baby was crying and Stevie was heard to say, "Never you mind; when we get to Heaven I'll show you which one is *our* daddy." Was the price too great?

To the world at large this was a sad waste of five young lives. But God had His plan and purpose in all things. There were those whose lives were changed by what happened on Palm Beach. In Brazil, a group of Indians at a mission station deep in the Mato Grosso, upon hearing the news, dropped to their knees and cried out to God for forgiveness for their own lack of concern for fellow Indians who did not know of Jesus Christ. From Rome, an American official wrote to one of the widows: "I knew your husband. He was to me the ideal of what a Christian should be." An air force major stationed in England, with many hours of jet flying, immediately began making plans to join the Missionary Aviation Fellowship. A missionary in Africa wrote: "Our work will never be the same. We knew two of the men. Their lives have left their mark on ours."

Off the coast of Italy, an American naval officer was involved in an accident at sea. As he floated alone on a raft, he recalled Jim Elliot's words (which he had read in a news report): "When it comes time to die, make sure that all you have to do is die." He prayed that he might be saved, knowing that he had more to do than die. He was not ready. God answered his prayer, and he was rescued. In Des Moines, Iowa, an eighteen-year-old boy prayed for a week in his room, then announced to his parents: "I'm turning my life over completely to the Lord. I want to try to take the place of one of those five."

Letters poured in to the five widows—from a college in Japan, "We are praying for you"; from a group of Eskimo children in a Sunday school in Alaska; from a Chinese church in Houston; from a missionary on the Nile River who had picked up *Time* magazine and seen a photograph of her friend, Ed McCully.

Only eternity will measure the number of prayers which ascended for the widows, their children, and the work in which the five men had been engaged. The prayers of the widows themselves are for the Aucas. We look forward to the day when these savages will join us in Christian praise.

Plans were promptly formulated for continuing the work of the martyrs. The station of Arajuno was manned to be ready in case the Aucas should come out for friendly contact. Gift flights were resumed by Johnny Keenan, so that the Aucas would know, beyond any doubt, that the white man had nothing but the friendliest of motives. Revenge? The thought never crossed the mind of one of the wives or other missionaries.

Barbara Youderian returned to her work among the Jivaros, with the two little children, and I went back to Shandia with ten-month-old Valerie to carry on as much as I could of the work of the Quichua station. Another pilot, Hobey Lowrance, with his family and a new plane, were sent to the mission airbase in Shell Mera, while Marj Saint took up a new post in Quito. After the birth of her third son in the United States, a few weeks after the death of her husband, Marilou McCully returned to Ecuador with her boys to work in Quito with Marj. For Olive Fleming, who had spent only two months in the jungle when her husband died, the problem regarding the future has been more difficult. But for her, as for all, one thing is certain: her life belongs to God, as had her husband's, and He will show the way.

In the months since the killing of the five men, Nate Saint's sister Rachel has continued with the study of the Auca language, working with the Auca woman, Dayuma. Many flights have been made over the houses of the Aucas. The first group of houses was found to have been burned, a common Auca practice after a killing, but not far away new houses were discovered, and gifts were dropped to the waiting Indians. When Johnny Keenan swoops over, "George" appears, jumping and waving the little model plane given him by Nate Saint. "Delilah" also seems to be there with him. Patches of bright yellow fabric from Nate's plane adorn the roofs of some of the houses.

Thousands of people in all parts of the world pray every day that "the light of the knowledge of the glory of God" may be carried to the Aucas, a people almost totally unheard of before. How can this be done? God, who led the five, will lead others, in His time and way.

From among the Quichuas with whom Jim, Ed, and Pete

worked, several have surrendered their lives to God for His use, to preach to their own people—or even to the Aucas, if He chooses. They have carried on the work begun by the missionaries, speaking to their relatives of Christ, reading the Scriptures that have been translated for them, traveling sometimes in canoes and over muddy trails to teach the Bible to others who do not know its message. A converted Indian, formerly a notorious drinker, came to me one day and said, "Señora, I lie awake at night thinking of my people. 'How will I reach them?' I say. 'How will they hear of Jesus?' I cannot get to them all. But they *must know*. I pray to God, asking Him to show me what to do." In the little prayer meetings the Indians never forget to ask God to bless their enemies: "O God, You know how those Aucas killed our beloved Señor Eduardo, Señor Jaime, and Señor Pedro. O God, You know that it was only because they didn't know You. They didn't know what a great sin it was. They didn't understand why the white men had come. Send some more mes-sengers, and give the Aucas, instead of fierce hearts, soft hearts. Stick their hearts, Lord, as with a lance. They stuck our friends, but You can stick them with Your Word, so that they will listen, and believe."

For the wives and relatives of the five men, the mute longing of their hearts was echoed by words found in Jim Elliot's diary: "I walked out to the hill just now. It is exalting, delicious, to stand embraced by the shadows of a friendly tree with the wind tugging at your coattail and the heavens hailing your heart, to gaze and glory and give oneself again to God—what more could a man ask? Oh, the fullness, pleasure, sheer excitement of knowing God on earth! I care not if I never raise my voice again for Him, if only I may love Him, please Him. Mayhap in mercy He shall give me a host of children that I may lead them through the vast star fields to explore His delicacies whose finger ends set them to burning. But if not, if only I may see

Him, touch His garments, and smile into His eyes—ah then, not stars nor children shall matter, only Himself.

"O Jesus, Master and Center and End of all, how long before that Glory is thine which has so long waited Thee? Now there is no thought of Thee among men; then there shall be thought for nothing else. Now other men are praised; then none shall care for any other's merits. Hasten, hasten, Glory of Heaven, take Thy crown, subdue Thy Kingdom, enthrall Thy creatures."

Epilogue

Nearly three years have passed since that Sunday afternoon. Today I sit in a tiny leaf-thatched hut on the Tiwanu River, not many miles southwest of "Palm Beach." In another leaf house, just about ten feet away, sit two of the seven men who killed my husband. Gikita, one of the men, has just helped Valerie, who is now three and one-half, roast a plantain. Two of his sons have gone to the forest, shouldering their skillfully-made blowguns in search of meat to feed the fifteen or twenty Auca Indians who are at present in this clearing.

How did this come to be? Only God who made iron swim, who caused the sun to stand still, in whose hand is the breath of every living thing—only *this* God, who is *our* God forever and ever, could have done it.

After the death of the five men the pilots of the Missionary Aviation Fellowship continued making gift-drops to the Aucas. Apparent friendliness on their part was unchanged, but we know now that we could never base our judgment of their attitudes on that.

Rachel Saint, sister of Nate, the pilot, patiently keeps on with her study of the Auca language with the help of Dayuma, who came to know the Lord Jesus and began to pray, with thousands of others, for the entrance of the Light to her tribe.

One day in November, 1957, I was at the McCullys' former station, Arajuno, when two Quichua Indians from the Curaray River arrived to tell us that there were two Auca women at their house. I went with them immediately, and there at the Quichua settlement where the rescue party had spent a night, I met Mankamu and Mintaka. Mintaka was the older of the two women who had come to "Palm Beach."

Later these two women went with me back to Shandia, where I began the study of their language, praying constantly that the Lord would take us into their tribe. His answer came first in a promise which He gave from Nehemiah 9:19 and 24—"Yet thou in thy manifold mercies forsookest them not in the wilderness: the pillar of the cloud departed not from them by day, to lead them in the way; neither the pillar of fire by night, to shew them light, and the way wherein they should go. . . . So the children went in and possessed the land, and thou subduedst before them the inhabitants of the land . . . and gavest them into their hands."

When Rachel and Dayuma returned from a visit to the United States, we went to see them, and the three Auca women—united after more than twelve years—started to talk of returning to their people together. This they did, on September 3, 1958. Remaining among them for three weeks, telling them of the kind foreigners they had come to love, the three returned once more to Arajuno where Marj Saint and I were waiting for them. They brought with them seven other Aucas, and an invitation for Rachel and me to come and live with them in the tribe.

Thus, on October 8, 1958, we arrived. The longed-for entrance had been made. The Aucas were friendly and helpful, receiving us as sisters, building us houses, sharing their meat and manioc. They say they killed the men only because they believed them to be cannibals. Basically it was fear that led them to what they now regard as a mistake.

But we know that it was no accident. God performs all things according to the counsel of His own will. The real issues at stake on January 8, 1956, were very far greater than those which immediately involved five young men and their families, or this small tribe of naked "savages." Letters from many countries have told of God's dealings with hundreds of men and women, through the example of five who believed literally that "the world passeth away, and the lust thereof: but he that doeth the will of God abideth for ever."

So, with this entrance we ask that those who have helped us by prayer will continue. We would remind you that it is only an *entrance*. Besides this group of fifty or so with whom we have contact, there is a "downriver group" who are the mortal enemies of these. Will God also lead us into that "strong city"?

"Thou art worthy . . . for thou wast slain, and hast redeemed us to God by thy blood out of every kindred, and tongue, and people, and nation."

THE McCULLYS: Visiting Marilou in June 1980 are her three active sons (from left) Steve, Matt, and Mike. Marilou served in the administrative offices of Auburn Hospital in the Seattle area for over seventeen years.

THE YOUDERIANS: (Top) Barbara and Roger Youderian's son, Jerry, is an auditor for the Bank of America; he lives in California. (Bottom) Barbara Youderian, spending time with her daughter, Beth Kachikis, and granddaughter Helena Marie in 1980.

THE SAINTS: (Top) They call her "Mom Saint"; Marj Saint Van Der Puy alongside her second husband, Abe Van Der Puy. Marj has spent over thirty years of her life as a missionary and is a valuable helpmate to her husband, former president of HCJB World Radio. (Middle) Associated with Missionary Aviation Fellowship in Honduras are Kathy Saint Drown and her husband, Ross, with sons Brent and Daron. Ross is the son of the missionary who led the ground rescue team searching for the bodies of the five martyrs. (Bottom) Neighboring Saints in Minnesota, brothers Phil (far left) and Steve Saint (far right) with their families: Phil's wife Karla holding their first child, son Karl (two months old in August 1981); Ginny, Steve's wife, with year-old Stephenie and the three boys, Jesse (age 3), Jaime (age 4), and Shaun (age 6½).

THE FLEMING/LIEFELDS: Olive Fleming Liefeld with her family (from left) Beverly, husband Walter, a former seminary professor at Trinity Evangelical Divinity School, son David, Olive, and their youngest daughter, Holly. Olive is the youngest of the Palm Beach widows. She is still accepting speaking engagements to tell of the incidents and meeting up with people whose lives have been changed.

THE ELLIOTS: The one who wrote the story and shared it 25 years ago, and continues to see its impact, is Elisabeth Elliot Gren, with her husband, Lars. Lars is Elisabeth's third husband; her second husband, Addison Leitch, died of cancer. Lars works closely with his wife, as her manager and agent, and also assists in managing a private foundation. (Bottom) Daughter Valerie Elliot Shepard and her family in December of 1979: Husband Walter, Jr., holding Walter III with Elisabeth on her mother's lap. Mr. Shepard is a church pastor.

Epilogue II

This time it's not a leaf-thatched hut on the Tiwanu River but a small house with big glass windows and real walls high above the Atlantic Ocean on Massachusetts' rockbound coast.

I sit at my desk looking out at a nearly pure white sea reflecting a white sky, with no horizon to divide them. A winter sun makes a pale, shimmering pathway on the calm water where two little boats idle as the lobstermen pull their pots. It is a long way from the jungle.

Although the pathway of my life has taken many unimagined turns since I wrote this (my first) book, I have not been allowed to forget the story. I would not have wanted to forget it, but there have been times when I have wondered if others might. Perhaps they have tired of it. Should I continue the retelling as I am so often asked to do? I spoke of my misgivings to Miss Corrie ten Boom who, as an old lady, indefatigably traveled the world to tell her own story over and over again, of her family's providing refuge to Jews in Holland during World War II, of their being betrayed and imprisoned in a concentration camp, and of the deaths of her sister and aged father as a result.

"Sometimes," she told me, "I have said, 'Lord, I must have something fresh. I cannot go on telling the old story.' But the Lord said to me, 'This is the story I gave you. You tell that one.' " So Corrie encouraged me to go on telling mine.

Readers will want to know what has happened to the people in this book. It is easy enough to answer the questions about the widows. Two of them are still in Ecuador. Marj Saint is now Mrs. Abe Van Der Puy, wife of the former president of HCJB World Radio in Quito. They have six children between them and an impressive crowd of grandchildren. Barbara Youderian ran a missionary guest house for the Gospel Missionary Union before returning to live in Orlando, Florida. She has two married children, Beth and Jerry. Marilou McCully is retired as a hospital accounting supervisor and lives in Bonney Lake, Washington. All of her sons are married—Steve, who is a schoolteacher, and Matt, a sportswriter. Mike, the middle one, travels around the country working with racehorses. Olive Fleming married Walter Liefeld, who is now retired as head of the New Testament Department at Trinity Evangelical Divinity School in Deerfield, Illinois. They have three children: David, Beverly, and Holly. Rachel Saint died of cancer in November 1994 and was buried in the Waorani settlement where she had lived for a number of years. My third husband (the second died of cancer) is Lars Gren, who, when he is not "managing" me and our travel and book sales, works for a private foundation. My daughter, Valerie, is the mother of several children. Her husband, Walter D. Shepard, Jr., is a pastor.

It is difficult not to grasp after thrills. The publicity surrounding the deaths of the five men focused what has sometimes seemed to be undue attention on that small jungle group, deflecting (some said) much interest from other vital kinds of missionary work. There can be little doubt that the drama of the story awakened many to the existence of "harvest fields" they had not thought of. At least hundreds were jolted by the sacrifice of five young men for whom obedience to their Lord was quite literally a matter of life and death. In a civilization where, in order to be sure of their manhood (or, alas, even their "personhood"), men must box, lift weights, play football, jog, rappel, or hang-glide, it was startling to realize that there was such a thing as spiritual commitment as robust, as total, and perhaps more demanding than the most fanatical commitment to physical fitness. It was a shock to learn that anybody *cared* that much about anything, especially if it was invisible.

On January 8, 1996, my husband, Lars Gren, and I, along with my daughter, Valerie, her husband, Walt, and eldest son, Walter, were with the Waorani. Steve Saint, pilot and son of pilot Nate, and his wife, Ginny, kindly entertained us in their jungle home on the Curaray River. We sat in hammocks as the Waorani crowded in to see us, to laugh and shout about how much I ("Gikari") and Valerie ("Mangari") had aged. They did their best to pronounce "Lars," "Walt," and "Walter," welcoming them with great glee, powerful handshakes, and deepest interest. Together we reminisced about the years 1958–1960 that Valerie and I had lived there. Minkayi and Kimo, two of those who had speared the five, talked and talked, telling me of events over the decades since I had seen them. They are Christians now. The New Testament has been translated into their language.

The name Auca is a Quichua word meaning "naked" or "savage." It is no longer used. Waorani is what the people call themselves. Their story, at the time of the death of the men, later when I lived with the Indians themselves, and during all the years since as I have recounted it and reflected on it in the light of my own subsequent experience, has pointed to one thing: God is God. If He is God, He is worthy of my worship and my service. I will find rest nowhere but in His will, and that will is infinitely, immeasurably, unspeakably beyond my largest notions of what He is up to.

This is the context in which the story must be understood—as one incident in human history, an incident in certain ways and to certain people important, but only one incident. God is the God of human history, and He is at work continuously, mysteriously, accomplishing His eternal purposes in us, through us, for us, and in spite of us.

There is always the urge to oversimplify, to weigh in at once with interpretations that cannot possibly cover all the data or stand up to close inspection. We know, for example, that time and again in the history of the Christian church, the blood of martyrs has been its seed. So we are tempted to assume a simple equation here. Five men died. This will mean x-number of Waorani Christians.

Perhaps so. Perhaps not. Cause and effect are in God's hands. Is it not the part of faith simply to let them rest there? God is God. I dethrone Him in my heart if I demand that He act in ways that satisfy my idea of justice. It is the same spirit that taunted, "If Thou be the Son of God, come down from the Cross." There is unbelief, there is even rebellion, in the attitude that says, "God has no right to do this to five men unless . . ."

Those men had long since given themselves without reservation to do the will of God. So far as they knew, they were to be plain ordinary missionaries—Roj to the Atshuaras; Jim, Ed, and Pete to the Quichuas; Nate to serve all the jungle stations with his airplane. But small things happen (Nate found some inhabited Waorani houses). Small decisions are made (he told Jim and Ed), which lead to bigger ones (they began to pray with new vigor for an entrance into the territory), and ultimately a man's individual choices become momentous. Plain, ordinary missionaries with wives and children whom they loved found themselves faced with a life and death decision. They were not looking for anything bigger to do, let alone for fame. The need of the Waoranis simply became the categorical imperative.

For us widows the question as to why the men who had trusted God to be both shield and defender should be allowed to be speared to death was not one that could be smoothly or finally answered in 1956, nor yet silenced in 1996. God did not answer Job's questions either. Job was living in a mystery—the mystery of the sovereign purpose of God—and the questions that rose out of the depths of that mystery were answered only by a deeper mystery, that of God Himself. The Lord answered Job out of the tempest:

Who is this whose ignorant words
cloud my design in darkness?
Brace yourself and stand up like a man;
I will ask questions and you shall answer.
Where were you when I laid the earth's foundations?
Tell me, if you know and understand.
Who settled its dimensions? (Job 38:1-4, NEB)

On and on the unanswerable questions went, overwhelming the man on the ash heap with proofs of divine control, origin, generation, legislation, authority, and wisdom. Job's only reply was that he had none. "What reply can I give Thee, I who carry no weight? I put my finger to my lips" (40:4).

Again God told him to brace himself, stand up like a man, and answer. "Dare you deny that I am just or put me in the wrong that you may be right?" (40:8).

Job stood the test. He recognized who God is. He "melted." But he then became the intercessor for his friends, and God restored to him more than he had ever had to begin with.

I believe with all my heart that God's Story has a happy ending. Julian of Norwich wrote, "All shall be well and all shall be well and all manner of thing shall be well."

But not yet, not necessarily yet. It takes faith to hold on to that in the face of the great burden of experience, which seems to prove otherwise. What God means by happiness and goodness is a far higher thing than we can conceive. John Oman said that "a true belief in Providence cannot be held either as an instinctive trust that God is kind or as an inference from life that He is benevolent, but only as the last and highest victory of a faith which has won a vision of a true and abiding good, which is not of the world, even while things in the world become a new creation to forward it" (*Grace and Personality*, p. 126ff.).

The massacre was a hard fact, widely reported at the time, surprisingly well remembered by many even today. It was interpreted according to the measure of one's faith or faithlessness—full of meaning or empty. A triumph or a tragedy. An example of brave obedience or a case of fathomless foolishness. The beginning of a great work, a demonstration of the power of God, a sorrowful first act that would lead to a beautifully predictable third act in which all puzzles would be solved, God would vindicate Himself, Waoranis would be converted, and we could all "feel good" about our faith. Bulletins about progress were hailed with joy and a certain amount of "Ah! You see!" But the danger lies in seizing upon the immediate and hoped-for, as though God's justice is thereby verified, and glossing over as neatly as possible certain other consequences, some of them inevitable, others simply the result of a botched job. In short, in the Waorani story as in other stories, we are consoled as long as we do not examine too closely the unpalatable data. By this evasion we are willing still to call the work "ours," to arrogate to ourselves whatever there is of success, and to deny all failure.

A healthier faith seeks a reference point outside all human experience, the Polestar which marks the course of all human events, not forgetting that impenetrable mystery of the interplay of God's will and man's (e.g., "He did not do many miracles there because of their unbelief"; "Jesus was handed over to the power of men"; "Thou hast set me *free* to range at *will*").

I think back to the five men themselves, remembering Pete's agony of indecision as to whether he should join the others in the venture; Ed's eagerness to go even though Marilou was eight months pregnant, his strong assurance that all would be well; Roj's depression and deep sense of failure as a missionary; Nate's extreme caution and determination; Jim's nearly reckless exuberance.

I think of the tensions that developed after the men died among those who had to try to "pick up the pieces" of the work they had left behind. There was misunderstanding between some of the mission boards as to what part each was to play in continuing efforts to reach the Waoranis.

I think of how, when Rachel and I finally arrived in the Waoranis' jungle clearing, we found that what she and Dayuma had been using as the Waorani language was not readily understood. Dayuma had forgotten a large part of it, and had unwittingly jumbled up Waorani, Quichua, a smattering of Spanish, and a little English intonation for good measure. Then gradually I saw, to my dismay, that Rachel's approach to linguistic work, her interpretation of what the Indians did and said, and the resulting reports she sent out were often radically different from my own.

I think of the Indians themselves—what bewilderment, what inconvenience, what disorientation, what uprooting, what actual disease (polio, for example) they suffered because we missionaries got to them at last! The skeptic points with glee to such woeful facts and we dodge them nimbly, fearing any assessment of the work that may cast suspicion at least on the level of our spirituality if not the validity of our faith.

But we are sinners. And we are buffoons. I am reminded of an occasion in Bible school when I nearly laughed aloud in the middle of a prayer. Following a long session in which one student after another had confessed his sins, real and imaginary, our principal, L. E. Maxwell, stood up and boomed out, "O Lord, *deliver* us from our sad, sweet, stinking selves!"

It is not the level of our spirituality that we can depend on. It is God and nothing less than God, for the work is God's and the call is God's and everything is summoned by Him and to His purposes, the whole scene, the whole mess, the whole package—our bravery and our cowardice, our love and our selfishness, our strengths and our weaknesses. The God who could take a murderer like Moses and an adulterer like David and a traitor like Peter and make of them strong servants of His is a God who can also redeem savage Indians, using as the instruments of His peace a conglomeration of sinners who sometimes look like heroes and sometimes like villains, for "we are no better than pots of earthenware to contain this treasure[the revelation of the glory of God in the face of Jesus Christ], and this proves that such transcendent power does not come from us, but is God's alone" (2 Corinthians 4:7, NEB).

We are not always sure where the horizon is. We would not know which end is up were it not for the shimmering pathway of light falling on the white sea. The One who laid earth's foundations and settled its dimensions knows where the lines are drawn. He gives all the light we need for trust and for obedience.

THE STORY CONTINUES....
Turn the page for two exciting sample chapters from *End of the Spear*

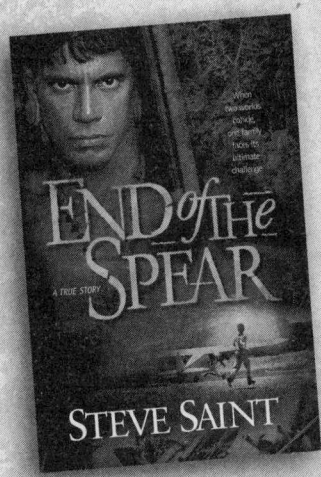

As a boy, Steve Saint lived among the jungle tribe that had murdered his father. During those years, his aunt Rachel taught these primitive people to walk God's trail; they taught Steve to live as a Waodani, one of the "real people."

Years later, after building a life and career in America, Steve Saint was compelled to take his family and once again live among the Waodani in the jungles of Ecuador.

The true story of an American family, a jungle tribe, and the healing and redemption they find...at the end of the spear.

End of the Spear by Steve Saint
Hardcover $22.99 – 978-0-8423-6439-3 • Softcover $14.99 – 978-0-8423-8488-9

AVAILABLE NOW AT A BOOKSTORE NEAR YOU.
Now a major motion picture from Every Tribe Entertainment

CP0278

Chapter 1

BACK TO THE STONE AGE
November 1994

The head flight attendant had given us the customary briefing before takeoff. It was obvious that her first language was not English. I couldn't help but feel a sense of excitement as the powerful engines on the 757 pushed me back in the seat.

We were a cosmopolitan bunch. Experience (and numerous Goofy hats) told me that some on board had been to Disney World. Others, apparently from the upper socioeconomic end, had probably come to the land of malls and shopping extravaganzas to update their wardrobes. But there were also some who had the coarse hair and weathered skin of the mestizo, those born from the mingling of Spanish conquistadores and descendants of the Inca Empire they conquered.

I love to fly, but not back where I was sitting. I like the front left seat, where I can select my destination through my smallest deflections of the controls. My stomach goes queasy every time a pilot I don't know—with my life in his hands—pulls back the power levers and we begin to decelerate while still pointed up at an alarming angle. In the small aircraft I fly, reducing power with the nose pointed at the sky is an invitation to stall and spin. But my mind was on other things this night. I tilted the seat back and closed my eyes.

On the other end of this flight I would spend a short night in the Andes Mountains. I hoped I would not get that crazy, suffocating sensation that had kept me awake in Quito's thin atmosphere on recent visits. Years before, when I lived and went to school almost ten thousand feet up in the mountains, I could play a full game of basketball and feel fine. Now, twenty-five years later, I had begun to understand what tourists complain about: "I can't catch my breath" or "I wake up gasping for air."

If they have Aunt Rachel's body ready, I should be on my way down to the jungle early the next morning, I thought.

Just the day before, I had been sitting at home after a long day of the same old, same old—driving around, talking on the cell phone, haggling over a few cents now that could make a difference of thousands of dollars down the road—the usual knock-down, drag-out life of a businessman. When the phone rang, I almost didn't answer. At home, Ginny answers the phone. She is a lot nicer to telemarketers, and after a day with my hand to my ear, I didn't want to talk into a machine anymore.

We had been expecting the call, but I still was not ready for it. "Hi, is this Steve?" I could tell the voice on the other end was calling from overseas. "I'm sorry to have to tell you that your Aunt Rachel died this afternoon. I think it would be good if someone from the family could come down. Remember, down here we have to bury within twenty-four hours. I can ask the doctor if he can do some embalming, but that will only buy us a few hours. If we take too long, the authorities will make us bury her in Quito."

Aunt Rachel had been in Quito to receive treatments for cancer. But I knew she had wanted to be buried at home in the jungle, with the people she loved—the Waodani. Mom and my stepdad, Abe, were out of town. I knew they wouldn't be able to get down to Ecuador in time. I would have to represent the family and help bury "Star," as the people there called her.

As we cruised high over Cuba, I wondered how to best get my dear old aunt's body down to the jungle. And I contemplated how I could keep the Waodani who had loved her from being overwhelmed by "outsiders" wanting to get in on this historic event.

I woke up to the same voice that had put me to sleep: "Pleeze fosten yur-e seat bels fur ourr londing in Quito." Now I was glad that I wasn't sitting in the left front seat. Quito lies in a tight valley rimmed by Andean mountain peaks. The city spreads right to the runway threshold, and on this night there was a heavy fog hanging over the valley floor. If we couldn't make a landing on our first couple of tries, we would have to divert to the coast and spend the night in Guayaquil, and I would almost certainly miss the reason for which I was coming. But thankfully, we made it.

ॐ

By the time I got to the Quito airport early the next morning, Aunt Rachel, wrapped in sheets, was already lying on the floor of the Cessna bush plane that would take us home. I took the seat beside her body. As we flew down the Avenue of the Volcanoes, regal snow-capped peaks rose above our flight altitude and disappeared into the high overcast above us. Normally, we would have made a fuel stop on the edge of the great Amazon rain forest, but we were in a hurry. I heard our pilot request that another plane deliver the casket and bring extra fuel for him. I watched as we flew over the little town where I had spent my most formative years. Aunt Rachel had been a big part of those years. I felt a yearning to just once more tell her how much I loved her and respected her willingness to risk everything for what she believed. She was the most humble, but also the most stubborn, person I had ever known. Without the humility, she never would have been willing to live in a thatched hut in the middle of nowhere. Without the stubbornness, she never could have survived living in the midst of the violent cultural chaos that characterized life among the Waodani, known to the outside world as "Aucas"—savages. Without her, it is possible that there would have been no one left to welcome us at our destination.

The Waodani heard the plane coming and were standing by the short gravel and grass strip when we landed. The makeshift runway was surrounded on all sides by a sea of dense jungle. Dayumae, Aunt Rachel's closest living "relative" in the tribe, was the first one I saw after I opened the plane door. She greeted me and then saw what was left of the *cowodi*—foreigner—she had adopted as her sister more than four decades before. Her reaction was chilling. She began to wail, taking me by surprise. The Waodani, her own people, don't do that. But Dayumae had spent fifteen years living with the Quichua, a neighboring tribe, and had adopted much of their culture. Their death wail is a dark window into the excruciating agony of a human soul that has little control over its own destiny. The rest of the group retreated from Dayumae's grief.

Finally, the pilot and a couple of Waodani and I unwrapped Aunt Rachel's shroud and lifted her body from the plane into the simple plywood box that would serve as her coffin. It seemed appropriate for this old Saint who had never worried about luxuries or her own comfort. Its rustic simplicity matched her house, which sat just a hundred yards down the trail. We carried her there for final preparations.

No one had thought to tie Aunt Rachel's mouth shut before rigor mortis set in. So the doctor had tied a head scarf around her head and under her chin to keep it closed. The Waodani women surrounded the coffin to get a last glimpse of this woman who had become as much one of them as her ruddy complexion and white skin would allow. Immediately, they began an animated discussion. They spoke much too rapidly for me to catch the details of what they were saying, but it was clear that they were not pleased with the doctor's choice of scarf. They untied it to find a replacement, but when they did, Rachel's mouth opened just as though she were going to speak. A gasp ran through the crowd, and they instinctively recoiled. But not even mismatched accessories were going to bring Star's eighty-two-year-old, cancer-ravaged body back to life.

I retied Aunt Rachel's mouth shut with the piece of bright cloth that the Waodani women finally settled on. We carried her body over to the rustic little church just a few feet away. I was surprised to see that there were quite a few foreigners mixed in with the Waodani. But these were Aunt Rachel's close colleagues and friends, who had made flights for her, kept her two-way radio working, and helped her help the Waodani. I could not object to their presence, although I did ask them to let the Waodani bury Star their own way.

The Waodani, however, have no chief or other recognized authority. Over the past forty years, they had become accustomed to giving decision-making power to the *cowodi*, who can fly and make little metal boxes talk, who have little seeds that make diseases go away, and who perform a myriad of other unimaginable feats. I realized they were waiting for one of the foreigners to take charge. I stepped in.

I handed a nail for the coffin lid to each of the people who constituted Star's closest family.

Brave, impetuous Dayumae had adopted Star and given her the name of her young sister, Nemo, who had been hacked to pieces in a spearing raid when she and Dayumae were just girls. It was because of Dayumae that the tribe had invited Aunt Rachel to live with them, along with Elisabeth Elliot, whose husband, Jim, had also been speared when my dad was killed. Rachel and "Aunt" Betty were the first outsiders ever to receive such an invitation.

I also handed nails to handsome Kimo and nubile Dawa, the first ones to believe what Aunt Rachel and Dayumae taught them about a new way to live, a way without hating and killing. Kimo had taken a big risk in building a house for Aunt Rachel. Others in the tribe had been displeased and told him it would be his grave.

I gave a nail to Mincaye, who didn't take well to allowing foreigners in Waodani territory. He had threatened to spear Aunt Rachel and Aunt Betty. Then one day, Mincaye mysteriously had a change of heart and told Rachel that he had decided to follow God's trail. After that, Mincaye became jovial and almost happy-go-lucky.

Old Dyuwi also received a nail. When Dayumae had first returned from the outside world with the two foreigners, he was already a seasoned killer at age twenty. But he went from hating and killing to peacemaking almost instantaneously.

I kept the last nail for myself.

Just before we carried Star out to the hole that had been dug between her house and the little tin-roofed church with chicken-wire windows and chainsawed boards, Kimo offered an impromptu eulogy.

Waengongi Taado ante odomoncaete ante Nemo pongantapa— "Teaching us to walk God's trail, Star came."

Aunt Rachel was large by Waodani standards and had grown stouter as she aged. When we reached the burial site, several of the Waodani men jumped into the grave to help lower her coffin. I was moved to see the care and almost reverence with which they handled the old shell that had been so precious to those of us gathered in that little clearing. This was the second member of my family to be buried here.

Yowe missed the signal to jump out of the grave and found himself alone, under the coffin, as it was lowered the last couple of feet. In desperation, he struggled to extricate himself. In doing so, he tipped the coffin, and we all stood horrified as we heard Aunt Rachel's body roll to the side. With all the weight on one side, the box fell to the bottom of the grave with a thud. No one moved.

I could almost hear Aunt Rachel giving instructions, with Dayumae passionately countermanding them. At first, we reacted like schoolkids whom the teacher had caught cheating. Were we in trouble again? But I could tell that Mincaye was trying to keep from bursting out laughing. Finally he let out a little involuntary snort, and we all broke up. Even Star would have enjoyed the irony of her mourners laughing at her interment.

ॐ

Strange circumstances, combined by providence, had led this silver-haired old woman to spend half of her long life in the wilds of the Amazon jungle with an egalitarian and violent Stone Age people. Aunt Rachel's mother had been a daughter of wealth, growing up with luxury and pampering. Her father was a well-known stained-glass artist.

Rachel was Lawrence and Katherine Saint's third of eight children and their only daughter. Because her mother was frail, Rachel became something of a second mother to her younger brothers, including my dad, Nate.

As a young girl, Rachel caught the attention of a wealthy Philadelphia widow with no children of her own. That woman lavished Rachel with the accoutrements of prosperity that Katherine had rejected but her daughter had never tasted. Coming home from a summer in Europe—as was the custom of the old moneyed families in New England—the wealthy dowager informed a teenage Rachel that she had decided to make Rachel her heiress.

Such an inheritance would have ensured the care her mother so desperately needed for tuberculosis, fine educations for her brothers, and the opportunity for Rachel to be the financial protector and provider for the family she already nurtured.

But Rachel refused the offer because it would require her to be a companion to her wealthy benefactress until her death. "I have already made a prior commitment to do whatever God wants with my life," she told the woman. "I cannot make any commitment that might cause me to compromise what I have promised to God."

Unaccustomed to rejection of any kind, the wealthy mistress scolded Rachel harshly for her lack of gratitude and her idealism. She summarily cut off any hope of help for Rachel and her family. "You will not receive a cent from me, you ungrateful girl," she informed Rachel; and she meant it. When she died years later, she had her executor send Rachel a set of inexpensive cuff links. "It was the only cheap possession she owned," Aunt Rachel told me.

Feeling rejected and uncertain about what her family would think of her hasty but principled response, Rachel sought privacy in the bow of the passenger liner on which they were voyaging home. In the mid-Atlantic she poured out her heart to the One to whom she had betrothed herself emotionally and spiritually.

"This never happened to me before or since," she told me on one of my extended visits with her in the jungle. "But while I was in the bow of that ship, I had a vision of a dark-skinned tribe of people who had never heard that the Lord Jesus loved them. And God promised me that if I continued to be faithful to Him, He would one day allow me the privilege of being the one to take His precious Word of love and peace to them."

She went on to finish high school and then spent the next twelve years working in a Christian center for drug and alcohol addicts. The family needed help financially if her brothers were to get adequate educations. She was content that when her responsibility to them was satisfied, she believed God would keep His promise to her.

Although Rachel was past the normal age limit, Wycliffe Bible Translators accepted her as a candidate translator and sent her to Peru to temporarily replace a translator who had been working with a head-hunting tribe there. On the way she stopped in Ecuador to visit my parents, Nate and Marj, who were missionaries there. Dad flew her to several jungle stations, carefully skirting Auca territory in the process. Rachel was keenly observant and asked why Dad avoided flying over that area.

"That part of the jungle is inhabited by people who have killed everyone from the outside world who has ventured inside their borders," Dad explained. "If we had a forced landing there, we might survive the crash, but we would not survive the Aucas."

"As soon as Nate told me that, I knew that they were the very ones God had promised to let me take His Good News to," Aunt Rachel told me. She never wavered in her confidence, even when tragedy struck several years later and the Aucas speared the little brother she loved like a son.

თ

I watched as the Waodani filled the grave. Kimo and Yowe were watching me.

I had been near this spot years before. Kimo and Yowe had been watching me then, too. I was only fourteen. Of course, there was no village and no airstrip back then. We had trekked over from the next valley to the south with a group of Waodani.

My sister, Kathy, had decided she wanted to be baptized. Because our own dad was dead and could not do it, Mom suggested that Kathy choose a couple of men who had influenced her life spiritually. Only two years younger, I decided it was time for me to take this step too.

I understood that baptism was a symbolic, though important, gesture that signified my determination to live by a standard that *Itota*, the Creator's Son, had established for his followers. My hunting buddy, Iniwa, and Oncaye, a Waodani girl about Kathy's age, said they wanted to be baptized as well.

Mom had always wanted to see where my dad and his four friends had been killed, so she and Aunt Rachel decided to do so on this trip. We would trek over to the Ewenguno River to visit Dad's grave for the first time in the nine years he had been gone. And we would be baptized there.

We slogged over muddy jungle trails for several hours and then poled down the Ewenguno in dugout canoes, arriving just before dark. There was a set of jaguar tracks on the beach to inspire my imagination, and there was dinner to be caught. I helped with the fishing while many men and women gathered materials to make shelters for the night. I never ceased to be impressed by how little the Waodani took with them and how much they had when they arrived.

Since Aunt Rachel had started living with the Waodani, I had looked for every chance I could get to stay with her and the tribe. That is, after Aunt Rachel figured I could visit without being killed. The Waodani had a long history of killing outsiders and being killed by them. I was just a ten-year-old kid when I first visited Waodani territory, but I was almost as tall as some of the adults in the tribe, though pitifully skinny.

By the time the evening mist began to settle over our little encampment and the night sounds began their serenade, the shelters had been made, the fires were going, and fish and monkey were in the pot. It didn't get much better than that in my book—and there was always the possibility that the jaguar would come back. That would add some excitement for sure.

The next morning, after drinking the Waodanis' customary breakfast of plantain mashed in warm water and finishing the meat from the last night's meal, we were ready for the baptismal service. Kathy wanted Kimo and Yowe to baptize us. They were both warriors I had learned to respect, and they treated me like family. Kathy's choice was good by me.

Kimo spoke to *Waengongi*—God—as some of us bowed our heads: "A long time ago we came to this place to do a bad, bad thing. But now, speaking your name well and keeping you in our hearts, we have come back to do a good thing. Taking these four young people into the water, they will die to the old way of living and will show that they truly want to walk your trail now, following *Itota*, your only Son, who marked your trail for us."

It didn't occur to me until Kimo was praying that he and Yowe knew this sandbar well. The men we had chosen to baptize us were two of the very same men who had speared my father and the others—at this very same place. It seemed strangely out of character that such kind and gentle men whom we all liked so much and who obviously liked us could have done such a terrible thing. I hadn't forgotten the pain of losing Dad, but I couldn't imagine not loving Kimo and Yowe and all the other Waodani who had come to visit this terrible, wonderful place with us.

Then Kimo and Yowe took Kathy, Oncaye, Iniwa, and me into the water and lowered us into it as though they were burying us. When they lifted us back up, they told us to live happily and at peace, following God's trail.

We all gathered back on the beach while Yowe prayed. Yowe, normally a man of few words, covers a lot of territory when he talks to Waengongi. I opened my eyes, wondering why we should keep them shut when there was so much to look at. On the sand, right in the middle of our circle, was a bright yellow butterfly that looked an awful lot like my dad's little Piper cruiser.

When Yowe finally finished his address to our Creator, the butterfly was still there, in the exact place where "56 Henry," as Dad's plane was called, had died. I wanted to ask Kimo and Yowe why they had destroyed the plane, but I didn't know how. And I was sure Aunt Rachel would disapprove. I also wanted to know why they had speared my dad and our other friends. But again, I remained silent. I was too young to realize how strange it would seem to other people that Kathy and I were baptized at the same place and by the same men who had speared our dad and hacked his body with a machete. These were people Aunt Rachel loved and Mom had been praying for since before they killed Dad and the four others. Following their example, it had never even occurred to me to hate them.

When we finished praying, the Waodani warriors took the four of us into the jungle beside the beach to show us the stump of the tree where "the five foreign God-followers built their sleeping house when they came to bring us God's carvings and teach us how to live well." The bodies had been buried right here. We had no idea at the time, however, that one of us would also die and be buried in this same place. Nor did we have any clue that 56 Henry would one day reappear here.

As we prepared to leave the grave site, Mom noticed four bright red flowers clustered together nearby. It seemed almost odd that there were not five of them. Then, Aunt Rachel noticed one more just a short distance farther back. I remembered then that Ed McCully's body had not been buried with Dad, Jim, Roger, and Pete. His body had been found too far downriver to safely bring back for burial. Surely that fifth bloom was for "Uncle" Ed.

Chapter 2

CAN COWODI HUNT?

The Mission Aviation Fellowship planes left, taking all the visitors with them. I was finally alone with the Waodani. There was a group of Aenomenani in the village, members of the downriver part of the tribe, whom I had never met. They were part of the same tribe, but they and the upriver Waodani had killing vendettas that went back as far as anyone could remember. Apparently, the Aenomenani had heard that the foreigner who was Star's "son" was visiting. They wanted proof that I was that foreigner, the one called "Babae."

No problem! Mincaye grabbed one of the Aenomenani's nine-foot blowguns and prepared to give them proof. I could understand only a little of what he was saying, but it was clear that he was bragging about what a great hunter I was. "Just like one of us, only with white skin," he said. They all laughed. Using the blowgun as a prop, he started demonstrating how I could creep up on the wiliest of jungle fauna. But the Aenomenani did not want to hear Mincaye's stories; they wanted to see me prove myself.

While I was busy thinking of excuses that would work in this particular setting, a young boy returned from hunting. He had a tiny bird tucked under his G-string. One of the Aenomenani warriors grabbed the little bird and climbed up a nearby tree where he tied it to a limb. I could see what was happening and began to protest. My authenticity and the credibility of my mentors were about to be tested. I could hardly see the bird way up in the tree, and most of what I could see was just feathers. Unless I happened to hit the scrawny body hidden under all that feather fluff, the dart would fly right through. Besides that, I had not been blowgun hunting for about twenty-five years. I had a blowgun at home in Florida that I used to discourage raccoons and other varmints from getting into our garbage. The poison on my darts was too old to be very effective, but the varmints in our neighborhood quit patronizing our garbage anyway. But I hadn't used a blowgun for serious hunting since I was a boy.

The Amazon jungle covering the six thousand square miles of Waodani territory is like a sea of green poured over the badlands of North Dakota. The terrain is rugged and wet. The precipitation there can reach thirty feet per year as the warm, humid ocean air pushes up against the Andes Mountains to the west. Some of the moisture is carried up those steep slopes, forming glaciers on the perpetually snowcapped peaks that overlook the jungle. There, the air is cold and dry enough that Incas buried on those high slopes can still be found in amazingly well-preserved condition—freeze-dried.

In these rain forests the foliage is so dense that the jungle floor is a world of semidarkness. It is in this mysterious and wonderful world that I learned to hunt the exotic animals that make up a significant portion of the Waodanis' diet.

The Waodani impale large animals that live in and on the jungle floor with hardwood spears they have developed into highly effective weapons. But a warrior must be swift enough to get within a few feet of a tapir, wild pig, or deer in order to spear it. It takes a powerful thrust to plunge a pointed hardwood shaft deep enough through tough skin and muscle to make a kill. Pride and hunger are a Waodani hunter's greatest assets.

Young boys in the tribe who are not yet strong enough to spear start their hunting careers with the ingenious and inspiring Waodani blowgun. When I was a boy, my first challenge had been figuring out how to maneuver a nine-foot blowgun through dense foliage at a dead run. Whenever I tried to creep up noiselessly on a nesting toucan or a large macaw, I always seemed to bang one end or the other against something. My ineptitude frequently scared away my intended prey.

Monkey hunting presented another challenge. We could usually hear monkeys long before we could see them, because they yell and scold each other as they graze in the upper canopies. I would follow the Waodani boys through the jungle, and when we heard game nearby, they would begin to talk in their special hunting voices that carried well but, surprisingly, would not startle jungle wildlife. Their voices became high-pitched as they called to each other in clipped staccato outbursts of sound rather than individually identifiable words. I learned to discern what they were communicating from pitch and inflection before I actually understood what they were saying.

Once we were in position, our next challenge was to drive a poison-tipped dart a hundred feet or more on a straight trajectory toward the bird or animal. This requires much practice and incredible skill. The dart, made from a soft palm frond stem, must be whittled aerodynamically. Heat from the fire hardens the darts, which look like sharp, foot-long toothpicks. Monkeys and other tree-dwelling animals are much too large to kill with a single dart. For them, the dart is merely the vehicle for delivering *oomae*—poison.

The Waodani taught me to make the poison from shaving the thin bark of a special vine. The poison, which causes muscle paralysis, is the same drug used for surgery in many developed countries. Once a patient is put to sleep, this "poison" is used to temporarily paralyze the patient, ensuring that he or she won't twitch or move during surgery.

The Waodani boys were patient and persistent. I'm sure I provided great entertainment for them. And in exchange for what they taught me about hunting, I taught them about airplanes, screws, paper, radios, and other mysteries from the "outside world."

In the outside world I was always chosen in the first round for pickup softball, football, or basketball. In the jungle, it was embarrassing to be such a klutz. But after much patient coaching by my young Waodani friends, I finally started to get the hang of hunting. I only now realize that they never would have allowed me to scare off so much game if they didn't like me. I realize now, too, that Mincaye, especially, encouraged his boys to teach me these critical jungle skills. I think he was hoping, even way back then, that I would choose to stay and live with him and his family. He was certainly treating me like a member of the family.

During one particular hunt, we shot a fairly large monkey. A monkey can reach almost fifteen pounds, which provides a lot of meat, though it tends to be a bit tough. (People often ask me what monkey tastes like. To be perfectly candid, it's a lot like chicken.) The monkey reacted to being shot by screeching and dramatically clawing at his side. The dart broke off almost immediately, leaving the poisoned tip to do its work and paralyze the monkey.

The tip didn't just happen to break off. My Waodani friends had taught me to twist the dart in a piranha jaw that hangs from every authentic blowgun dart-holder. This creates a groove that weakens the dart right behind the poisoned tip so that when a monkey tries to pull the dart out, it breaks off.

Instead of running, the other monkeys gathered around their injured companion to see what had happened to him. By the time the monkeys realized they were under attack, we had hit three or four of them. With a thrashing of leaves and rapidly diminishing crashes, the troop of monkeys fled, jumping from the branches of one tree to another. The boys disappeared after the fleeing monkeys, and I found myself completely alone.

I was scared and helpless. I didn't know it yet, but these were feelings I would get used to. This sense of dependency would help me understand how my tribal friends would feel years later when they had to learn to deal with another world as strange to them as theirs was to me. When confronted with elevators, moving sidewalks, bathrooms, cars, and grocery stores, they would feel helpless too. Remembering what it was like to be lost in the jungle, I would determine never to let them feel that way when I understood the surroundings and they didn't.

When my friends disappeared after the monkeys, I didn't have the vaguest idea of how to get back to the village. Even if I could have found the trail, I still could not have found my way back. The Waodani waste little effort in unnecessary tasks. Their trails are merely the elimination of obvious obstacles that require the expenditure of unnecessary energy to efficiently move from one part of their domain to another. They don't actually cut a trail. They just use it, and if it gets used often enough, a path eventually becomes distinguishable from the surrounding tangle of undergrowth. Hunting trails never became that apparent.

The first few times I was left behind, I feared for my life. Even the Waodani don't like to spend a night alone in the jungle. If it intimidated them with their PhDs in jungle survival, it sure as anything was too much for me. I was just in kindergarten, but I knew enough to realize that if they didn't find me, I would never find them.

Finally, it dawned on me that it would actually be almost impossible for them *not* to find me, no matter where I went or what I did. If they could follow the trails of animals that wanted to elude them, surely the sign that this barely initiated *cowodi* left behind would be like a AAA map.

☙

Now, I knew that my standing with the downriver members of the tribe hung on the impossible challenge of hitting a tiny bird with a blowgun. I had never used this blowgun before. Each blowgun, like everything else made by the Waodani, is one of a kind. I didn't even know the size of the hole running through this particular weapon. That would determine how much cottonlike kapok I would have to twist on the dart so the explosion of breath I was about to release into the blowgun would propel the dart through the long barrel, then through the air, and into the meager flesh of my tiny target.

I prepared my dart, adding kapok until the fit felt just right. I remembered to choose a fairly straight dart, flexing it to take out a slight curve. I think the Aenomenani were surprised to see that I at least knew how to properly spin the kapok on the dart. Even this minor step in the process requires practice. If the wad of kapok is not aerodynamic in shape, the dart won't fly straight or far.

When I had stalled as long as I could, I gave in to the inevitable. I held the long weapon as I had learned to do long ago, with my hands only about eight inches apart. This seems awkward but is necessitated by the fact that we almost always shoot up at a forty-five-degree angle or greater. My audience realized that I had done this before. Maybe they would give me the benefit of the doubt if I at least came close to the target.

I took a huge breath, cheeks puffed out, both eyes open, and let go with all the pressure that my out-of-practice diaphragm could muster. "Tae, tae, woo-tae." Mincaye immediately started jumping around, exercising the traditional "I hit it, I hit it," bragging rights used by Waodani hunters. I hadn't even seen where my dart hit. It didn't appear to be sticking in the bird, but it must have come very close, because the tiny fowl was spinning slightly on the string used to secure it. Then it twisted back and I saw what Mincaye was bragging about. My dart was sticking right through the center of the bird's scrawny neck.

It is not the Waodani way to be modest at a time like this. Showing the traditional arrogance, I handed the blowgun back to its owner and challenged him, "Bito diae?"—"What about you?"

A half hour later, everyone was still trying their hand at duplicating my feat of marksmanship. They kept offering me more tries, but I wasn't going to tempt fate. It seemed providential that I hit it the first time. There was no way I was going to take a chance on ruining a perfect score.

The Waodani do share one characteristic with all other hunters of the world. The more they tell their stories, the bigger and more dangerous the quarry gets and the more magnificent their own role in bringing it down. I could only imagine what was going to be told around the Aenomenani cooking fires that night. Chances are Mincaye would make the rounds to make sure I received adequate credit for my incredible shot—and that he got credit for teaching this white-skinned foreigner to be so *Waodani-bai*—Waodani-like.

جيم

Many of the Waodani from the original Gikitaidi clan had gathered at the Tonampade village to bury Star.

While the younger men were finishing the blowgun tournament, members of the clan I had belonged to invited me to Dayumae's cooking hut to eat some wild pig and manioc. They seemed to have something serious on their minds. I thought maybe it was just the somber occasion of burying Aunt Rachel. Finally, my tribal grandmother Dawa raised the issue that was on their minds: "Now Star who is dead—being buried, we say you come live with us!"

What was this all about? I thought I might have misunderstood part of what she said, but I did understand the part about "come and live—with us."

It was a nice gesture, but I realized that these people who had become like a part of my family could not possibly know what they were asking. I couldn't just leave my business; I had struggled for twenty-some years to learn how to live in North America. After years in the jungle, it really had been tough for me to get an education, competing against contemporaries who grew up in business families with connections and venture capital. And what about my wife, Ginny? Her biggest adventure had been leaving Minnesota at age twenty-two to visit South America for a two-week excursion with a singing group. Dawa and my *inanani*—jungle family—could not possibly know what Ginny and our four children would think of such an outlandish request. Shaun was starting college. Jaime was finishing high school. Our youngest son, Jesse, and only daughter, Stephenie, had well-established friends and were busy in high school jazz band and other activities of young teenagers. *No. What you just asked me to do is impossible, but thank you for asking,* I thought to myself.

"You sending a message to me; I will come and visit," I countered, quite sure that this would end the conversation. I couldn't have been more wrong.

"We say come again to live with us, bringing your wife and children." I tried sweetening my offer: "Star, who is dead, being gone— her house is now mine. You calling me; I can come and live here with you from time to time when you need me."

Dawa was intransigent. "Bringing your family, we say come and live here."

I was surprised. Adult Waodani don't tell other adults what to do. They rarely tell small children what to do in a demanding way. They are probably the most egalitarian people on earth, with everyone doing whatever he or she wants. So what was Dawa, obviously coaxed by the others, doing? Surely she was not telling me what to do. But there could be no mistaking that she was telling, not asking.

Then I realized what was happening. Once Aunt Rachel had explained to me that when an individual Waodani clearing, usually consisting of two warriors and their families, felt an attack against them was imminent, they would move to another part of the jungle to elude their enemies. The alternative was to invoke a cultural mechanism that allowed one family group to demand relatives from another clearing to temporarily live with them. The increased concentration of warriors in one house reduced the risk of being attacked.

The group being asked to join could refuse, but in doing so, they risked severing familial ties that are important to the Waodani both emotionally and practically. When families stick together against their mutual enemies, their life expectancy is increased. Even when they do stick together, extreme, unimaginable violence within the tribe makes their life expectancy unbelievably short. No one would invoke the right of assimilation lightly, but neither would anyone object without a very good reason.

It finally sank in: The Waudoni weren't asking me to come. They were telling me to do so! They were also paying me a high compliment in doing so. They considered me to be family. But none of that could eliminate the fact that I had another life with another family who knew little of the Waodani and their unique culture.

I couldn't deny my Waodani family's demand lightly, but neither could I casually accept. I decided to use an old excuse: "Speaking to Waengongi, if He sees it well, then I will come live with you." English translation: "I'll pray about it." But what I really meant was, "I don't want to do what you have asked, but I don't want to say no either, so I'll pretend to seek God's will in the matter and will give you *my* answer later—which I hope you actually believe is God's answer, to which you can hardly object."

The Waodani show their cleverness in a thousand ways living off the unforgiving land they know as home. But I had learned the obfuscating ways of the foreigner, where sleight of speech, like sleight of hand, is a skill much to be prized.

They were not deterred by my prevarication, however. Dawa merely turned to the group gathered in the little smoke-filled hut and declared, "Already having spoken to Waengongi, I know He sees it well." How could I, of all people, have so easily underestimated my Waodani relatives? Just because Dawa and most of the others could not read the Book, it did not mean they were not a people of the Book. Nor did it mean she couldn't understand what it taught about the Creator and His desire to talk with his creation. I felt bad about my condescending attitude. It was unintentional. But I still needed a good reason to turn down what they wanted me to do.

"Speaking to Waengongi and my wife, Ongingcamo (Ginny), if

they both see it well—then I will surely come." The Waodani might be able to talk to God, but I knew none of them could get in touch with Ginny. The nearest telephone was days away by trail, and no one would know how to use it if they got there. Nor did they have phone cards or money to pay for it.

I felt relieved and slightly smug at my ability to handle such a sensitive cross-cultural situation.

Dawa was neither intimidated nor stumped. "Ongingcamo, being a God-follower," she declared to the gathering, "if God sees it well that Babae come, how can Ongingcamo not see it well?" I was taken aback, but I was also moved. I remembered what a close friend would often say when faced by a difficult decision: "A hundred years from now, who will care how successful we were or how comfortable our lives were? What will matter then is what we invested our lives in."

I couldn't imagine how I would explain to my gentle and loving, but unadventurous, wife and our four children that I was even contemplating what the Waodani wanted. I wasn't about to give in, but neither could I think of any way to resist. The clan's demand put me in a precarious position between my two worlds. Either choice would surely alienate people who were critically dear to me. And if I wasn't careful, I could alienate both sides. *God only knows*, I thought, *how I can come out of this dilemma a winner.*

꒰

I needed to get away. But where? I knew the jungle around the Tiwaeno village where I had lived with Aunt Rachel, but I didn't know any of the trails around Tonampade where we had buried her. *Hey*, I thought, *no one has told old Gikita that Star is dead.* Gikita needed to know. In the tribal kinship, Gikita was Aunt Rachel's uncle. He was also the warrior who had led the spearing raid at Palm Beach. I could get Mincaye to trek over there with me to tell him. I hadn't seen this charismatic and imposing old warrior for a long time, but I knew he lived at the headwaters of the Tzapino River, just north of where we were.

There was a group of young bucks standing around between Dayumae's house and Aunt Rachel's—no, it was my house now. I noticed that some of them were wearing *nenkinga*—sun things, watches. I had only one full day before the plane was scheduled to come back to fly me out of the jungle. If I was going to go tell Gikita about Star, I would have to be sure that I could make it there and back the same day.

Time means little to the Waodani. They don't divide life up into segments of work and play. They don't have weekends off. They don't take vacations either. There is nothing in their lives to take a vacation from. For them, everything is simply *cae*—doing. Asking the Waodani if I could make it to Gikita's house and back in one day would seem like a ridiculous question. In their mind, it would depend solely on me: how fast I could walk or run and how long I was able and willing to keep at it. They would want to know if I was going to be carrying a heavy load or just taking food and my *tiamo*—killing stick.

But since these young guys had watches, I knew they must be attending the high school there in Tonampade. I was sure they could tell me how many hours it would take.

"Aepodo nenki, Gikita weca, gote pomoi?" I asked, pointing to my watch. "How long, going to Gikita's place and coming again, will it take?" They looked at each other, building up the courage to answer my inquiry. Finally, one of them bravely answered as spokesman for the group. He raised his arm, fingers outstretched, to a forty-five degree angle above the horizon.

That is the way the Waodani indicate where the sun will be when something happens. But I didn't want Waodani time; I wanted to know how long it would take in "gringo time." I tapped my watch and asked again. They whispered nervously, glancing at their watches, and then lifted their hands in concert and pointed to where the sun would be at about three o'clock in the afternoon.

I wanted to know how many hours it would take to get to Gikita's house and back. Besides, they had not asked what time I was going to leave. How could they know what time it would be when I returned? They looked so sure of themselves and so proud that I had asked them, I hated to reveal what I was really feeling.

How can you all spend so much time going to school without even learning how to tell time? I wondered critically. I had already noticed that Waodani young people who attended high school at Tonampade seemed to have a cocky attitude that was an aberration of Waodani comportment. I had also realized that around Tonampade, the young people let the old people do all the heavy work. But a nagging feeling told me that my frustration was due to something I had forgotten rather than their poor answer. Then it occurred to me. They *did* know what time I would leave.

Waodani wake up at about six and bathe quickly in the river while it is getting light. By six-thirty, they are having their breakfast of manioc or plantain drink and whatever might be left in last night's cooking pot.

If you are going anywhere, you are on the trail when the sun is "there," just over the eastern ridges—seven o'clock.

They were telling me that if I left at seven in the morning, I would be back from Gikita's house at about three in the afternoon. But now I realized that I needed some clarification. The Waodani have three trail speeds: fast, which is about as fast as foreigners walk when they are late to catch a plane. They use this speed when they are carrying a heavy load and going a long distance with lots of climbing and descents along the way. Faster is approximately a slow trot, which they use to cover two days' worth of walking in one day. All-out is what they do when word comes that there is a herd of wild pigs or a fiesta someplace off in the jungle. It is a run that they can keep up from sunup to sundown. This speed requires powerful legs, the stamina of a marathoner, and a high pain threshold.

I asked more questions, determined to find out which speed and how much pain it would require to get back by three o'clock the next day. The old people who had taught me to walk their trails weighed in on our conversation, claiming that I would have no trouble making the trip. I reminded them that I had lived like a foreigner for a long time. But I got the impression that they were bragging again about how much I was like them. With the blowgun, their boast just required a lucky shot. On this test, proving them right might kill me.

Mincaye said he would go with me, and I was grateful. Since he was twenty-some years older than I was, I mistakenly figured that I would finally be able to keep up with him.

I was up with the sun the next morning, ready to hit the trail. Half an hour into our excursion, we came to our first big ridge. I was tired within five minutes of climbing and slowed down. A few minutes later I was totally winded. It was so steep that I could as easily pull with my arms as push with my feet—and I was hardly bending over. The last couple of hundred feet up "heartbreak ridge" brought sheer agony. At the top, I swallowed the remnants of pride that were poking through the pain in my muscles and lungs and asked Mincaye to carry my pack.

By the time we started the long descent into Gikita's valley, my legs were quivering. Climbing down ridges under such circumstances is just as painful as climbing up. By the time we saw Gikita's house nestled on a triangle of land where the Tzapino and another small river join, I was numb with exhaustion. *The plane might come,* I thought, *but I'm not going to be there unless Mincaye can drag me back.*

Gikita's wife, Mangamo, handed me a gourd full of plantain drink as soon as I plunked down in one of their hammocks. I started to drink just to be polite. But I quickly remembered why the Waodani don't go anywhere without drinking manioc or plantain and why they always drink as soon as they arrive. By the time I had downed a full quart, I was feeling better. Not good, just better. Mincaye was on his third quart, and he and Gikita laughed when I made it only partway through my second. The Waodani can drink nearly four quarts of the thick drink. I was ready to explode after my first.

Gikita showed no emotion when I informed him that Star had died and we had buried her. This old warrior had spent his life as head killer of the Gikitaidi clan that bore his name. He grew up in a culture of death and had achieved its highest accomplishment. He had become *tempo*—a remorseless killer. By the time the two *cowodi*, Star and Woodpecker (the tribe's name for Aunt Betty), came with Dayumae to live with his clan, Gikita had outlived every other man in the tribe. He was the old man—in his early thirties.

The only way to reach such a ripe old age was to kill your enemies before they killed you. Gikita had distinguished himself in that. But I had come to know him just after he gave up killing and forgave the vendettas he had yet to avenge. I looked up to Gikita in the jungle like one might look up to the chairman of a large corporation in the outside world. In his world, Gikita was top dog, the best of what mattered most in Waodani life—killing.

After digesting the information about Aunt Rachel, Gikita responded. "Babae, being old I, too, am soon going to die. Going to live, then, in God's place, I will wrap my arms around your father whom I speared first. There we will live happily together.

"Before, we lived very badly, hating and spearing all the time. Now, the young people, well, they are living badly again. Wanting many things and not sharing, they, too, are living angry.

"Star already dying, and me dying soon, I say, you come and teach the young people how to live well." End of speech. Short and sweet, for him. Difficult and convicting for me. One of my reasons for making this grueling trek was to get away from the turmoil caused by the demand that I return to the jungle. Now Gikita had added to it.

Mincaye picked up my pack for the return trip to Tonampade without my even asking. Fortunately, we surprised a badgerlike animal on the return trail, and since my hands were free, I hit it. We would return with meat. I felt a bit wimpy having Mincaye carry my gear for me, but by bringing game back to the village, I felt my honor was at least partly redeemed. Mincaye carried my animal, too.

I asked Mincaye why Gikita lived way over on the Tzapino, so far from everyone else. He explained that two of Gikita's daughters had been married to a young warrior. One day, the husband killed two pigs while out hunting. He carried one of the pigs to his clearing and told his older wife to fetch the other. She refused, demanding that he send the younger wife. As she stormed off, he became angry and shot her in the back with his muzzle-loading shotgun. "She bled, threw up, and died," Mincaye finished.

Gikita had had enough. He had grown up hating and killing. Then, after becoming a God-follower, he gave up all the hatred and fear that had haunted the first half of his life. Seeing the old ways creeping in again in a new form, he moved deeper into the jungle with his wife, Mangamo, and sister, Mintake.

There seemed to be no end to the chaos and violence contained within this small, isolated tribe of people. I had learned to love them before I reached the age when I felt I had to understand them. Now I wondered if I ever would. It would be several years before I would see the Waodani struggle with the same thing as they tried to understand the "civilized world," a world in which the cowodi killed each other with great killing machines.

As Mincaye and I neared Tonampade, the sun was somewhat lower than the young Waodani men had estimated. I had forgotten to tell them I wanted to drink plantain and talk. All they had factored in was the time needed to trudge there and back.

A half hour out, I heard a bush plane land at Tonampade. Oh, no! They had come for me early. There were no flights planned into Tonampade that Mincaye knew of, so I coaxed my rebelling body into one final agonizing sprint, knowing that the pilot would not be able to wait long.

When Mincaye and I reached the airstrip, the Waodani told me that the plane was parked at the other end of the strip. Four hundred extra yards to go.

I grabbed my things and walked to the strip, followed by a small entourage of Waodani. As we walked down the strip, we met a couple of obvious gringos coming the other way. The plane had not come for me. It had come to bring visitors. Clean clothes and lack of proper jungle attire made it obvious that this was their initiation into the world of mud and mildew.

I was too tired to expend unnecessary energy on elaborate greetings. "Hi, who are you?" I asked.

"Who are you?" they asked back, as though *I* were the intruder. I was sure they would be embarrassed when I told them who I was. I belonged here, after all. I answered, "I'm Steve Saint."

They might not know who I was, but surely they would recognize my last name and its association with the Waodani. I was wrong. They continued on past us before turning around. "Did you know that these are the people who killed the five missionaries?" they asked me. "We just came back from the beach where they did it."

I was aghast at what I had just heard. *How dare such callous people come here and strut around like they own the place!* I thought. They had apparently come to see a sandbar and add an adventure badge to their experience vest. They would go home and tell their friends that they had visited the famous Palm Beach, where savages had killed the missionaries. They probably had even taken some sand home as a memento.

"Who let these cowodi come?" I asked the Waodani. We don't know, they responded with shrugs. "Always coming, they just want to see the sand where the missionaries died," they informed me. But I could see the resentment and frustration behind their response. What they hadn't said was, "To the foreigners, we will always be the people who killed the missionaries," but I could tell they were thinking it.

I was seething with emotion. I was feeling protective. Someone had just threatened my family, and the fight-or-flight reaction had automatically kicked in. If I felt this much emotion, how must the Waodani feel? What the Waodani had done made sense within their warped culture of hate and fear. What they had done to the five foreigners was reasonable in their minds. At the time, they couldn't understand the extravagant overtures of friendship these foreigners had made. But I knew my other world was just as warped, and just as full of hate and fear. In the outside world, we just had more rules to keep the killing in check. And we had a lot of police and soldiers to enforce those rules. Otherwise, both worlds were pretty much the same.

The Waodanis' reasons for telling me to return and live with them were probably as complex as the group that was asking. But when I asked them why they wanted me to come, I was given three reasons. They wanted me to help them protect themselves; they wanted me to teach them; and they wanted me to help them to get medicine. None of those reasons had seemed urgent or had made much sense to me when I first heard them less than twenty-four hours before. But now the reasons had become personal. Someone needed to put a stop to people rubbing my "family's" face in the fact that members of their tribe had killed my dad and uncles. They needed to be protected from this type of insensitive intrusion.

What the Waodani had meant for evil, God used for good. Given the chance to go back and rewrite the story, I would not have been willing to change it. Sure, it was painful, but over time I had begun to see the pain of Dad's death in a different light. If I could have changed things, I could have kept my dad. But then Mincaye would not have adopted me. Yowe and Kimo would not be my spiritual mentors. I would not have been part of this mysterious and wonderful Waodani world. Dawa would not be my grandmother, and Dayumae would not be my aunt. And in the outside world, thousands and thousands of people would not have dedicated their lives to helping take teachings of peace and hope and comfort to people like the Waodani in frontiers scattered all over the world.

I would soon find out that the Waodanis' requests were a lot more complicated than I could have guessed that afternoon in Tonampade. What I realized, however, was that if I couldn't help, who could? And if I wouldn't, who would?

Palm Beach was about people, not sand. It was about giving life, not death. Without knowing it, I had just crossed the fine line of decision.

FREE Discussion Guide!
A discussion guide for
Through Gates of Splendor is available at

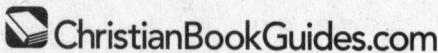